JOURNEY
AMONG HEROES

BOB GREER

ISBN: 978-1-4269-9611-5 (sc)
ISBN: 978-1-4269-9612-2 (hc)
ISBN: 978-1-4269-9613-9 (e)

Library of Congress Control Number: 2011916976

Trafford rev. 12/21/2011

 www.trafford.com

North America & international
toll-free: 1 888 232 4444 (USA & Canada)
phone: 250 383 6864 ♦ fax: 812 355 4082

Dedicated to

Nguyen Thi It
Pham Thi Tuyet
The memory and family of the late Nguyen Thi Thu
Dinh Thi Que
Nguyen Thi Huong
Nguyen Thi Ha
Le Thi Meo
Duong Thi Sam
Nguyen Thi Chau
The memory and family of the late Le Thi Gom
Dinh Thi Chuy

CONTENTS

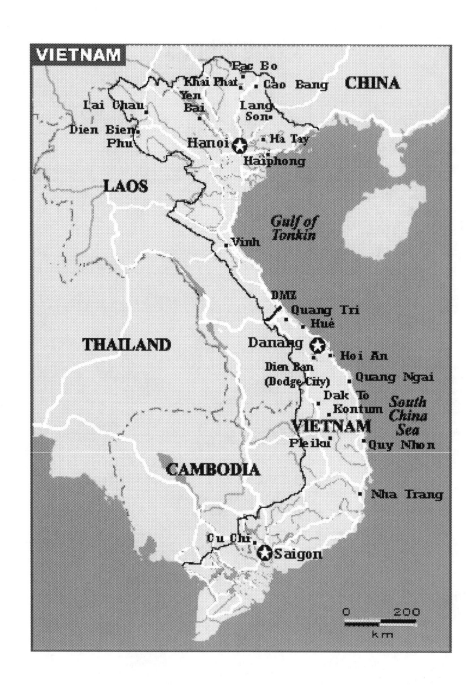

Acknowledgements

The writings of French-American scholar and historian, the late Bernard Fall, proved inspirational as I kept returning to Vietnam in an effort to come to grips with what happened there in 1944-1975. *Hell in a Small Place* and *Street without Joy* were my closest travel companions. I was always conscious that Fall logged his miles under conditions that were often trying, uncomfortable and dangerous until the day he was tragically killed while on patrol with US forces in 1967 at the age of 40 years.

Trinh Thu Lan, a Press Officer at the Department of Foreign Affairs in Hanoi at the time, helped me obtain consent from the authorities to interview the Hero Mothers despite my visa violation. Without her assistance there would have been no journey.

Nguyen Quynh Huong was the Press Officer assigned to assist me. She arranged meetings with Hero Mothers, made travel arrangements and accompanied me to interviews. Huong was instrumental in arranging my brief interview with legendary General Vo Nguyen Giap and others who were prepared to help. She traced Ha Hung Long, one of Ho Chi Minh's original soldiers, and arranged for us to travel to Tuyen Quang to meet him. Her personal insights and sensitivity made for pleasant and informal meetings wherever we went. I found out by chance much later that Huong normally travelled somewhat better than my meagre budget permitted, but not only did no complaint escape her lips, she was always an enthusiastic fellow traveller.

Professor Le Van Lan, an eminent and busy Hanoi historian, twice spared me time to explain about the horrors of the starvation under the Japanese during World War 2 as well as the remarkable role of

Vietnamese women during times of national crisis over the last two millennia.

Professor Tran Duc Phan and Mac Thi Hoa, Director and Deputy Director respectively of the Vietnam Red Cross Society Agent Orange Victims Fund, helped me understand a little about the extent and nature of problems caused by that terrible chemical.

Eng Dang Vu Dung, Vice Director of the Friendship Village in Hanoi, allowed me a tour of that marvellous facility. The unusual rendition of the Hokey Pokey song in a classroom we walked by will remain with me for the rest of my days. I am in awe of both the courage of all the victims I met and the dedication of those who help them.

Many others contributed to a wonderful journey in five parts. My thanks go to the mountain men who on occasions helped repair my old Minsk motorcycle, and to the many along the way who shared information, tea, food and humour. I have never felt safer whilst travelling off the beaten track. The twelve Police, Army and Immigration officers who once charged me with an impressive variety of offences later withdrew them. I am obliged to them for endless cups of tea, an interesting lunch, a good few laughs and the return of my motorcycle after a brief hearing the next day.

In Washington, Dorothy Fall, artist, writer and widow of the inspirational Bernard Fall invited me to dinner at her home. It was a marvellous end to one trip and encouraged me to embark upon another.

Cristina Giordano, librarian in charge of the General Reference Unit at the UNOG Library, Geneva, kindly supplied a copy of the text of the Geneva Accords noting that the Conference was "an event from the quiet shores of Lake Leman that cast a long shadow on the XX th century history . . . and led to very dramatic events, with serious consequences for the world order."

In 2011 I visited Ngo Thi Tuyen, one of the great heroines of the American War who features in the chapter "Those Viet women", and the chapter that follows. Her back causes her discomfort these days because of those wild exploits, but she nevertheless accompanied us to the Dragon Jaw Bridge so that we might better understand her courage under extreme pressure. I am grateful to her for reliving tough times around her village of Nam Nam all those years ago.

And then, of course, there are the Hero Mothers. Sadly, two of the most charming of these delightful women have passed on: Le Thi Gom of the heavily scarred legs from her days as a fifty-year-old infantry soldier, and Nguyen Thi Thu, the old matriarch. The others are mostly in the autumn of their years, while a couple are certainly well into winter. One was slightly hunched, and has a little trouble with her chest as a result of a few beatings too many. Another took the time to show me around her award-winning little fish sauce factory, run from the kitchen of her home. Uneducated peasants, they were personalities all, and shared their war with me, with tea, humour and the occasional tear. They spoilt me with their hospitality, courtesy and kindness and I will forever savour the pleasure of meeting them.

Bob Greer
Brisbane, Australia
August 2011

Introduction

These pages are about two parallel journeys made by a wide-eyed tourist who was caught up by a small museum exhibit during a holiday visit to Vietnam. The physical journey commenced in 2001, with annual trips thereafter until a final visit in 2005. It was a matter of following a ball of string as it unravelled, only to learn after my return home of yet another large ball. There is always much more to be seen and learnt, but sadly this part of the journey has now ended after nine months spent in Indochina. The spiritual journey commenced at the same time, but will last the rest of my life and quite possibly well beyond.

The story is not really about the Vietnam War although references to that conflict intrude regularly: the War is after all the backdrop to a combination of tragedy, love story and fairy tale, laced with an improbably massive measure of sheer courage, with the lot drenched in such amounts of blood and suffering as would make Macbeth pale by comparison. It is as unlikely a tale as can be, considering it features the triumph of illiterate peasants in a third world country over the super-power of the day. It is the equivalent of David versus a gridiron team of Goliaths with the big fellows favoured by a blind referee. History records that it did happen—I was just privileged to glimpse tiny facets of some of the events.

The chapters do not appear in chronological order. I did not plan on writing a book at the outset of the journey, lurching about Vietnam in pursuit of leads that somehow kept landing at my feet. Nor had I any idea about what else might appear to be followed up. The need to establish a fact, an attempt to picture a scene or make sense of what appeared to be senseless might lead to a train trip, a speedboat journey down a river, a motorcycle expedition or a backside-numbing bus journey.

A promise to a couple of aged women to do my best to tell their stories to their counterparts in the West turned out to be rashly made, requiring as it did my resignation from a comfortable financial position, the sale of my house and ultimately the liquidation of my superannuation fund. However, promises made to Hero Mothers are to be taken seriously, and I can now look any of them in the eye.

Readers not familiar with events in Vietnam may find the historical background at the end of the book helpful. It is necessarily broad. Detailed histories are found in bulky volumes, some of which appear in the bibliography. The perception of the war being about the forces of good fighting the evil Communist hordes is somewhat dated and inaccurate. It is also self-serving, a sort of palliative for those who might otherwise be mildly troubled by events there.

A few terms used throughout might need a little explanation:

The Vietminh fought against the French in 1944-1954. They were led by the Communists, but being by and large uneducated peasants determined to see the French leave Indochina, they were not all Communists. In 1941 Ho Chi Minh organised them into the Viet Nam Doc Lap Dong Minh (Vietnam Independence League)[1], shortened to Vietminh. They fought the French throughout Vietnam—they were not limited to the north.

The NLF (National Liberation Front), an organisation formed in 1960 in the south by largely middle class patriots[2], had a fighting arm to whom President "Diem's publicist gave a pejorative label, the Vietcong, or Vietnamese Communists, and the name stuck"[3]. Locally sourced and based, many came from villages throughout the south. They were irregular forces and specialised in "hit and run" operations. Many of their fighters had previously fought as Vietminh. The NLF was dominated by the Communists in the late 1960s, especially after the heavy losses sustained by the Vietcong in the Tet Offensive of 1968 required reinforcements from the North.

The PAVN (People's Army of Vietnam) was the regular army of the Communist government of North Vietnam. It later moved about the South in larger formations after infiltrating the country via the Ho Chi Minh Trail, and fought a more conventional style of war.

The ARVN, also known as Arvin, was the Army of the Republic of Vietnam. That is, it was the army of the theoretically-democratic government of South Vietnam. It acquired a reputation for being highly skilled at avoiding combat, with corruption endemic in its upper ranks.

The Ho Chi Minh Trail was a network of trails starting around Vinh, a vital rail junction and port facility in North Vietnam, and leading down to South Vietnam via the neutral countries of Laos and Cambodia in an effort to avoid American bombers. In an attempt to deny forest cover to Communist forces and convoys, the Americans sprayed large tracts of the area with Agent Orange, a herbicide that causes major problems in Vietnam still, and could do for generations to come.

Tet is the Lunar New Year and the biggest festive date in the Vietnamese calendar.

The Tet Offensive of 1968 saw the Vietcong violate a truce to attack over a hundred towns and cities in South Vietnam in the mistaken belief that locals would join them in an uprising against the government. Vietcong losses were very heavy, and the Offensive was a major military defeat for them, but Americans back home were shocked to see an enemy they had been told was on the brink of defeat mount such an attack. It seriously dented the credibility of the military and caused many to question continuing US involvement in Vietnam.

Indochina consists of the former French colonies of Vietnam, Laos and Cambodia.

Bao Dai was the last Emperor of Vietnam. A dissolute character, he was at different times a French puppet and a lackey of the Japanese. He enjoyed the company of women and spent a great deal of time abroad. He spent his last years in Paris.

There were in effect two wars in Vietnam during the period of the American War, as the Vietnamese termed that conflict. The Americans withdrew in 1973 and left the South Vietnamese to continue the war until they were finally defeated in 1975.

It should be noted that the United States never declared war on Vietnam.

With a group of friends, the author has launched Platypus, a charitable organization to lend a helping hand in Vietnam. Interested readers can look it up on the internet at www.platypus-charity.org

1. Le Thi Gom

It was the morning before New Year's Eve 2003, and nature had laid on overcast weather around Cu Chi, South Vietnam. Rain threatened, but always retreated; it was windy and looked cold, but I removed my jacket in the car. The place is about fifty kilometres from Saigon, or Ho Chi Minh City, as it is now known, and achieved notoriety not only for the violent conduct of the war in the area, but for the network of tunnels that Communist fighters used to torment the French military. When the French were defeated in 1954, the American military succeeded them and suffered heavily in the same area until their departure in 1973. The locals, of course, suffered a great deal more, whether they were civilians, Vietcong or Southern sympathisers—when B52 bombers come a-calling, there is pain aplenty for everyone.

Cu Chi was along the route to Saigon from a stepping off point of the Ho Chi Minh Trail in Cambodia, near an area aptly known as the Iron Triangle. The Communists could and did send fighters and military hardware from the distant North to the suburbs of Saigon along the heavily camouflaged Trail and tunnels. Control over this area was vital to both sides. That flat, hard country saw torrid military action over three decades: if hell had been located anywhere in Vietnam during the war, this would surely have been one of perhaps half a dozen logical sites. Hamlets and villages dot an area that was nevertheless subjected to destructive B52 high-altitude bombing raids, Agent Orange spraying and random interdictory fire, in addition to exposure to the very full suite of weaponry and combat systems that an overwhelming modern superpower could command. Cu Chi was also a "free-fire" zone—anything that moved could become a legitimate target for US forces.

We were on our way to the penultimate step (or so I thought at the time) of a very special journey, travelling to meet the tenth of eleven remarkable old women. On our way to the home of Hero Mother Le Thi Gom we passed by part of the Cu Chi tunnel complex, now one of the most popular tourists attractions in the country. Visitors can fire the legendary Russian AK47 assault rifle or the American M60 machine gun for US$1 per round. They can feel like Rambo without risking heavy return fire, although I suspect the former soldiers who prepare the weapons for tourist use must sometimes be sorely tempted. Tourists can and do walk and crawl through sections of tunnel that have been enlarged and sanitised, or watch demonstrations of a chilling array of booby traps used in the tunnels.

We made the obligatory stops at a couple of government offices in order to make ourselves known to the local Peoples Committee and produce our authorisations from Hanoi to interview Le Thi Gom. One does not move far from the main roads of Vietnam before coming to the attention of the Committee, in this case the executive arm of the local government. Introductions and pleasantries complete, we were joined by an official who skilfully navigated along back roads and short cuts until we drew up before a new house on the outskirts of a quiet hamlet. We were in agricultural territory, surrounded by rice paddies.

The house was compact, a double-storied home of modern design, painted beige with darker brown highlights. We strolled towards a tiled forecourt, and as the entrance to the house came into view we saw a sprightly figure sitting cross-legged on the front verandah, weaving a small container of sorts from what looked like thinly split bamboo. As soon as she saw us, the woman leapt to her feet with enviable agility, wiped her hands against her skirt and moved to meet us at the front door.

Huong introduced me to an elderly woman with silver hair tied tightly back in a bun. Despite a gaunt, deeply lined face, Ma Gom had lively, shining eyes that darted about constantly. She wore a purple top with a white flower pattern, over khaki baggy trousers with square motifs. Introductions dealt with, she happily led us into her home.

The floor in the living room was tiled, as were the walls to about waist height. Thanks to many large windows, the room was bright and inviting. There was little about by way of decoration, but the old woman explained that she had just moved in and had not yet settled in properly.

She spoke to a teenage girl who hovered about in the background. Ma Gom had scarcely assumed a lotus position on her wood high-back chair than the youngster arrived with a tray and all the makings for extended rounds of fresh green tea. Whilst tea was being poured I could not help noticing our hostess's heavily-scarred legs: the wounds were clearly not caused by a fall from a bicycle. I forced my eyes away from her legs, concerned with issues of modesty, but wondered how I might find out about her injury.

The old woman reached for a small cube of leaf, and offered it to me; when I declined, she smiled and popped it into her mouth. Although I was unable to detect any sign of teeth, she enjoyed a vigorous chew as she chatted happily to Huong. Thereafter she relied on superb communication with the teenager, who turned out to be a delightful grand-daughter and talented gum maker, to ensure a steady supply of chewey treats.

The youngster remained within earshot as we could hear her moving about beyond the wall throughout the interview. The old woman was at ease now as she related her story.

Le Thi Gom was born in 1921, in the village where she still lives, to poor farmer parents. The fifth child, with four brothers and two sisters, she worked at home while a brother attended primary school. She married at twenty in 1941.

"Was yours an arranged marriage?" I asked her.

"Yes. Our families did the matchmaking and arranged the wedding. My husband, Bien Van Diet, was one year older than me."

"Were you happy with their choice?"

"Oh, yes. He was handsome and kind."

The young bride became something of an activist. Vietnam was under the oft-times brutal control of the French at the time, until the Japanese moved them aside 3 years later. The young Le Thi Gom formed a women's group to demonstrate against the Japanese; I would not have thought one could survive such an activity, given the record of the Japanese wherever they went during World War 2. Like her remarkable peers, she did not allow her clandestine activities to interfere with her family responsibilities but somehow juggled her way through the years.

"How did you manage your women's activities, raise a family and look after the home during such difficult times?"

"There was a shortage of clothing and food, but I managed to do some clever business to cope with the problems." By clever business I suspect she meant she had done a little trading, probably smuggling goods past French and Japanese forces.

Her parents started supporting the Revolution against the French presence in the late 1940s in a community of divided loyalties. Ho Chi Minh, based in the far north, enjoyed considerable support in the area, but this far south the French had a strong presence until 1954. After that, the dominant forces were South Vietnamese, and after 1964 they were joined by large numbers of US soldiers. Diem and the succession of presidents who followed him in Saigon in the south, held sway here, nominally at least.

"What became of your brothers and sisters?"

"My brother, Le Van Tay, died nearby in 1949 fighting the French. We recovered his body when the French left the battle scene. Le Van Quei died early due to ill health, while Le Van Quan moved north before the battle at Dien Bien Phu. He survived the wars and is now a police officer near Vinh in the north. My fourth brother, Le Van An, was killed in 1969."

"How did he die?"

"We do not know. He did secret work, but we have no details about his death."

It was not clear if the old woman even knew where her brother had died; he might be one of the 300,000 who died or disappeared and were Missing in Action. I did not press her for more information.

It had been a family war effort. Her sister Le Thi Beo supported the soldiers and survived the war, but has since died of ill health. Her other sister, Le Thi Xa, also supported the soldiers and was politically active. She, too, survived the war and now lives in Saigon with her son.

Ma Gom's father was a secret supporter of Ho Chi Minh's revolution, and was shot dead by the French in 1952 when he was returning from a meeting. Her mother stayed home to raise the rest of the family, but died in 1954 of illness. That was the year Ma Gom started supporting the Revolution; although she had a family of her own to care for by then, she ran messages when she could. When the French left and were replaced by the Americans, her family as a matter of course once again supported Ho Chi Minh. Ma was able to do secret work during the American war, reporting troop movements.

She had lost her father and a brother to the French, but the American war was to extract a much heavier toll. Her secret work made her an enemy agent eagerly sought by the other side.

Her husband Diet had joined a local Volunteer Group before they married, and he continued his secret work after the French left. He stayed around the Cu Chi area and was in charge of local volunteers. He was shot dead by soldiers of the Army of South Vietnam in 1963. Ma Gom and family were able to retrieve his body and bury him properly.

"You had a family of your own. What happened to your children?"

"We had four sons and three daughters. My oldest son, Bien Van Giup, was born in 1948. He went to primary school and never married. As a Vietcong security man, he was looking after the safety of the villages when he died in 1968."

"Do you know how he died?"

"It was during a B52 bombing attack not far from here. Some body parts were found that were accepted as belonging to him."

In a nation that practices ancestor worship, remains of the deceased are important, but a B52 bombing raid lacks such consideration and leaves little for the bereaved. Sometimes a little leeway was required in identifying remains so that families could complete the grieving process, and sometimes families had to settle for less-than-perfect identification methods.

"Another son, Bien Van Nuoc, was born in 1951. He was also a Vietcong security officer, and he died nearby, fighting against US forces in 1969."

The old woman looked unhappy, and I guessed she either knew little about his death or found something about his passing particularly disturbing. It was not a time for questions. Nevertheless, she continued.

"Later that year, Bien Van Son died. He was only thirteen years old, and did not even have the opportunity to join the Vietcong. He was on his way to school one morning when the area came under artillery fire. Someone took him to a safe spot, but he did not want to stay there and was killed by artillery fire after continuing his walk to school."

He and his brother had died in the same year as their uncle.

I could not help wondering if an observer, seeing a child walking in a "free fire" zone, had called in a few rounds. It was known to happen. Perhaps the youngster was a victim of random fire.

An incident in one of my reference books concerned a senior US officer who wondered at unauthorised artillery fire at strange hours within his area of responsibility. When he had someone investigate it, it turned out that a senior South Vietnamese officer had a deal going whereby he sold the casings of artillery shells to a local recycler. He had a good deal going and was anxious to shell the area to keep his cash flow going. There was no way of knowing how many lives his little side-line had cost and I wondered if Son had been a victim of such a scheme.

"Bien Hoang Than was too young to fight. He now lives in Saigon, but his young daughter lives here with me, and goes to school in the nearby village." It was she who prepared the gum for Ma's enjoyment.

The daughters of Le Thi Gom were as feisty as the rest of the family and were all actively involved during the war:

"Bien Thi Gop was born in 1942. She was a nurse at a Vietcong hospital that was sometimes located in tunnels. She was shot dead in 1963, the same year her father died."

I had read about the high mortality rates among the medical teams who sometimes operated under atrocious conditions in rooms scooped out along the tunnels. They had to cope with American attempts to flood or gas the tunnels, along with the usual bombing and infantry attacks.

"Bien Thi My was a Youth Volunteer. When she was old enough she joined the army but was injured by aerial rocket fire whilst transporting supplies in the area." She now lives with her own family, across the road from Ma. I was to meet this delightful woman soon.

"My daughter Bien Thi Khanh was a Youth Volunteer. She survived the war."

Of her seven children, one had been too young to become involved, one daughter had survived with wounds and another daughter seemed to have survived intact. I looked at Ma's scarred legs, but the question was stillborn. She had more she wanted to tell me.

"In 1968 US troops came looking for me, but I escaped and joined the army."

"When you say you joined the army, do you mean you became a fighter?"

"Yes." She had signed up for combat at the age of forty-seven years.

"How did your war go?"

"Fine, until I was shot." She could have been discussing the weather, but a great number of people were shot around that area, so she may not have thought her fate to be newsworthy. The Viet are in any event inclined to understatement.

Her role at that stage was partly political, offering suggestions and advice to women wanting to support the Resistance effort.

"In 1971 I went to fetch food and special orders from a tunnel in the area. Villagers loyal to the South identified me to US forces who were looking for me. When I saw them I escaped, but they shot me in both legs."

Ma showed me her lower legs. Somebody had spent a lot of time on them, for long cuts ran almost the whole length of both shins. Her left knee seemed to have had a great deal of attention and scars ran above the knee, higher than modesty would allow me to question. The old woman was anxious that we understand that she did not waste the recovery period, but spent it tracking troop movements and establishing contacts.

"Once I climbed a high tree to see where one of my sons died," she told me.

"Did you ever just want to give up?"

"Giving up was impossible. I knew we must keep going. My children had died for their country, and I had seen boys too young for war moving down from the north to help. I knew we must not cry—we must get rid of the Americans. I was so sad when only one of my four sons returned from the war, but I have family, and I have been well supported, better than after the war." By that, I guessed she meant that a crippled economy, wrecked infrastructure and many clashing economic priorities left hundreds of thousands of needy people in desperate straits for many years after the war. Some wasteful and inefficient government and corrupt officialdom had not helped. Nixon's withholding of $3.25 billion of reconstruction money did not help. It took nineteen years to implement the Hero Mothers programme, and her house had only recently been completed.

She was happy to pose for a few photographs, and asked if I would care to meet her daughter. I had for the moment lost track of Bien Thi My, the injured daughter who lived across the road, and jumped at the opportunity. We stepped across the lane to a delightful house with a large courtyard paved with thick terra cotta tiles. Sheds to shelter the farm animals adjoined her home and the whole setup was immaculate and professional. Once inside one of the sheds we met a smiling, cheerful woman on crutches who had been supervising a lively bunch of piglets under the watchful eye of a very large sow.

Ma Gom had told me her daughter had been injured—she had in fact lost a leg. Yes, she would be happy to pose with her mother. Bien Thi My is a strapping, photogenic woman and sometime later, as I consulted my notes, I was shocked to realise that she was probably approaching sixty years of age.

She was anxious that the photograph be just right, so we selected a suitable spot with perfect light. She turned for the photo so that her missing leg was not so noticeable and flashed a sunny smile. I took a few photographs, noticing during the process that My's remaining leg is somewhat less than perfect, and will probably trouble her in her winter years. Not that it will faze her unduly.

Ma Gom and Bien Thi My, pig farmer extraordinaire

It was time to return to Saigon. We had enjoyed warm hospitality and very good company, but something about Cu Chi bothered me. It still does. I have returned twice to the district since first interviewing Ma Gom, but there always seems to be a sense of desolation about the place. Perhaps it's the mental picture of an old woman climbing a tree to glimpse the spot where she lost a son, or of a thirteen-year-old killed by artillery fire on his way to school. Perhaps it is the knowledge that the whole province was just a human abattoir, where the value of a human life was on a par with that of a chicken.

Three generations of Ma Gom's family saw us off with waves and an open invitation to call again. The road back to Saigon seemed different somehow; the story of Le Thi Gom lent gravity to the sense of depression I had felt at the start of our day.

Back in my hotel room, it was review time. I drew a few time lines, reshuffled my notes, and re-examined the Vietnam War as it had touched Ma Gom. It had certainly been disastrous for the old woman. Her mother had died of natural causes in 1954. Of her four sons, only the sole survivor reached his twenty-first birthday. The intermingling of generations and genders in the death toll struck me as being horrific. A father killed, three years after a brother; a husband and daughter in the same year; two sons and a brother six years later. Two brothers killed, twenty years apart. What a hell of a war.

Ma Gom must be one of the more unusual tough, gun toting warrior/ spy / political activist types to have graced the planet.

A few months later, a friend in Perth pointed out that the old warrior is also missing a toe, but I told her that Ma had probably been too busy to notice such a minor discrepancy. She probably would not dream of raising it at the next women's function for fear they would think she is growing soft.

In most western cities or towns, any grandmother with war wounds who once toted a gun in battle would be both a rarity and a celebrity. In Vietnam, it merely gains you admission to a very large club. God knows what you have to do for bragging rights; perhaps bringing down a helicopter might get you a moment in the sun.

In September 2004 as I was doing some follow up interviews, Huong and I learnt of Ma Gom's death. I had hoped to meet up with the Cu Chi family once more, so we decided to call on Bien Thi My again. I was keen to see her anyway, for she was delightful, and I thought she might be able to clarify a few things for me. I wanted a little more information about the medical treatment Ma Gom's legs had received. I was a little puzzled too at the number of family members who seemed to be fighting simultaneously and wondered if I messed up my charts.

Her husband, Nguyen Van Ut, joined us, as did Ma's granddaughter and former chewing gum maker, Bien Tu Hoang Nhung. Several photographs of Ma Gom now adorn the family shrine, and the special cakes that we brought along ended up there also. They would be removed and enjoyed later, although I was pleased at the thought that Ma would have first go at the cookies. We presented young Nhung with an enlarged photo plaque of her with her grandmother, and handed My one of her with her mother. Sadly, the timing was right for such pictures.

Ma's leg wounds had remained a mystery to me. They did not look like the result of rifle or even machine gun fire. As it turned out, they weren't. Bien Thi My explained that although an M79 grenade round had narrowly missed Ma Gom, she had been hit with many pieces of shrapnel, hence the numerous scars and perhaps even the missing toe.

"How did she manage to get treated? Somebody worked very hard to help her." What I was getting at was that Cu Chi was not known for its surgical facilities, and Ma Gom had received a hell of a lot more than first aid. I wondered if she had been treated in the tunnels.

"She was treated at a US health centre in Saigon!" My told me.

"She was Vietcong, shot by US soldiers. Why would they treat her? Surely they would imprison her? She was the enemy," I told her.

"The medical people did not know that. She was an old woman: anything could have happened to her."

I had overlooked her age—Ma Gom was wounded at fifty years of age. Bien Thi My explained to me that her mother had been betrayed by supporters of the Southern cause, and soldiers had been on the alert for her. Presumably in the confusion that often follows such skirmishes Ma Gom had been able to pass herself off as a civilian casualty.

My's husband Ut was from the same village. He joined the army in 1968, the same year as his mother-in-law. He served in the main Vietcong office in a forest in adjoining Binh Duong Province, assisting a commander. It sounded very much as though he was at Vietcong HQ, the highly sought after COSVN complex, in a very heavily bombed area. He married My in 1972, and they have a son and two daughters, the first born in 1974 as the civil war approached its final year.

"It was a very busy period for you. Ut was in the army in the forest, and you told me you were sometimes transporting supplies; your mother was recovering from her combat wounds. Finding the time to marry and start a family must have been terribly difficult." The couple looked at me blankly.

"It was normal," said My. There can be no normality within a society that has become caught up in a thirty-year war, especially not a civil war that so deeply divides communities.

"Carrying ammunition, weapons and other supplies in free fire zones must have been dangerous. How did you carry them?"

"By water buffalo. We would carry crops, with more interesting goods underneath."

Once again, I had this feeling that they thought I was being petty.

"Did you sometimes wonder if the war would ever end?"

"Sometimes it seemed as if the war would go on forever. The war plans were kept a close secret so it was impossible to know what was happening, and it was hard to get news," said My.

I was surprised to see granddaughter Nhung there, expecting she would have returned to her parents in Saigon once Ma Gom died in May. She told us later that living with her grandmother for all those years had changed her life: she now feels like a village girl, and is uncomfortable in the city. Nhung loves where she lives and will stay. The young woman hopes to become a school teacher and is awaiting an acceptance letter from an institution in Saigon. After graduation she will return to Cu Chi to live in her grandmother's house; she has it all worked out and from the look of her she will follow it all through—this is a young woman with a firm sense of direction.

She is a fit and attractive young woman with a sunny personality, but there was an underlying impression of great strength about her. I believe that given a cause to fight for she would be as tough as an old boot.

"This is one fighting family. How does it feel to be part of a family with such a history?" I asked her.

She is happy and proud. Nhung may be just seventeen years old but anybody wishing to harm the village will have to pass by her first. Then pass the house next door, and the next. It will be a very difficult passage, for Nhung has that Hero Mother look about her, and genes that military commanders would die for.

We bade our farewells to young Nhung, Aunt My on crutches, Ut, and the photograph of Ma Gom on the shrine and it occurred to me that they are all chips off the old block. The block being the Trung sisters, those diminutive warriors who tormented the Chinese two thousand years ago.

As to the purpose of the journey that meandered so much more than I had foreseen, well, it was connected to a holiday trip that spiralled out of control and changed my life in so many ways forever.

2. The Beginning

It was during my first visit to Indochina in 2001 that I visited the Army Museum in Hanoi, North Vietnam. The Museum is small and understated, and since it is located at a very busy road junction one could easily miss the place, but for the assortment of military wreckage scattered around the yard. Large American artillery pieces, a helicopter and miscellaneous aircraft wreckage, a French Quad 50 (.50 cal four-barrel machine gun) and the like attract your attention as you approach.

That was where I first saw The Board. It was made of wood and attached to the feature wall in a large, airy room on the ground floor of the Museum. Deep red in colour with gold lettering, the Board listed every province in the country and allocated a number to each, totalling around 41,000 although there was nothing to indicate what it all meant. A guide with a little English explained that the Board showed the number of Hero Mothers in each province. These were women who had lost at least two family members during the war. (I probably misunderstood her, for this turned out to be only partly correct. I also assumed that the numbers referred to children who had perhaps been civilian casualties of war, such as schoolchildren who had perished during bombing raids; this turned out to be tragically incorrect).

The Board featured in a subdued display among photographs of old women, some of whom were being pushed in wheelchairs by senior army officers at some sort of function. Most of the photographs were captioned in Vietnamese, with a few translated into English, but the captions seemed to be wrong. They indicated that a number of the women had lost eight or nine family members to the War, and one had

13

lost a round dozen. That surely couldn't be correct; besides, there were just too many of these old war victims.

Walking around the hall, absorbing the pictures and the captions, I came across the first bronze bust I had seen in any of the numerous museums visited. It was of an old woman with a heavily lined and worn face, who was said to have lost nine sons, a son-in-law and two grand-daughters during the war. It was a stark introduction to Nguyen Thi Thu, matriarch of the Hero Mothers.

I assumed her family had lived at My Lai, the village involved in the major massacre by US troops, or had been victims of the bombing of Hanoi—how else could one lose so much family? There was no-one about to tell me more about the old woman, other than that she was from Central Vietnam, near Danang, and would be very old if she was still alive.

Some of the translated captions referred to casualties of the French War. I knew the French had been defeated at the Battle of Dien Bien Phu in 1954, but had always assumed that the final battle followed a number of minor skirmishes. In the country highlands area of South Africa where I grew up the struggles of the colonial French in Vietnam were not exactly hot news; the French War had in any case been a little before my time. Thus, the display in the Hero Mothers Hall left me with a great deal of food for thought, and the bronze bust remains firmly in my mind's eye even today, eight years later.

A couple of other displays in the museum also made a great impression: maps and diagrams told of the three defeats of the Mongols by the Vietnamese, and there were accounts of major victories over the Chinese. The Viet have a very rich and proud military tradition. Something nagged at me and, as I sipped on a cool drink in the courtyard afterwards, watching coach loads of visitors arriving, it finally came together: it had taken the Mongols three attempts at invasion to realize that Vietnam was a tough conquest prospect.

The Chinese had later learnt the lesson, also at great cost. The French had left badly scratched and dishevelled. Had the powerful men in Washington been aware of this and, if so, why they had not factored this into their deliberations before they set out to do what those unfortunate invaders before them had been unable to achieve: subdue the Vietnamese? Perhaps they did not bother learning about the history of minor nations.

The Board—Army Museum, Hanoi

The Board offered a glimpse of a human aspect of the Vietnam War that had been missing from the material I had read. The bust of Nguyen Thi Thu and photographs of the old surviving Mothers reached out to me, for this was a side to the War I had never considered. These old women clearly had a great deal to tell if they were prepared to talk. They would mostly be very old and it could be a race against time to record their experiences, but I left the Museum with a very strong urge to look behind the board—perhaps I could lift it, or flip it over and see what lay underneath. In the metaphorical sense, of course.

I spent the remaining week in the north visiting beautiful places like Halong Bay and the mountain resort area of Sapa. It was strangely disturbing, for it was difficult to imagine savage, modern warfare being waged in such idyllic country although I had been assured the war was fought on practically every hectare of Vietnamese soil. All too soon, though, it was time to return to serene Perth, Australia, where I had lived for over a quarter of a century. Another visit to the Museum for a final look at the Board made me wonder if the French war had been quite as romantic as the little literature I had read about it seemed to suggest. My Beau Geste images of gallant French officers performing daily heroics started to blur.

A few months after my return to Australia, finding the Board somewhat intrusive, unable to erase the image of it from my mind, I wrote to the Vietnam Consulate for permission to meet a few Hero Mothers, perhaps even interview them. The response was crushing: permission to meet the women was denied. The tone of the letter seemed to be that the Hero Mothers were an issue for the Vietnamese people and did not require the attentions of a foreigner. I could hardly dispute that. The letter writer also advised that 31,584 of the 44,716 Hero Mothers had themselves died during the war.

The Board I had seen showed some 41,000 Hero Mothers, and was clearly either wrong or somehow out of date, although it was hard to see how the numbers could increase. I was depressed at the thought that so few of these women had survived the war, saddened that a marvellous opportunity to learn a little oral history had slipped away, but I resolved to meet them if an opportunity ever arose.

3. Success

I realised I would be unable to place what the old women might tell me in meaningful context since I knew little about the whole Vietnam picture. In order to conduct any sort of intelligent interview, I needed to do some research. There appeared to be two separate wars: the French War of 1946-1954 and the American War, as the Vietnamese call it, which followed.

Websites kept throwing up the name of a French scholar and author who had written with great authority on the French conflict and who had opposed US involvement in Vietnam: Bernard Fall. His *Street without Joy* had been required reading for US officers destined for Vietnam, and *Hell in a Small Place* is considered by many to be the definitive record of the battle of Dien Bien Phu. Both books also happen to be very good reading, and by the time I had digested them and a few other books it was time to return to Vietnam and research the country for the novel I intended to write.

During my second visit in 2002 I spent two months travelling around Vietnam and Laos, visiting old French battle sites, checking topography against Fall's maps and coming to grips with the war. The Vietnam War was emerging as one great, unlikely tale, with a certain romance interwoven with major destruction and tragedy. The idea of peasants defeating two modern foreign armies, including that of the major superpower, the most powerful military force ever assembled at that time, seemed absurd.

I visited battlegrounds from South Vietnam through the Central Highlands to North Vietnam, from the coastal plains to the borders with Laos and China. By the time I visited a remote site in Laos accessible only by speedboat I was amazed at the geographical breadth and depth of the war against the French. The peasants' military leadership had been extraordinary and warranted more research.

A further visit to the Army Museum in Hanoi led to a more detailed examination of exhibits such as household utensils used to support the revolution started by Ho Chi Minh. I had visions of young mothers raising families, feeding communist fighters, placing signal lamps around their homes at night or becoming fighters in their spare time. It all seemed a little far-fetched. Then, of course, there were the pictures of the old women. I had never seen such communicative faces.

Aspects of the French military culture were perplexing, so I travelled to Aubagne in the South of France to visit the home of the French Foreign Legion, where I began to come to grips with the history, strange culture and tradition of that force. Then I travelled on to Washington DC where I visited Dorothy Fall, widow of the historian whose accounts of the struggle against the French had inspired me.

I found a different, exciting world, and upon my return to Perth I took advantage of an early retirement option. Local libraries proved inadequate, so I ordered a pile of books on the Vietnam War, and acquainted myself with the facts of life in Indochina 1941-1975.

A year later, in 2003, rather better informed on the war, it was time to return to Vietnam for the third time on a three-month tourist visa to seek locations for my first novel, a rather complicated and unlikely tale that had not progressed much in all this time. In hindsight, I know now that I simply missed the country and its people. The information I had been digesting since my last visit caused me to view the Vietnamese of the Central Highlands and the North with a new and enormous respect.

A consignment of books had arrived from Amazon just before my departure so I took a couple with me, including *Even the Women Must Fight* by Karen Gottschang Turner with Phan Thanh Hao. On the flight over, I started reading about the experiences of Vietnamese women who supported the Communist effort during the American War and their contribution to that conflict. It was stirring stuff.

By the time I arrived in the old capital city of Hue in Central Vietnam I had resolved to meet some of the Mothers with a view to perhaps having a newspaper article published about them. The earlier denial of permission was unfortunate, but in my state of ignorance I felt this was probably a mere technicality.

The reception crew at the hotel where I had stayed on my previous two trips was surprised to see me back so soon. I boldly announced my intention to interview Hero Mothers, and the grapevine started humming as typically helpful hotel employees tried to help me find a few of the old women. They seemed a little apprehensive about my approach, but I thought we would soon settle into a comfortable work pattern.

There was deep silence for three days as my little network, as I liked to think of it, spread its tentacles. This had proved far easier than I would have dreamt possible, and a heavy scent of self-congratulation hung about Room 207 at the Thai Binh 2 Hotel in Hue. Then a telephone call cast a pall of gloom over proceedings: an official from the Vietnam Department of Foreign Affairs in Hanoi had received word of my intentions. I had violated the terms of my tourist visa, and he wished to interview me in Hanoi.

The receptionists took over the call and gave me a blow by blow translation. The trip to Hanoi would be a very good idea, they suggested.

Things then came to a grinding halt as my little network disintegrated: somebody had hacked the tentacles off my octopus with a single blow. Heading for home via the nearest airport crossed my mind but, if the authorities were displeased that would be futile. Besides, flight would mean the end of the Hero Mothers and Vietnam for all time. Deportation or being barred from visiting Vietnam in future would be a bitter blow—the place had taken a serious hold on me and I thought I was just getting the hang of things.

I flew to Hanoi where, with help from hotel employees at an establishment I had also stayed at previously, I dealt with the official from the Department of Foreign Affairs by telephone. He seemed pleased that I had arrived so quickly but communication was again a problem, so he handed me over to a lady named Trinh Tu Lan from the Foreign Press Centre, an arm of the Ministry of Foreign Affairs. Things looked up immediately, and I was pleasantly surprised to receive what seemed to me to be a sympathetic hearing as she invited me to state my case by facsimile.

Trinh Tu Lan called me in for an interview. Highly educated and articulate, she had studied for her Master's degree in Australia for two years and obviously understood the Aussie mind-set. She clarified my situation courteously but firmly, leaving no room for future misunderstandings. I should have applied for a work visa, for starters. Foreigners could not just be let loose among the ageing Hero Mothers as there had been cases of clumsy questioning in the past that had distressed some of the old women. If I were allowed to continue, a Press Officer would accompany me on my travels and would act as translator at all interviews.

Perhaps Lan accepted that I had no ulterior motives in meeting the Mothers, or perhaps she realised I was simply too inept to be a real problem. My lack of Press credentials, or the fact that I was not a journalist may have helped, but whatever the reason, three days later issue of my Press Visa was approved, as was assistance from the Press Office for the duration of the interview component of my project.

This was fabulous news, but there was a small glitch: I had arrived shortly before the commencement of the 22nd South East Asia Games (SEAGames) and the Press Office was gearing up to accommodate the requirements of several hundred foreign sports correspondents. I would receive assistance as soon as the Games were over, in mid-December, some six weeks hence, having unwittingly ended up in competition for Press Office assistance with the regional equivalent of the Olympic Games. Vietnam expected to do well and excitement around Hanoi was palpable. Everyone was far too polite to tell me I was in the way.

The next six weeks were spent building a foundation for the interviews. I bought a 1955 Minsk motorcycle and clocked up 5,000km in the countryside, visiting Dien Bien Phu in the North West before looping back via Lai Chau, Sapa and Yen Bai. There was time to describe a circle via Cao Bang and Lang Son back to Hanoi—divine, mountainous country where the fate of Colonial France was decided. A trip south followed through Vinh, a city destroyed by the United States Air Force, past Quang Tri, a city that disappeared under bombs and that is still reluctant to make an appearance. Then down through Hue, stopping in to visit the scene of the massacre at My Lai near Quang Ngai, visiting Pleiku and Dakto before returning to Hanoi via the mountain passes of the Truong Son, the mountains near the Lao border. Part of the famed Ho Chi Minh Trail passed through this region.

A slight problem arose near Pleiku when my motorcycle was confiscated and Immigration, the Army and local Police laid charges against me for unwittingly straying into a restricted area. I had tried to visit Plei Me, site of the battle immortalised in the film *We were soldiers once, and young,* not realising that the absence of roadways to the site on my map indicated the place was out of bounds. Cleverly using my ancient military skills, I gradually neared the place until a local shopkeeper agreed to take me there. I had then happily followed him into the grounds of the local military HQ where to my disgust he dobbed me in to the officer on duty. The concern seemed to be that I might provide money and other resources to help minority tribesman escape to Laos. During my unsolicited but extended guided tour of the army's garden by a young officer my Minsk was thoroughly searched. A Minsk is the most rudimentary of vehicles, being of 1930s design, and offers few concealment options for gun smuggling or other nefarious activity, but proceedings would clearly be protracted.

Everyone was polite and respectful, but I was concerned at the attitude of one young army officer who clearly believed he had a miscreant in his sights. As far as I could make out, he saw something in my eyes that demonstrated my villainy. As it turned out, his view did not prevail.

Senior officials kept arriving from Pleiku until they numbered a round dozen and the interview commenced. Language was a problem, but this was resolved when a young school teacher was found to act as interpreter. After an hour of robust questioning followed by a fair amount of banter, pots of tea and an interesting lunch, I was allowed to return to Pleiku in a military vehicle, with hearings scheduled for the next day.

I watched in dismay as a police officer rode off on my motorcycle after I had explained a few of its idiosyncrasies to him—every Minsk has a number of quirks that need to be accommodated. I drew some comfort from the spray of oil that was staining his immaculate uniform trousers.

A young tour guide with a degree in tourism heard of my plight and intercepted me en route to the hearing. I took an instant liking to him and hired him as my defence counsel. He most ably represented me the next day as charges were dropped and my Minsk was returned to me. Apparently my main defence was that I was a prominent journalist setting the scene for an important documentary. My young guide had done me proud. A grinning police officer informed me that my polite conduct had been viewed favourably. No doubt pleased to be rid of the smoking, smelly Minsk, he waved me off as I hastily continued my journey and left the province post haste.

There could have been no finer introduction to the country and the people of Vietnam. Every place I visited had a recent connection to war and yet the people were warm and friendly, always happy to enjoy a joke with an overweight, balding Westerner with a grey beard, mounted on an old Minsk. By the time I returned to Hanoi, I was ready to meet the old women.

During this period a few tourists suggested that I was allocated a Press Officer so that the government could influence my writing: it would be a sort of propaganda conspiracy with a twisted translation resulting in the publication of a Communist viewpoint. This bothered me briefly, but I dismissed such notions after the first interview. Such an exercise would have required an extraordinary amount of work and coordination at short notice—it would have been far easier for the authorities to simply deny permission for the interviews. Besides, I was not exactly an international literary figure.

The original agreement with the Press Office had been that I would select those Hero Mothers most appropriate for interviews from a list someone would compile. Calls would then be made to see if they were available and if they could travel to Hanoi for the interview. Unsaid, of course, was that the war had ended almost thirty years ago and many of the Mothers were very old. Some would have fallen into ill health and others would have passed away. I put in two special requests: I was desperate to meet Nguyen Thi Thu, the woman of the bronze bust in the Army Museum, and a Mother in Cu Chi who had clearly had a dreadful war.

The trouble was that by the time the SEAGames finished there was insufficient time for all that. The whole project was self-funded and I had already sold my house and cashed in my superannuation in order to conduct meaningful research; I could not afford delays. I wanted stories about how foreign occupation had affected the lives of the Mothers. The French had been there in the 1930s-1940s, the Japanese during World War 2, the French again when they returned to their former colony in 1945 until their defeat in 1954, and then the Americans shortly thereafter, resulting in the arrival of significant US forces in the south in 1965. I wanted to establish what all this had meant to those old women, and would happily to travel to anyone prepared to see me.

I had also suggested to Trinh Tu Lan that a female Press Officer might be more appropriate for the interviews since she might enjoy a greater empathy with the old women, helping to settle their nerves. As it turned out, mine would be the only nerves on edge but I had the courage of ignorance on my side. One evening I received an email from a Nguyen Quynh Huong, who was to be my Press Officer. A friend at reception told me the name indicated I had been allocated a female officer. Huong, he told me, was a romantic name, that of a very special flower.

Something about the email suggested to me that I would be travelling with a serious, older bureaucrat, probably of domineering demeanour. I had visions of being escorted around the country by an old, grim faced and decorated war hero, perhaps a woman who had shot down American fighter planes on weekends and tinkered with heavy artillery on Thursday nights. When we met a few days later to review our programme, I met a shy, twenty-six year old woman, obviously very keen to do the best job she could. A couple of years out of university, she was steeped in the culture and history of her country, and was intrigued at the thought of meeting Hero Mothers.

I was pleasantly surprised at her youth, but still a little wary—we probably both were at the start of our first meeting. I had expected to be allocated a tough minder, a sort of wolf in lambs' clothing, and she was a young, traditional woman who had not travelled about with a Westerner on his own. By the conclusion of the meeting we were on the same wavelength and looking forward to the journey as the project was new territory for both of us.

We would have to travel to interview the old women on their home turf, she told me, as there was insufficient time to arrange transport for them all. I was relaxed about that, so Huong called provincial authorities to track down Mothers who were prepared to receive us. I never asked her about her selection criteria, but I had expressed a preference for a little geographical variety and we ended up interviewing in six locations. I resisted the temptation to select Mothers who had lost the greatest number of family members as I wanted to interview a cross-section of women. As it turned out I met a few marvellous old Mothers who would not have been fit enough to travel, so it worked out very well in the end. There was a meeting with Huong and Lan to review the project. I would pay the Foreign Press Centre US$50 per day for Huong's services, and all her travel costs. Wherever possible I would be pleased to dine with any Mothers prepared to join us. I had become aware that some of the old women, particularly those who had lost their entire families, were doing it very tough, so I had set aside about US$100 for each woman as a gift. This information was not passed on to the Mothers, but was left to our discretion, so it was not a payment for the interview. I would have loved to be more generous, but I knew I had a long road ahead and limited resources.

Huong had a final list of eleven Hero Mothers for my approval. Two lived around Hanoi, five around Hue, two near Danang and two in the region around Saigon. To my delight, Nguyen Thi Thu, she of the bronze bust in the Museum, would see us: her health was poor, but she lived with her daughter near Danang. The other Mother I had hoped to meet had lived in Cu Chi, but had recently passed away. Mother Le Thi Gom lived in the area and had made herself available.

I happily approved all Huong's arrangements and packed for the trip as nerves set in at the prospect of meeting a matriarch aged one hundred years whose family had suffered so dreadfully at the hands of Westerners of my vintage, some of whom may have been of my nationality.

4.   The Board

A few days before our trip was due to commence, Huong arranged a meeting with Phanh Thanh Thao, the official responsible for the welfare of Hero Mothers in Hanoi. He took the time to elaborate on the whole concept of the Hero Mothers for me.

A Decision signed by President Le Duc Anh in 1994, nineteen years after the end of the war, led to the start of the Hero Mother programme in which the government made a concerted effort to address living standards of thousands of women, many of whom were at an advanced age, who had been severely disadvantaged because of their support of the Communist war effort.

Thao explained that the major prerequisite for official recognition was that each Mother had supported the war effort, and that family members had also died in active support. Those conditions satisfied, there were three ways of becoming a Hero Mother.

The loss of an only child, regardless of gender, qualified a Mother. In a society where children are treasured this reflects the high value placed by the Vietnamese on the family unit as a whole.

The loss of three immediate family members—a husband, wife or child qualified, but not siblings, parents or grandchildren. Thus a Mother who lost a husband and one child, and was herself killed whilst supporting the war, would be eligible for Hero Mother status, albeit posthumously. As previously noted, three quarters of the Hero Mothers, over 30,000 in all, were recognised posthumously.

Hero Mother status was also conferred upon a mother who lost two or more children.

There were cases where families were politically divided, and we would meet two such families during our journey; if children went to war against the wishes of their mother who did not support the Revolution, Hero Mother status would not be granted should those children die for their cause. Support might not involve direct combat. Women provided food for transient fighters, accommodation and intelligence about hostile forces. They ran messages or had their children act as messengers or guides. It is important to understand that only deaths arising from active support were recognized. The loss of, say, three children during a B52 bombing raid while attending school or playing in the village would not count towards eligibility. If such deaths had been taken into account there would be far greater numbers on the Board.

Sadly, this type of event was not as rare as one might like to think. Truong Thi Le lost nine members of her family during the My Lai massacre, but did not become a Hero Mother as a result since My Lai was a slaughter of peaceful civilians. I had assumed that Nguyen Thi Thu, the Matriarch of Mothers who lost nine sons as well as other family members, had suffered at My Lai. It seemed inconceivable that they had all died fighting. But a few weeks later I would find that that was indeed the case.

The Board covers the period commencing in 1930 when the struggle against the French can perhaps be said to have really started as the nationalist and communist movements gained momentum. During that early period, dozens of patriots were beheaded by the French after an uprising in Yen Bai, and there was brutal suppression elsewhere in the country. Ho Chi Minh's was not the only nationalist movement in Vietnam, nor was it the first. Peasants represented over ninety per cent of the population in the 1940s, and were for the most part very poor and uneducated. They had no technology to contribute, so they contributed their lives and those of members of their families.

The children who died could have been youngsters helping with the war effort, or adults fighting as soldiers. The dividing line was blurred, making it difficult to distinguish between the two, as I would discover soon enough.

The medal awarded the Mothers is a five-pointed star with red ribbon. The flag appears on the medal with the words Anh Hung, meaning Hero, and Ba Me, Mother. There are other benefits for these women including a number of means of recognition and support. They are accorded a special status within the community, which looks up to them. They address gatherings of young people who are respectful of their elders anyway, and who admire them and are pleased to listen carefully to their advice. The Hero Mothers have been added to a colourful list of those who have helped save their country during periods of crisis, and care is taken that sacrifices during war and the ghastly price of victory are not forgotten.

By the end of the French War in 1954 Vietnam had been damaged; by the end of the American war in 1973 it was wrecked. By the time the Civil War ended in 1975, the country's very fabric and structure was fractured and seriously disrupted, so there was no vast treasure chest for everyone to dig into, to somehow make things better. There can in any event be no adequate compensation for the Mothers, but a little recognition and care in their old age does make a noticeable difference to the old women, as we would see for ourselves.

Those Hero Mothers able to travel are invited to special functions where their sacrifices are honoured. There are usually prominent dignitaries in attendance, sometimes the President himself, or legendary General Giap who by 2004 was in the autumn of his years but does his best to attend.

Housing is provided for the Mothers where required. The eleven Mothers we visited had comfortable homes in pleasant areas. With one exception they were very close to where they had lived during the times of conflict, mostly within a stone's throw of their birth-places where their ancestors are buried. Ancestors are revered and they most reluctantly part company with them. A cynic might argue that perhaps I interviewed the few Mothers who had good accommodation, but I can think of no reason why Hero Mothers would be dealt with on a discriminatory basis.

In a country where the poorest peasant households in 2001 had a monthly cash income of US$3 in addition to a modest food surplus, each Mother receives a monthly grant of about US$30. She also has an outside sponsor who takes an interest in her welfare and provides extra benefits according to her needs. Gifts of US$16 are paid on each of five holiday occasions during the year, as well as other benefits. Their maternal instincts are astonishingly strong and from my observation most of the money probably goes into education or necessities for any grandchildren they may have, or may have adopted.

The authorities do not lightly confer Hero Mother status. Many women are not recognized because of difficulties in substantiating losses: family missing in action cannot be taken into account without some sort of corroborative evidence, and there are some 300,000 Missing in Action. As more records come to light the numbers on the Board will increase.

A Canadian woman I met near Vinh asked me if I was going to interview American mothers in order to deliver a sense of balance. I had not commenced the interviews at that stage but I told her that my journey was about the Board in Hanoi. I did not get the opportunity to explain to her that, as I expected the scale was hopelessly lopsided, I could not hope to obtain any sort of balance. Having met the Mothers I now know that to be the case.

No group of mothers in the US suffered losses such as the group of Hero Mothers I met. This is not intended in any way to belittle the loss of a single family member, for one is too much, but the scale of suffering bothered me throughout the journey and still disturbs me greatly. Whole generations of Jewish families perished during Hitler's holocaust. The same thing surely happened when the Huns and the Mongols swept forth on their terrible journeys of conquest, but the difference between those atrocities and what happened in Vietnam seems to me to be twofold:

Firstly, the Huns and the Mongols roamed a long time ago. We are theoretically far more civilized today. We also have far better means of gathering intelligence and much more accurate weaponry that is supposed to allow us to target with greater discrimination. Yet in Vietnam not much effort seems to have been directed at limiting "collateral damage", that lovely euphemism for civilian loss of life.

Those napalming a village in some verdant area in Vietnam seem hardly any more civilised than those barbarians who beheaded residents in some ancient European town some one or two millennia earlier. The French were of course enthusiastic beheaders of Vietnamese dissidents, thoughtfully often even sparing them the ordeal of a trial; both Western powers were at times happy to look away as a little institutionalised torture obtained desired information.

Secondly, we regard the Huns and the Mongols, as well as the Nazi regimes, as barbarians whereas France, Japan and the USA would be offended to be thus described.

Initially I had some difficulty with the Hero Mother concept. At first it seemed very Soviet, an exchange of a fistful of certificates and a medal with a red ribbon for perhaps six children and a husband. There seemed to be a suggestion that one acquired Hero status simply by losing a number of children. I wondered if the Board was a sort of palliative to prop up some lonely, devastated old women in the final years of their lives.

My misgivings were founded on ignorance, and it would not be long before a remarkable collection of old women demonstrated that emphatically.

5.   Nguyen Thi It

Two years after first sight of the Board my journey was about to commence. I worried about how best to conduct myself in the presence of those old women. Some of them might be bitter and angry, some might refuse to answer questions, and some could have accusatory villagers and relatives with them. There was bound to be the odd hostile reception. I kept my fears to myself because I suspected Huong was not as confident as she appeared.

Nguyen Thi It lived in Ha Tay Province, in a hamlet about ninety minutes from Hanoi. Huong had arranged the hire of a car and driver who knew the area intimately and it was a cool, overcast morning as we set off for this attractive region. Ho Chi Minh, father of modern Vietnam, had started his campaign for liberation in a cave at Pac Bo near the Chinese border. He had later built a weekend retreat in this most pleasant part of the province. An abundance of rivers and mountains, and an agreeable climate make Ha Tay a popular weekend destination for city dwellers. There was a bustle, an air of prosperity about the place.

Huong was armed with documentation from Hanoi that included the necessary authorization for our interview, but permission from local authorities was also required. We needed clearance from officials of the Peoples' Committee, the executive arm of the Communist government, at provincial level as well as at village level. That meant calling on officials at two locations around Ha Tay.

Little escapes the attention of the Committee, and I suspect it was they who first detected a clumsy tourist attempting to secretly interview Hero Mothers in Hue. In spite of this, throughout the journey the officials we met were helpful and cheerful once bona fides were established, and they seemed to care for and about the old women. There was plenty of mutual respect in evidence during the interviews, perhaps because most of the officials were war veterans themselves, and had almost certainly suffered their own bereavement. They often sat in on the interviews, assisted with their detailed knowledge of the Mothers' files, and displayed endless patience in assisting with the occasional communication glitch.

On this first visit we sipped tea with two officials while Huong explained to them the purpose of my trip. I had no command of their language, so she explained that I had visited French battle sites during previous visits to learn about the war, and that I had conducted considerable research into the war. The atmosphere gradually became relaxed, and my confidence in Huong grew in leaps and bounds. After many cups of tea the officials supplied a little documentation and we proceeded to the premises of the village Committee some twenty minutes away. There, the tea ritual was repeated before two officials accompanied us to the house the Peoples' Committee had built for Mother It due to her impoverished state.

Of brick construction, plastered and painted pale blue, the house had a tiled roof, with shutter doors and windows, and seemed comfortable enough although a little maintenance was overdue. As we approached the house, a middle-aged man met us in the hard earth courtyard, and, once we had discarded our shoes as peasant custom demands, ushered us into the main room. This room had a wooden bed in the far corner, with a thin bamboo rollup mattress, and as is usual in homes in Vietnam, the family shrine occupied pride of place. The old woman was out, but as we took our seats somebody set off to fetch her. We indulged in a little small talk, and established that the man who had met us was a distant relative, although we could not determine the exact relationship.

We learnt that the old woman lived on her own, with the relative and his family for neighbours. He and his wife looked after her with a little help from the hamlet—we were to find that Hero Mothers at times seemed to be community property. After a few anxious minutes, there was movement outside and someone helped Nguyen Thi It into the lounge area.

Our first Hero Mother was something of a shock to the system. Very small in stature, she presented a wraith-like figure. I estimated her body weight at about thirty kilograms. Slightly stooped, a little hunched up with age and wear, she stood about 1.5 metres tall. She wore narrow black trousers that nevertheless seemed unfilled, and a white satiny top from beneath which could be seen a couple of layers of other garments, for it was considered quite chilly in late December. The old woman also wore a warm wrap that she later discarded, and a green and black woven scarf tied in jaunty fashion around her head that gave the impression of an impish but ancient elf.

Nguyen Thi It

She appeared a little confused as to the purpose of the meeting and it finally dawned on me that she was unusually old. She had a way of peering up at people—a sort of myopic squint—that looked a little odd. I was seldom able to see eyes that sometimes seemed veiled.

Huong ran through what became our standard introduction, explaining that I had lived in South Africa until I moved to Australia with my young family in 1974, by which time all Australian troops had left Vietnam. She also told everyone I had visited Vietnam for the first time in 2001. This served to break the ice a little, and also satisfied the curiosity of the women about me, for most of them had never dealt with a Westerner before. She also explained that I was not a Vietnam

Veteran, although I doubt that would have bothered any of them. Huong then explained my interest in Hero Mothers and my resolve to find out more about what had happened to them, as well as my hope of producing something that would be published so that Westerners could learn a little more of the effects of the war. That seemed to meet with the old woman's approval.

My eyes roamed around the room. Cement floor and walls, simple and sparse furnishings. The Vietnamese are sensitive to cold, so the total lack of floor furnishings always puzzled me. The temperature was comfortable but I somehow felt no warmth in the room. It was as though nobody really lived there—there was a feeling of bleakness in that house I never shook off.

When an official indicated that the old woman was ready, the interview commenced, with me asking questions through Huong. A small digital recorder invariably allowed me to focus my attention on the faces of the Mothers. They were mobile faces, sometimes deeply lined, always fascinating.

"Would you please tell me how old you are, Ma?" It may have been stage fright—I had forgotten my manners already. I had been taught at an early age never to ask an elderly woman her age, but my childhood training in tiny Clocolan in the highlands of South Africa had not prepared me for this situation. It took a little discussion before she spoke to Huong.

"110."

"Could we have that again, please? 110?"

"Yes." There was nodding from the locals present, who had known her for a long time.

Having a birth date to work with, I was able to start some gentle probing. Ma had a hearing impairment, but one of the officials had developed a method whereby he spoke very loudly about two feet from her ear, at an elevation and angle that obviously carried his voice to her clearly. That was how some of the story of Ma It emerged. It was nowhere near as complete as I had hoped for but she had suffered greatly, so I was grateful for what she told me.

She was born in nearby Thai Binh Province, and had two brothers and a sister, which made for an unusually small family for peasants in those days. Her parents were poor, and worked on farms in the district. She had to contribute to the family income, as was a daughter's duty, and did not attend school. When she was fifteen years old she travelled to Dong Nai to work on a rubber plantation.

There was a little murmuring from the officials, so I hauled out my map. With a little help from Huong, I saw that Dong Nai Province was close to Saigon in the far South. Almost a century ago, she had travelled perhaps twelve hundred kilometres, nearly the length of the country, as a teenager to find work to help her family, and had found it in an infamous industry.

Her story about her years working in the rubber plantation reminded me of something I had read about conditions in those plantations.

The recruiters employed assistants known as contracting foremen who obtained signatures on the contracts, often tricking the illiterate peasants into signing documents they did not understand.

Contract violations commenced almost immediately after signature, even as they were awaiting transport to the south. Small personal allowances due under the contract were reduced; food was often about half the amount promised. This occurred at ports like Haiphong where they were assembled prior to departure. They were shipped to Saigon in cramped conditions, and upon arrival were treated like cattle. From there they were transported north to the plantations.

They were assembled into groups of ten to work under a Vietnamese foreman, who reported to an overseer, usually half French. I came across an extract of a study by Tran Thu Binh, details of which I could not find for accreditation purposes but which bore out snatches of others' experiences. Binh wrote of conditions on a Michelin plantation, where an intimidatory beating would be administered on the first workday. This was to instil a sense of hopelessness in each worker, and was repeated regularly. Morning roll call would often be handled by a blow to the head during the head count. The regime was brutal due to efforts to dominate the workers from the outset, and the death toll from beatings was substantial.

Brutality was only one of a number of hazards the workers faced. Others included malarial mosquitoes, ox flies and a nasty variety of army ant. Dysentery was a problem due to poor diet and drinking water that was not boiled.

Women had a particularly bad time. They were regarded as being available to everybody from the chief overseer down to the Vietnamese foremen. It would be a matter of weeks before a remotely attractive new female arrival would be reduced both physically and mentally. On occasions medical personnel sexually abused those reporting for medical treatment, and there were accounts of bestial managers. Women workers who fell pregnant would return to work two months after giving birth. I had heard about cages in Saigon factories where children were required to be kept while parents worked and I wondered if that was how Ma It's first two children grew up.

Plantations had their own security staff and could also call on the military and gendarmes for assistance. In addition, they offered a bounty to the tough mountain people of the area, the montagnard, for any escapee captured, dead or alive. That sometimes led to severed heads being produced to support a claim for payment, a procedure that probably kept escape attempts at an acceptable level from the plantation manager's perspective.

According to Tran Thu Binh, a group of seven escapees were recaptured, and beaten to the extent of having soldiers tramp on their ribs. Binh heard their ribs snapping. Afterwards, they were locked in a darkened building with their legs in shackles. After a week, another worker was due to be incarcerated and it was only then realized that they had forgotten about the seven men, who had died in their shackles. The brutality of the Vietnamese toward their own surprised me, but this tendency was utilized by both the French and the Americans.

Based on confidential reports that colonial administrators forwarded to Paris, seventeen per cent of workers at Phu Rieng plantation died in 1927. Inspectors were well briefed by workers, but their tours seldom resulted in changes to conditions. Sometimes they used information gained from their inspections to extort money from the plantations.

Vietnamese and French/Vietnamese who dealt harshly with their own people filled lower level supervisory positions while at the higher levels were Western managers who were aware of these conditions. Then, of course, the colonial authorities would also have been familiar with plantation practices. It was brutal territory for a fifteen-year-old peasant girl from the far north.

I had found, as I travelled about on my Minsk, that even today many villagers' lives revolve around their hamlets and perhaps a few nearby villages as travel is not easy for them, but this old woman had in her vulnerable youth undertaken an extraordinary and dangerous journey.

"How did you travel to Dong Nai?" I asked her.

"By boat. With other recruits."

"How were you treated during the journey?"

"It was all right, but we were treated roughly when we arrived in Saigon. Then they took us to the plantation by truck."

"Please tell me about life on the plantation".

"Life was hard, but I fell in love at the plantation, with Nguyen Van Dien, and we married. I became pregnant, but continued work for a further seven months."

"Who cared for your baby while you were at work?"

She could not remember and was vague about how she raised her daughter, for rubber plantations are not healthy places for babies and there were no child-care facilities available. I realised later that this had happened almost a century before, many family tragedies ago.

Her first child was a daughter. Her oldest son, Nguyen Nhac, was also born at the plantation. They eventually returned to their northern homelands, where they bought a small boat. She and her daughter My ferried people across the Da River to earn some money. In time she had three more sons, Nguyen Chuong, Nguyen Khanh and Nguyen Nien. Her husband Dien tended a small farm to support his family.

"There were many French in this area, and during the 1940s the Japanese were in charge. Did this cause you any hardship?" I asked.

"Life was tolerable, but we resented having so many French here. When Ho Chi Minh started his revolution, we supported him."

Suddenly there was a lot of discussion and I left it to Huong to work through what was being said, as the officials and the relative all joined in. Huong turned to me.

"In the early 1940s, Mother It lost her sons," she told me.

We had reached this point effortlessly—things had seemed to be looking up for Ma and her family and I thought we were proceeding to the American war. There was a rather loud silence as Huong and I digested this news.

"All of them?" I asked her. She turned to the old woman, and there was more discussion.

"Yes."

"How did they die?" I asked.

There was a good deal of talking, but the exact cause of the tragedy seemed elusive. It had something to do with a problem with food during the Japanese occupation. They had either starved or eaten contaminated food.

We had no idea where to go from there, but Ma confirmed that she lost all four of her sons in one year. The oldest was in his early twenties, and they all lived at home, as they were still single. By the time the Japanese left in 1945 Ma's daughter was the sole survivor of her five children.

Producing a son is a major wifely duty in Vietnam, Ma told us, and so she was desperate to be a good wife despite her age. She finally produced yet another son in 1946 at the age of fifty-three years.

"I produced a son when I was sixty years old," she told me, clearly proud of this extraordinary feat. There was a chronological problem that I was not inclined to probe, for we had a discrepancy of seven years that was of no particular importance. She looked tired, and I was suddenly conscious of her age; I was loath to subject her to close questioning, but there was this nagging feeling that her story was not yet complete. The absence of children in the household was ominous—her son should have been living with her.

"Then," she told us, "the Americans came to Vietnam." Under normal conditions, only sons were exempted from military service, and under the circumstances her sole surviving son was regarded as an only son. However, the late 1960s were the most brutal years of the war, and the war machine had developed an enormous appetite. Families had to dig deeper still to help win the fight. The family discussed the situation and her remaining son went to war.

Her baby of 1946 was killed in the south in 1968. That was the year of enormous slaughter at Khe Sanh, and huge losses during the Tet Offensive, the worst year of the war for both sides, but Ma It could not remember details of his death. Nonplussed at the tragedy in her life I desperately cast around for a silver lining.

"Could we talk about your daughter?" I asked her.

"She died of illness," she replied.

"She is a Hero Mother too," offered one of the officials.

Ma It's one surviving child from a brood of six was Hero Mother Nguyen Thi Luong. The price she paid for admission to the Club? A husband and one son. In order for her to be a Hero Mother, it had to be her only son, so I had no need to ask the question. The Japanese occupation and the French and American wars had cost Ma all her sons, her only grandson and her only son-in-law.

Confronted with all this tragedy, I asked a couple of questions about her siblings. One brother had died as a civilian bombing casualty during the French period at Tay Binh. The other brother was killed in action as a Youth Volunteer in a battle against the French.

It was getting to the stage where I was loath to ask a question for fear of the answer. I would grow tougher as the journey continued but at that point I could think of nothing else to ask. Ma It was getting tired and communication was becoming difficult. Even the official with the knack of speaking to her was growing restless. I interpreted that as an indication we should conclude the interview.

She held up her hands.

"This is all I have. Two hands. I would like to die," she told me. We found out from the others present that her husband died of natural causes at seventy-nine, and her daughter had died some years before, so it was no surprise that Ma was weary and unhappy. It seemed best to leave rather than distress her any further.

I thanked her for being prepared to see me, and for sharing precious memories of her life.

"Could I please take a few photographs of you?" I asked.

It was when she shuffled outside that I really noticed the gnarled hands and feet. I should have expected that a woman of 110 years of age would be worn after probably a century of hard work and a great deal of suffering. I told her she was the only person I had ever met who had lived in three centuries but it did not seem to impress her much. She gave up milestones in the 1940s, I think, when she probably died.

When we stepped outside, she immediately reached for her home-made broom. I noticed she had another on standby, leaning against a wall. She started sweeping the little courtyard in front of her home, although it seemed immaculate to me. The officials told us that the old woman sweeps a lot nowadays. When her forecourt has been swept to her satisfaction, she moves about her hamlet to lend a hand to neighbours whose yards are not as tidy.

We thanked the family for their time, and Huong handed our gift to the male relative. I always left the matter of the parting gift to Huong. She would size up the financial position of the household and advise me as to what she felt would be an appropriate gesture. She felt that money would help Mother It and her family, so an envelope changed hands as we left.

My farewell felt inadequate, so I strode up to her and delivered a light peck to her forehead. This surprised her, as it did me, for I am not addicted to kissing ancient, strange women, but the Hero Mothers rapidly monopolised a special spot in my heart, and this became my standard farewell for the rest of the trip. Huong told me that my gesture would not be considered offensive, and on occasions, it provided considerable amusement, as well as what sounded suspiciously like earthy commentary.

I took several photographs. As far as she was concerned, all the fussing was over and she had to work, so I did the best I could. Interfering with her work routine would probably upset her, so the pictures were mostly action ones of Ma It and her broom. We bade the family farewell, but as we made to return to our car, I turned around for a final wave to this diminutive figure. She had her head down, sweeping imaginary leaves from the courtyard.

After we had dropped off the officials, Huong and I, both saddened at her expressed death-wish, had a good talk about what we had been told. We felt the old woman's body just would not stop functioning, but that she will be pleased when it does. She was clearly anxious to be with her family once again.

I calculated later that at age 110 years she should have been surrounded by her seven children, around thirty grand-children and perhaps a hundred great grand-children. She probably would have expected rather more. Tet, the Lunar New year, is the most important festival of the year and was one month away at the time of our visit. It is a time for families to be together and she would under normal circumstances have expected her home to be overcrowded with rowdy family. Her reality is that she has nobody, and even with my limited knowledge of Vietnamese society I could feel her desolation.

The cost of foreign occupation of her country was an empty house and a lonely existence where there should have been laughter and love. In statistical terms, she lost two brothers to the French, four sons to the Japanese starvation, and her surviving son, only grandson and son-in-law to the US war. No wonder the house felt empty and cold, or that maintenance had been somewhat neglected.

Back in my hotel room, I reviewed my notes and seriously considered quitting. It occurred to me that I might not be equipped to handle the sort of stories I was likely to be told. In the end, though, I decided that the authorities had not only given me special dispensation to make the journey, but had helped me undertake it. Huong had worked hard to come up with a workable programme and the Mothers had made themselves available for interview; it would be rude to give up.

The interview had gone well, I thought. Huong's organization had been first class and she had dealt very competently with all officials and relatives. Most importantly, Ma It had not been intimidated in the slightest by a strange Westerner.

In August 2004, I returned to Vietnam with a first draft of this book, and a few follow up questions to be posed. I had learned a good deal more about Vietnamese ways and one question involved Ma It. Normally a son would live with his mother in her old age to care for her and I wondered who the man we had met was. He had apparently lived in the house next door. Could he be a son she had not wanted to mention for some reason? I realise now I was hoping to find that she had another son, or had perhaps adopted one, as sometimes happened during or after the war. We made our way to her home, accompanied once again by Pham Tieu Long and Tran Quang Hao.

To our surprise and delight, Ma It was lively and looking good. She had been expecting us, and was bareheaded and casually dressed. Sporting a very short haircut, practically a crew cut, she seemed pleased to see us, and was ready for some lively conversation. It was an extremely hot day, and Huong felt the weather had perked the old woman up. We got into the green tea and small talk immediately.

"Ma, you are looking much younger than the last time we met, a year ago," I told her. She smiled, nodding enthusiastically.

"I think that if I return in five years' time I will be an old man, and I will find you playing football outside with the children," I suggested, and she laughed and nodded her agreement.

It was some time before she ran out of chatter sufficiently for me to raise my question: who was the family that lived next to her, that cared for her?

That brought forth a typically unlikely but true Viet story. Having lost all his sons in the mid-1940s, Ma It's husband sought replacements.

This was her responsibility, but she feared she was too old to oblige. She had suggested to him that he take another wife who might bear him sons. He had followed her advice and this new union had borne fruit. A son, Nguyen Vanh Trinh had resulted. In the meantime, Ma It had of course borne him the son they had hoped for.

The identity of the couple who lived next to the old woman was revealed: Mother It was living with Trinh, the son of her husband's second wife, and his family. Her husband's second wife has since died, so she does indeed live with family, even if it is not hers in the strictest sense. Huong and I wondered why she had not told us about Trinh during our first interview. Perhaps she had been embarrassed about her perceived failure after the death of her four sons to replace them at a ripe old age. Custom and tradition had set the old woman amazingly high standards which she had strained to achieve.

Conversation gently drifted back towards the four sons she had lost. I was trying to establish why all her sons were still living at home at the time of their deaths, surely an unusual circumstance, since at least one was in his twenties, when talk suddenly became quite animated between her and Huong. It transpired that they had died of disease, and not starvation, but we could not establish the cause of death other than that it had to do with the critical food shortage. Some time later I was to learn from Professor Le Van Lan, a historian with expert knowledge of that crisis who features later in this book, that cholera may have claimed the young men.

This time, as we prepared to leave, Huong produced a variety of foodstuffs suitable for a very senior citizen. A large, soft biscuit was extracted from a box and was eagerly sampled. There were sounds of approval as she gummed it with obvious relish, although she needed a glass of water afterwards to smooth the digestive process. The biscuit had perhaps been too tasty. The rest would be placed on the shrine as an offering to the ancestors, to be consumed after a decent interval, but it seemed to me that the ancestors would have to be quick to claim their rightful share. They would no doubt understand if proportions were imperfect on this occasion.

Huong produced a black silk scarf that immediately met with approval, and a thick jersey to help deal with the approaching winter. Ma posed for a few pictures, but these were not action shots. She did not need her broom this time—I had looked for it as we arrived, but it was missing. Firewood bundling seemed to be her current activity, for there were immaculate, tied bundles stacked in a corner of the yard, with loose piles awaiting attention by the front gate.

She told us again that she has lived for too long, that it was time she died. This time I got the impression that she was just afraid of running out of chores. The place seemed brighter, happier, but that may have been in my mind.

We had lunch with our official friends near a war memorial where I paid my respects. It was just the usual village memorial, commemorating the dead from the struggle against France, the USA, Cambodia and China, with dates ranging from 1930 to 1977, as far as I could see. There was provision for later additions—they do not take peace for granted in those parts.

6. Starvation

I realized after meeting Mother It that I needed to fill in some huge gaps in my knowledge of Vietnam, particularly in relation to the Japanese occupation. Huong set about finding an historian of impeccable credentials who could provide further information about this disaster, and came up with a delightful character who fitted the requirements perfectly.

Professor Le Van Lan, an eminent but very busy Hanoi Professor of History, kindly agreed to meet me at the Press Office. He was at that time deeply involved in an archaeological discovery of some significance in the Citadel in Hanoi. An 18th century site had been further excavated, revealing remains of buildings about seven centuries older that had his full attention, but he was able to spare me an hour before rejoining a student group from Minnesota.

The Press Office had closed for lunch when I arrived, and I was tearing around the place looking for assistance when I nearly collided with a Vietnamese of unusual appearance. A short man of medium build, he had relatively long hair, quite unkempt by local standards, and wore thick black-rimmed glasses. A crumpled, tweedy old black jacket had that disreputable look that favourite garments of academics sometimes acquire, and jeans with generous turn-ups completed the ensemble. His dress, together with a myopic way of looking at me, completed a picture of a warm, friendly and eccentric man; he reminded me of Peter Falk in the Columbo television series.

Since the main offices were locked, the security personnel in the gatehouse graciously cleared space for us in their room. Lan was quite happy for the interview to commence there and I was greatly impressed when the television set was turned off while a local major football match was in progress. This was a tribute to the presence of the Professor, I think, but within minutes someone arrived to let us into a meeting room and football viewing was restored in the gatehouse, to the relief of all present.

Lan told me Vietnam had a population of about 20,000,000 in 1943-45 during the Japanese occupation, some 6,000,000 to 7,000,000 of whom lived in the Red River delta, the area hardest hit by the starvation process. As about 95 per cent of the population were peasants they were heavily reliant on the food crops they grew. There was a main rice harvest in May of each year, and another in October.

The Japanese military decreed that rice be replaced in some areas with other crops useful to the military, such as jute. It was a death warrant for the normally self-sufficient peasants. Many were forcibly changed from producers of rice to buyers, in an inflated market. Worse was yet to come.

The Japanese then ruled that certain taxes were to be paid in rice. Although they had demanded significant volumes of crop substitution, they were nevertheless hoarders of rice for distribution throughout their Asian territories. The French were hoarders also, so the peasants were trapped between two major powers with voracious appetites for the reduced rice crop. Many former rice farmers now had to buy rice to pay their taxes, but at vastly inflated prices: rice was a very scarce commodity. Then the Japanese started using rice as fuel for some trains, instead of coal.

"Are you suggesting this was intentional?" I asked the professor.

He nodded.

"Yes. This was a way of eroding Ho's support base. South Vietnam did not suffer as much as the north, where some provinces such as Tay Binh lost half their population."

He has vivid memories of what happened, for he was a child in Hanoi at the time. The peasants walked from even the distant provinces to Hanoi in search of food. In reality, they came to die. They would congregate in a particular part of the city where those able to help might visit. His family had sufficient food, and was anxious to assist those in need. He remembers his mother rolling rice into small balls that he would carry, since he was a child and therefore less conspicuous and less likely to be attacked for the precious cargo he carried.

They would walk about, looking for signs of life among the starving. At a signal from his mother, he would drop to his knees and feed a rice ball to someone in need.

"We probably saved nobody, and perhaps we only prolonged suffering by a day or two, but we had to try," he said to me.

He remembers emaciated figures lying in the streets, and wooden carts being hand pushed around in search of bodies to be buried. He could see that some of those loaded on the carts were not yet dead but during that terrible period it made little difference. By the time they reached the burial point they would have expired.

"How do you Vietnamese cope with these disasters? You have visited Japan, you have lectured there. How do you deal with that, having seen what was done here?" I asked.

He smiled.

"We say there are two ways of looking at such things. You can feel it with a heavy heart or a light heart. We choose the light heart. We have a word for it—nhe da." I would learn as the journey progressed that the Vietnamese have their own methods of coping with disaster; perhaps a tough history over the past couple of millennia equipped them particularly well.

"It seems strange that a civilised nation such as France, with its proud history of pursuing freedom and civil rights, could behave so abominably in Vietnam," I said to him, thinking of the torture, executions without trial, public beheadings, beatings, rape and common thuggery, among other aspects of appalling behaviour I had heard and read about.

This brought forth another smile, although it seemed a little tight this time.

"In those days there were two Frances: Civilised France and Colonial France. We got Colonial France." That was the end of that; there was no ranting and raving. I had not yet learnt that while the Vietnamese have a very keen sense of history, they have this remarkable ability to put much of the tragic aspects of their own history behind them as they look forward. Perhaps, I thought, one of the benefits of being an old civilisation is that experience and scholarship helps you find simple explanations for complex issues; Hanoi's first university was established a thousand years ago. As I was digesting all this, he related another childhood memory.

"My family moved from Hanoi into the country during World War 2. I would sometimes accompany an adult on a weekly forty-five kilometre bicycle trip to Hanoi to purchase twenty kilograms of rice and some cooking oil. At that time, the United States was attacking Japanese targets throughout Vietnam." (Japan occupied China at that time. Vichy France had surrendered to Germany, so technically France and Japan were allied. The Japanese were happy for the French to continue administering Indochina for them, but it meant the Americans sometimes targeted Japanese assets in Vietnam). "As we approached an anti-aircraft position, American aircraft arrived to attack. I was a little slow in dismounting from my bicycle to seek cover and I still carry a small piece of shrapnel in my bottom," he laughed.

"Is the shrapnel American, French, Japanese or Vietnamese?" I asked him.

"I don't know," he said with a smile.

"Does it cause you problems when you travel? With metal detectors at airports, for instance?"

"No," he replied, grinning broadly.

It was time for the Professor to return to his students. I wished him good fortune with his archaeological project—he hopes to persuade the military to part with a sizeable chunk of real estate, which will take some doing. All the same, my money is on the academic.

Back in Perth between visits, I had scoured the library shelves for anything I could find on Vietnam, and Amazon was profiting handsomely from my research. A J Stor file [4] was most helpful I providing an insight into the starvation. The number of lives lost varies—there were not the facilities and resources for accurately recording the numbers of dead. Admiral Jean Decoux, the collaborationist Governor General of French Indochina until 9 March 1945, when the Japanese took over directly, is quoted as being in no doubt that one million Tonkinese (from the most northerly region of Vietnam) starved to death during the winter of 1944-5 alone.

Peasants would die by the side of a track leading to their destination, to be buried later by someone with priorities other than statistical precision. The usual amnesia that the Japanese experience when it comes to war crimes set in and they are reluctant to acknowledge what happened. Other descriptions of the disaster match what Professor Lan had told me. Stanley Karnow quotes Tran Duy Hung, Mayor of Hanoi at the time[5]:

"Peasants came in from nearby provinces on foot, leaning on each other, carrying their children in baskets. They dug in garbage piles, looking for anything at all, banana skins, orange peels, and discarded greens. The even ate rats. But they couldn't get enough food to keep alive. They tried to beg, but everyone else was hungry and they would drop dead in the streets. Every morning, when I opened my door, I found five or six corpses on the step. We organised teams of youths to load the bodies on oxcarts and take them to mass graves outside the city. It was terrifying—and yet it helped our cause because we were able to rally the nation."

There was no single reason for this starvation. Other possible causes such as changed weather conditions had happened before, without mass starvation resulting. Clearly, a little care about the welfare of the peasants could have helped avert a major tragedy.

The remarkable aspect of this suffering is that, as World War 2 ended, even after suffering such calamitous casualties, the peasants in the north supported Ho Chi Minh as they did. That they did so is not surprising—the indifference to their welfare on the part of the French, followed by the inhumanity of the Japanese probably ensured their support—but the extent of their support, commencing within a year of such a disaster must have been a shock to the French.

The starvation may have been the proverbial last straw, the one that would motivate them to fight for another thirty years to rid their country of foreigners.

7. Pham Thi Tuyet

The day after our first meeting with Ma It we set off to visit Mother Tuyet, who lives in an inner Hanoi suburb. Huong and I caught a taxi to the local offices of the Peoples' Committee, where officials scrutinized and approved our documentation and two officials responsible for Veterans' Affairs and Hero Mothers accompanied us to our interview.

While waiting for one particular approval, Phan Thanh Thao, the official who explained the criteria for Hero Mothers to me, surprised me by twisting his left arm behind his back and then up and over until his hand was resting on his left shoulder. Seeing my astonishment, he smiled and waved in a self-deprecating manner. He was wounded on the last day of the war, during the final hours as the Presidential Palace in Saigon was being taken. He seemed quite impressed with the replacement limb they had given him.

His wound was no big deal, he said; he had many friends who were less fortunate. Thao reminded me of the Monty Python Knight, who referred to the progressive loss of limbs during a sword fight as mere flesh wounds. The art of understatement was surely born in this country. The trouble with this tendency is that it is very easy for an outsider, or indeed the younger generation to forget just how bad things were.

Thao was cheerful and outgoing, and, although I was keen to learn if his new left arm performed any functions other than the party trick he had shown me, I decided not to ask for fear that he might unscrew it and hand it to me.

With our paperwork and permissions all in order, we travelled to a nearby suburb. We soon found ourselves walking up a narrow laneway past a few apartments, with Thao acting as navigator. He stopped and knocked on the last door on the ground floor. There was a brief conversation through an open window, and we waited until a face peered through at us. With our identification established, the front door opened, so we removed our shoes and entered the home.

A pleasant, elegant and diminutive woman smiled a welcome and showed us to small, low plastic chairs in the main room. It served as her bedroom, lounge, dining room and general living area, with a small kitchen off to the side. There was an upstairs room as well, for I saw her cat literally fly up the stairs to escape the large gathering. Her private space was probably up there.

She was a lively and articulate woman of solid build, immaculately dressed in slacks, covered by a light grey cardigan, with a black short-sleeved waistcoat over that. With her silver hair wrapped in a bun, this stylish woman looked much younger than her years.

The walls held numerous paintings and a few photographs in addition to a number of certificates. One was her Hero Mother citation, another testified to the bravery of her only son, and several paintings on the wall were by her late husband, a celebrated artist. A compact shrine occupied a prominent position in the room, with incense sticks alongside photographs of departed family members.

She poured tea as Huong completed introductions. The officials were old friends and there was chatter and laughter before we settled into the interview. The old woman really took a liking to Huong, so the interview was relaxed throughout. Ma Tuyet asked if I liked the tea, and I learned it was her own blend of lotus tea.

"Please tell me a little about your early life," I asked her.

"I was born in Hai Duong Province in 1920. I was the fourth child in our family, and I had two brothers and three sisters. My parents were farmers and we were quite poor."

"Did you have any school education?"

"No. I had to help in the house, but my brothers received a little education."

"How did you meet your husband?"

"When I was nineteen, I went to Hanoi to visit my aunty. My brother was visiting her also, and that was how I met his best friend, Luu Van Sin. He was an artist, ten years older than me."

"Was it love at first sight?"

She laughed.

"We married within six months."

She crept over the very low bed to fetch some news clippings about Sin and laid them out on the bed, sitting cross-legged behind them as she sorted them into some sort of order. There were a lot of clippings. She was now very low down and we could not hear her very well, so I crept onto the low bed and sat opposite her, lotus fashion. To the surprise of the officials, that was how the interview proceeded, and it worked well.

Pham Thi Tuyet

Luu Van Sin was indeed a very handsome man. A drawing on the wall, done by some former pupils when he was seventy-three years old, clearly showed a surprisingly young man who looked remarkably like a young Battle of Britain pilot, given the bomber-style jacket he was wearing, and the scarf around his neck. That required a short discourse of that battle, on my part. She knew a great deal about bombing raids, as I would find out soon enough.

"You did well to marry him before someone else did," I said. She smiled, and nodded.

"He was a fine artist, and also a very good dancer. I could not dance, but he loved it so I was happy for him to go to the discotheque alone. I trusted him."

"Did you ever go to the discotheque with him?"

"Yes, I tried it, but somebody asked me for a dance and I did not enjoy that. I was also happy to let him visit the romantic city of Hue on his own sometimes where he could spend time on the river and meet his artistic friends." Theirs must have been an unconventional marriage within that country, at that time.

They seemed a most unlikely match, but the uneducated peasant girl and her suave, sophisticated and urbane artist and dancer had lived the good life largely undisturbed by the French or Japanese occupation. They enjoyed a comfortable lifestyle and were in great demand socially. They must have been an elegant couple. Life was by no means easy, but they had enough money to manage even during the food shortages caused by the Japanese.

Their only child, a son named Luu Tat Dat, was born in 1940. They moved from Hanoi to the country, with workers carrying Dat. I did not query why workers carried the youngster, but guessed that an artist could not be expected to be thus burdened. Dat was concealed for safety reasons, probably because the territory was quite lawless at that time.

The French did not always treat women well, so Ma Tuyet tried unsuccessfully to buy a gun. Fortunately, she never needed it. This all happened towards the end of the good times in Vietnam, if one could call wartime occupation under the Japanese good times. But they probably felt like good times in comparison with the thirty years of war that commenced soon after the occupation.

"Did you have difficulties with the French after you moved to the country?"

"We were bombed by French aircraft in our temporary home in Tay Binh Province in 1946. My son never forgot the traumas of his early childhood and became a revolutionary at a very young age. My family decided to support Ho Chi Minh's revolution because of the hardships the French caused so many people. I was in Hanoi in September 1945, when Ho declared Vietnam independent."

Ma Tuyet's family had moved to the province worst hit by the starvation: Professor Lan had told us Thai Binh lost half its population.

In typical northern fashion, since the family supported the Revolution, both her brothers joined the army. They survived the war.

It emerged that her husband was something of a free spirit. The money from his paintings seemed to finance mainly his excursions to Hue, visits to the discotheque and tea for the family. Tradition places most family responsibilities on the shoulders of the mother so it is up to every Vietnamese wife to supplement the family income. Ma Tuyet was not found wanting in that respect.

"In 1950 I became the only northern businesswoman to use a motor vehicle," she told me; "I purchased a Tecracin, and employed Mr Binh as driver."

A Tecracin was apparently a small van of French manufacture.

"With this car I could travel to the country to buy goods to resell in Hanoi. I remember Mr Binh was a Christian and a good driver."

"Was it not dangerous at that time, Ma? There was a civil war in progress, with French and Vietminh soldiers killing each other."

"It was a bit dangerous as the French were everywhere. Once a car travelling behind us was hit by a bomb, but I was lucky. Sometimes we came upon casualties from bombs and land mines."

"Did the Vietminh ever stop you, perhaps to ask you for money, or to carry things, to smuggle guns or something?"

"No. The Vietminh were afraid in those days. They would come out only at night and I would travel only by day." Bernard Fall had described Vietminh night attacks on isolated two-man blockhouses manned by Vietnamese recruits. Soldiers could often hear their neighbours being over-run but were unable to assist. The French would clean up the mess the next day and bring in fresh crews to await their death.

I did a quick calculation, and realised that she had probably been in business just before the Vietminh began to enjoy success along the northern border with China, where within a few years they decimated French forces along Colonial Route 4. Those victories signalled the beginning of the end for French colonialism in Indochina, and, indeed, in North Africa as Algerians who fought for France in Indochina realised the French could be beaten in battle. Upon their return to their homeland, many Algerians joined nationalist forces to fight against France.

"I hope these trips were profitable for you, since they were so dangerous."

"I did very well with business in textiles, paint for wood and lotus tea. I bought this land in Hanoi with the proceeds and we built our house on it in 1951. I sold the van in 1952 and Mr Binh retired."

It seemed strange that her husband would stay home while she undertook such activities in the family interest. I got the impression that, as well as leaving business to her, her husband was also content to leave matters of family security and defence in her capable hands. I think he was a bohemian, probably not particularly gifted as regards practical matters. We got up to look at the paintings on the wall.

She told me that because of his love for her, he painted other women only in ethnic dress. It seems he steered away from nudes. He also liked to paint the highlands around Hanoi. She proudly showed me a thick, glossy book. There in *Painters of the Fine Arts College of Vietnam* were two pictures by Sin. The picture of a young woman in ethnic dress walking by a pond was particularly impressive.

Ma Tuyet then showed me a newspaper article about the set of five postage stamps her husband had been commissioned to design in 1964. The finely drawn fruits were not chosen at random: two were fruits exclusive to the north, two to the south, and one was common to both regions. The underlying message was clear: the North expressed hopes of a united Vietnam. One of his paintings on the wall was of a young woman releasing a white dove carrying a message. This symbolized sending a message of peace to the south.

I saw a photo of guests present at the ninetieth birthday of General Giap, the military legend who had so emphatically disproved any notions about the invincibility of Western powers. It was Giap who led the Vietnamese to victory over the French in 1944-1954, and who then successfully dealt with the Americans who followed. He is regarded by some military historians as the greatest living expert on revolutionary warfare. It was no surprise to see Ma Tuyet seated immediately on his right.

"My family disapproved of the divided Vietnam. It was one country, and the north did not need an aggressive southern neighbour. The US supported Diem in the south, trying to divide the people, and the north risked being overpowered. The south could not be allowed to become another Taipei. There was only a river to be crossed, so when Ho Chi Minh called for fighters another decision was made."

The river in question was the Ben Hai, which was once the demarcation line between North and South. The river itself was unremarkable, but the American fire support bases that abounded on the southern side and the constant United States Air Force sorties made the whole area one great death trap. Hell, I thought, it was not merely a matter of crossing a river. There would be over three million lives lost during the crossing.

"Tell me about Dat, please."

"He was twenty when he left his secondary school in 1960, as the war had interrupted his education. He was a good artist and had good hands also. As an only son, he was exempt from military service but he was keen to help with the struggle so a family decision was reached that he should volunteer."

His good hands must have come in handy when he was posted to 312 Division after joining the army, for he excelled at repairing guns. His multi-skilling seemed typical of that war: art, weapon maintenance and anti-aircraft gunnery. Dat had served with a great unit. The 312 distinguished itself at Dien Bien Phu, and participated in the 1968 Tet Offensive before fighting in Laos in 1968-71. It fought in the South later and participated in the final offensive of 1975.

"He served with an anti-aircraft unit but died during a US bombing raid in 1966 in Laos, helping to defend a bridge as part of a team operating five guns."

Given the location of his death, he would have been helping to defend the Ho Chi Minh Trail, regularly and heavily bombed by the USAF. Their B52 raids took a fearsome toll in those parts.

"How did you learn of his death?"

"He used to write home twice a month, so when letters stopped coming we contacted the Army Headquarters in Hanoi. Sin received confirmation of Dat's death about three months later but would not tell me the bad news. He was afraid the shock would be too much for me. He could not hide his sadness forever, and I could see that something was terribly wrong, but he would not tell me anything."

There was a secondary pain following the death of their son: the painter ceased painting.

"Something went wrong in his head. He developed headaches and started taking medication. I looked after him until he died in 1993." Sin had been concerned about the damage the bad news would have on his wife, but it appears he suffered in her stead.

"Hanoi was heavily bombed. Please tell me about it."

"During the bombing raids my mother-in-law was unwell so we hired two people to carry her about 120 kilometres away to Tay Binh Province, on their backs. I always think of the US bombing as a Dien Bien Phu of the sky, with gunners on the ground pitted against B52 bombers. The bombing of Hanoi was very bad, with bombs landing close by."

(The battle of Dien Bien Phu saw the French rely heavily on air power both to inflict heavy damage on the enemy and to resupply their own forces. The Vietminh absorbed the punishment as they reduced the French perimeter and effectively closed the airfield. They then slowly strangled the French garrison).

Ma Tuyet was immensely proud of her husband and son, for they are both still in some senses with her. Dat's superior officer still visits her on the anniversary of his death so that they can pray for him together. She mourns his death, but is consoled by the unification of Vietnam. Her view is that she lost one son, but others lost many more. I wondered how many house calls the officer makes each year on anniversaries—what a superb gesture after all those years.

"Would you like to have dinner with me?" she asked suddenly.

We had spent the day in her company and time had flown. Somewhere along the line the officials had departed. I was delighted at her sudden invitation, but loath to put her to the trouble of preparing a meal after such a long interview. As it turned out she had in mind a meal at a nearby outdoor eatery. As the officials had left us, Huong and I took up station on either side of the formidable old woman and escorted her down the road.

She was obviously very much a local celebrity as the number of waves and greetings indicated. She had lived in the area for almost sixty years. I wondered what tales the stall-holders around the café could tell, many of whom would have endured not only heavy bombing by the United States Air Force but starvation under the Japanese. Some of the elderly women were probably very handy with a grenade launcher, mortar or anti-aircraft gun in their prime.

Ma Tuyet maintained a lively conversation throughout the meal. It transpired that I was the first westerner to spend a day hearing her story, and she had enjoyed it. A Cuban delegation had called on her previously for an hour or so. We discussed my project and she asked me to do whatever I could to have the book published: mothers in the west should know of the experiences of the Vietnamese during the war. I promised her I would spare no effort.

She offered helpful advice to the café proprietors on how to improve the flavours of the *pho*, the noodle soup, and suggested improvements to the visual presentation of their establishment. They listened respectfully, although I gained the impression that they have been beneficiaries of her advice for quite some time and might have managed without it. Thus encouraged, she assumed a grandmotherly role with Huong, offering her a good deal of personal advice.

Huong listened attentively, as would any young woman of traditional upbringing. The three main duties of a wife were raised: to support the husband and family structure, to raise and teach the children, and to earn money and provide financial support. It occurred to me that Vietnamese men have got off quite lightly. As the journey progressed I would learn just how seriously the women took their duties.

Marrying a foreigner was not a good idea, she warned Huong. There would be too many cultural differences and the relationship would fail. I took this as a thinly-veiled reference to earlier jokes I had made with Huong about sending both my sons over to Vietnam to seek local brides. I was left in no doubt that Ma Tuyet would be desperately unhappy to receive a postcard from Huong Greer, postmarked Perth, Australia. Or anywhere else, for that matter.

We talked about the successful SEA Games that she had followed on television; she had watched everything. It turned out that this eighty-four year old is an avid follower of all football and David Beckham got an honourable mention. The English, Italian and Spanish football leagues are all familiar territory to her, although her favourite team is the Vietnamese women's soccer team that swept all before it during the Games.

Huong and I had difficulty in trying to decide on a suitable gift for the old woman, but when we returned her to her home we discovered that her television set was out of order and she had been unable to follow the football recently. We hired a couple of *xe oms*, motorcycle taxis, and set off immediately on an important mission. We returned an hour later with a colour television set with a remote control. It so happened that a young woman at the shop where we bought the set was the daughter of a Hero Mother, and Huong was able to negotiate an appropriate discount. We were anxious to have Beckham restored as soon as possible and much to our relief the technician arrived minutes later to tune it properly and explain the controls to her.

We bade our farewells at the end of a memorable day. Ma Tuyet extended an open invitation to me to visit at any time in the future, an invitation I have accepted twice. We departed knowing that she can now change channels or switch off the set without having to get out of bed. It will make Beckham so much more accessible.

Upon arrival at my hotel that night I mentioned the postage stamps that Sin had designed to Long Tuan Dat, a hotel employee who had helped me in many ways over the previous couple of years. I told him I would like to purchase a set for Ma Tuyet, since she had none of the stamps. The next day we set off on a round of philatelists, and although the stamps were old and in demand, I was able to buy two sets and have one mounted in a suitable frame. They are exquisite, and now reside near the photograph of her beloved dancer.

Ma Tuyet lost one son, as have so many mothers throughout the ages, but her loss was so much greater than it appeared to be at a glance. The family life they would have enjoyed without the intrusion of foreigners in their lives would have been so much richer—Sin and Son, artists, dancers and coffee drinkers, perhaps. The war had claimed her bohemian. She never complained, but did say once that it gets a little lonely on her own at night.

I revisited Vietnam a year later to check a few facts gleaned from earlier interviews. I had no outstanding issues with Ma Tuyet but she had issued an open invitation to me and I wanted to be sure Beckham was still around. And yes, I missed all the old Mothers.

When Huong and I called on her, an elderly woman was taking her leave. As she bade us farewell she extended her left hand to me, which took me by surprise. Ma Tuyet explained about her later.

"She is a traditional doctor who had a raging fever when she was very young. She lost the use of most of her right side. She visits me twice a week, and has done so for years, to massage my arms and legs," Ma told me.

"A one-armed masseuse and doctor?"

"Sure. She has a little machine that helps."

A while later a male visitor arrived, had a brief chat and left.

"He has just returned from studying in Russia for ten years. Many years ago he was a poor student who wanted to learn to paint. Sin had stopped painting by then and was not his normal self, but taught him what he could. We gave him a piece of our land, since he was so poor, and helped him build a house on it. One day I met a woman doctor at the local hospital, and I thought she would be a fine wife for Truyen. The young couple married and they remain my neighbours," she told me in matter of fact manner.

As if to complete what seemed to me to be a very unusual day of socialising, another neighbour dropped by.

"She was our neighbour during the war. There was room in our air raid shelter for four, so she and her mother used to join us."

The two women shared humorous recollections of those days.

"It was good that the Americans used to bomb us at the same time every day. That predictability gave us time to prepare for the underground stay of up to three hours."

"What did you do during the bombing? I have read that it was so severe that survivors would sometimes be driven insane."

"We dug an air raid shelter in our garden. This was a bit of a problem as the high water table restricted the depth to a maximum of 1.6 meters. You could not survive a direct hit or even a near miss but we were lucky. The shelter was just large enough for four. Sometimes it was not so easy. Dat had died a few years before and Sin by then was unwell. He did not want to be in the shelter, so I would take tea, cigarettes and biscuits into the shelter to get him down there. He would sometimes lie on his back so that things became quite cramped for everyone else, but we did not mind." This conjured up a very strange picture in my mind.

"With Sin smoking in confined space things would surely have been unbearable?" She laughed, nodded.

"I had to lure him into the tunnel with my sweet voice. A little smoke was bearable."

She had many other hardships to deal with. When Sin no longer painted there were financial problems. The spacious family home had to be sold for subdivision into smaller apartments, and she had retained the one she currently lives in. Her needs are modest, and with help from the Peoples' Committee, together with the Hero Mothers benefits, she gets by. She is sociable, gets out and about, and attends many functions, proving the value of the Hero Mothers programme.

I visited the Fine Arts Museum in Hanoi before returning to Australia after my first meeting with Ma Tuyet, and was pleased to see three of Sin's paintings on permanent display. I wondered if Dat's work might have hung there, had circumstances not ruled out that possibility in 1966.

8.   Nguyen Thi Thu

The sole bronze bust in the Army Museum in Hanoi is that of Nguyen Thi Thu. According to a plaque on the wall, she was ninety-seven years old when first I saw her image. Meeting her had somehow become a priority, and to my great surprise two years later, when I was interviewing the other Hero Mothers, Huong was able to arrange an interview with her.

We caught a flight from Hanoi to Danang, a coastal city around the centre of the country. Danang, known as Tourane to the French who maintained a strong military presence in the area, was also at one stage the site of the largest American military base in the world. It is something of a boom city, and not exactly a tourist magnet, but it is in a delightful setting with mountains, great beaches, and secluded fishing villages. It is now a bustling regional centre with an international airport and a very busy port, so tourism development is inevitable.

A thirty minute southerly drive took us to Hoi An, a picturesque former major port known about four centuries ago as Faifoo. Traders would sail from China, Indonesia and other ports to trade with Vietnamese, Chinese and Japanese merchants in Faifoo. It is now a tourist mecca, a laid back place where tailors will run up a pair of hiking pants or a three-piece suit to the latest London design with any modifications you may dream up. Up to date fashion catalogues from London and Paris are available up and down Le Loi Street and elsewhere. Hoi An is also home to artists of every ilk, from painters to woodcarvers, sculptors, makers of lanterns, fine furniture and ceramics.

Visitors can be forgiven for thinking that the war somehow passed by without touching Hoi An, but they would be wrong. The Vietcong were very active in the area, the fighting bitter and merciless: Quang Nam Province has some 6,300 Hero Mothers, by far the greatest number in Vietnam. A local tailor explained to me that the Americans were in charge of the area around the town by day, but the Vietcong ran things at night. That was of course true of much of the rest of the country.

Early the next morning, having completed formalities at the Hoi An offices of the Peoples' Committee, we drove with a couple of officials through flat rice paddy terrain to a bustling market town in Dien Ban District. This was part of an area dubbed Dodge City by the Americans because of the continuous gunfire they encountered. We made our presence known to the local office of the People's Committee, before travelling with officials to Ma Thu's neat pink house.

The old woman lived close to where she grew up in the Dien Thang community in Dien Ban district, a mere twenty minutes from Hoi An. Gardening was apparently not her favourite activity, for she had not much to show off to visitors in her front yard, but at her age messing about with flowers is probably not a priority. The grand old woman's daughter Le Thi Tinh was about and went inside with one of the officials to announce our arrival.

Ma Thu had been enjoying a nap. I offered to return later, but somebody assured us that she was delighted to meet us, even as they propped her up and made the introductions. She blinked for quite some time to get her eyes fully functional. Perhaps she did not like what she saw for her eyes remained shut for a significant part of the entire interview. There was no way of knowing how she felt about the interview and I never knew whether she had consented in advance or not, although the very elegant jacket she wore suggested we were expected.

I saw a very frail old woman with a scarf around her head framing a face worn with age, heavily lined with hard work and, I thought, with suffering. She clearly was not in good health. Her prominent cheekbones sat atop hollowed cheeks, and her eyes were rheumy; her daughter told us afterwards that she had an eye condition, among other medical problems. For all that, she had a marvellous face for both photographer and artist, and looked magnificent in her fine, multi-hued jacket and maroon trousers.

Her home was relatively new and in excellent shape. There were terra cotta tiles on the floor, with walls in a matching colour, and there was good light. It was a nice place to visit, cheerful, lived in. Pride of place went to the family shrine, surrounded by a massive assortment of certificates, photographs and citations.

Her hearing was a bit of a problem, but one of the officials had over time found a way of communicating with her and explained to her why I had come to visit. There was a little facial movement from the old woman to indicate that she understood. Behind her, one wall held a large and elaborate red banner, with gold writing and symbols: it was from the government, congratulating her on reaching her centenary, although she had some four months to go by my calculations. Huong explained to me that they follow a system whereby age is measured from date of conception, so a baby is born nine months old.

Nguyen Thi Thu with author

Huong directed my questions to Ma Thu, the officials often gently helped explain the question, and sometimes her daughter would join in the conversation. I could not take my eyes off the old woman.

Nguyen Thi Thu was born in 1904 to poor farmers. She was the sixth child, and had five brothers and two sisters. There was no opportunity for schooling and she took up household responsibilities at an early age.

"You have lived around here for your whole life?"

"Yes."

Peasants moved most reluctantly since they were loath to abandon their ancestors who were buried around the place. It caused the Americans major headaches: they wanted to move people to fortified villages to place them beyond the reach of the Vietcong and away from agitators and recruiters, and they wanted to deny the Vietcong food and support, but the people would not go. They were often moved at gunpoint, and many attempted to return, sometimes at the cost of their lives.

"When did you marry, Ma?"

"I married Le Tu Tri in 1922. He was a farmer; we moved to our own farm of 1500 square meters. It is here, where I still live. We had our first child when I was twenty-two years old."

Somebody pointed out that the first child was daughter Le Thi Tinh who had met us upon our arrival and who now lives with her. We would find that Tinh, too, experienced great loss. A sturdy woman of what seemed like middle age, she hovered about at a discreet distance, keeping a watchful eye on proceedings. She has chosen to be known now as Le Thi Tri, an adoption of her father's name, in order to honour him.

Ma Thu's memory was not acute and I realized this was not going to be a long and detailed interview. But she did have more to tell me.

"You had many sons."

"I had eleven."

"What was life like under the French?"

"The early years of French occupation were tolerable. So were the years of Japanese domination."

"Was there any fighting around here in the early days, after the French returned?"

"There was a French military base nearby, and sometimes we heard gunfire." Gunfire in that area was probably unexceptional. After the reoccupation of Vietnam by the French following World War 2, military activity throughout the country hotted up considerably as the struggle to rid the country of the French intensified, and Ho Chi Minh cranked up his revolution.

Men were called to arms as military operations against the French intensified. Women of all ages lent their support, as did youngsters barely in their teens. Occupation forces found themselves fighting not only enemy soldiers, but families and communities. I asked the old woman how she felt about Ho's determination to drive out the French.

"My family supported the war effort and joined Ho's movement."

At this stage she seemed to be tiring, so we pieced together a little more of her story with the help of her daughter and the others present. She lost four sons during the French war, but has no recollection of where and how they died—it happened almost sixty years ago. Later, she and her husband were angered at the loss of an independent and united Vietnam so they let their remaining sons join in the struggle. They felt cheated because a cornerstone of the agreement after the defeat of the French was that there would be free elections throughout the country by 1956 to elect a government to rule a united Vietnam.

The major powers of China, Russia and the USA never pressed for that election and it never happened. I did not initially appreciate the intensity of the outrage of several of the Mothers' families at the cancelled elections, but I should have since it led to the US war, a war that cost Ma Thu another five sons.

She had been coughing intermittently, a bowl nearby for the phlegm, and it was clearly time we brought an end to the interview. I did ask her though, "Did you know there is a bronze bust of you in the museum in Hanoi, the only one in the whole place?"

"Yes, a visitor once told me, but I have never seen it."

"I will send you a photograph of it, as well as prints of any photographs I take here. Huong will ensure that it reaches you."

Each Mother has since received a copy of all photographs taken during their interview.

She told me she never met Ho Chi Minh, but did once meet Pham Van Dong. He had been a cave dweller with Ho and Giap in the 1940s and was Prime Minister for thirty years. Dong rates highly in the all-time hierarchy, so Ma felt greatly honoured.

She and her husband, who died in 1989, had supported the struggle in any way they could, such as supplying food or cooking. All her sons and her daughter took part in the fighting. Without any prompting she told me she forgives the French and US forces for the pain and suffering caused her and her family.

I later obtained the names of her sons, and during another follow up visit in September 2004 I recorded birth and death details from official documents.

Her first born, Le Tu Chuyen, was born in 1926. He married and fathered eight children, but was killed on 30 April 1975. It was the very last day of the war, and he died during the final attack on Saigon, in sight of his fiftieth birthday.

Second son Le Tu Xieng was born in 1928. He was single and living at home when he signed up. He was killed aged twenty on 18 June 1948.

Third born, Le Tu Han, was born in 1930. He, too, was still living at home when he signed up with the Vietcong. He died aged eighteen during the French war in 1948, the same year as his older brother.

Ma's fourth son was born in 1931. As sometimes happens when siblings are born within a year of each other, he was given the same name as his older brother, Le Tu Han. He, too, answered the call whilst living with his parents. Tragically, he was killed at seventeen in 1948 also, within 10 days of his namesake.

Le Tu Lem was born in 1933, signed up whilst living at home, and was the fourth brother to die during the French War on 1 April 1954 at twenty years of age. The French War ended two months later and the family looked forward to peace and unification of their country under Ho Chi Minh, as the results of the election were a foregone conclusion. The elections did not take place and eleven years later US Marines landed at Danang and a far deadlier war commenced.

Born in 1935, Le Tu Nu married and fathered a son. He was killed on 5 September 1966 at the age of thirty-one, the first of Ma's sons to die during the American War.

Le Tu Muoi, born 1937, was also single and living at home when he joined up. He was killed on 14 April 1972 at age thirty-five.

Le Tu Thinh was born 1939. Another boy soldier, he was single and living at home when he signed up. He died at age thirty-five on 28 August 1974.

Le Tu Trinh was born in 1941 and was killed on 12 September1971 at age thirty. He had never married.

There was a very strong, ugly pattern here. Only one of her sons killed during the French war reached the age of twenty-one, and she lost three of her four oldest sons to war in 1948 at ages seventeen, eighteen and twenty.

She lost her sons over a period of twenty-seven years in this thirty-year war. There had been huge hurt early for her, as well as great pain late in the war. She had lost children in each of the four decades that spanned the struggle, and their ages at the time of the deaths ranged from seventeen to fifty years.

Back with Ma Thu it was obvious that she could talk no longer and needed to rest. Her daughter laid her down gently and covered her frail body with a couple of light blankets. Ever vigilant daughter Le Thi Tri had been present for parts of the interview and had shown an interest in proceedings. A pleasant, sociable woman, she was happy to tell us her own story, and while we were chatting with her, I realised that she was well past middle age, as one would expect since her mother is a centenarian. Tri was an octogenarian. Very smartly dressed, in a sort of silver blue jacket and yellowish trousers, she too wore a scarf around her head in the cool weather.

Born in 1924, she led an uneventful life until the Japanese forced her to work for them, helping to grow rice. The Japanese military was not renowned for its kind treatment of women, and she was threatened with beatings if she did not comply. In 1949, a year after the French War had claimed three of her brothers, she married a local farmer.

The young couple had an illegal radio, which could be a capital offence at the time, depending on the mood of the French officer present when such equipment was discovered. They listened anxiously to reports on the progress of the war against the French. In due course, the couple had four daughters. When their fears of US intervention were realized the family supported the struggle in whatever way they could. Their support was, of course, never half hearted, and inevitably came with a heavy price.

Her eldest daughter, Ngo Thi Dao was born in 1951. She was active in the struggle and survived the war.

Ngo Thi Cuc was born in 1953. She had been a Youth Volunteer, acting as a scout and guide, and was killed in 1973.

Ngo Thi Mai was born in 1954. A fighter who led a squad of 15, she survived the war, and lives with Mother Thu and her extended family.

Ngo Thi Dieu was born in 1956, and went missing in action in 1970, at the age of fourteen. There was no death notification, and no details of her fate were ever forthcoming.

"Please tell me about your husband," I said to her.

"He was an official of the Army Bureau. He was arrested one day and taken to the American military prison in Hoi An. There, he was beaten to death within a week. I was allowed to view his body, but I was not awarded custody and could not give him a proper burial. He rests somewhere around Hoi An, but I do not know where."

Had confirmation of the death of her daughter Dieu been forthcoming, Tri would have been a Hero Mother herself, having lost a husband and two daughters on active service. Documentation problems cost many mothers the recognition and support they deserve. Identification of recovered bodies remains a problem, for Vietcong did not wear dog tags. Sometimes it is possible through personal possessions found, or distinctive clothing such as belts or shoes, as would prove to be the case with a Mother we would interview soon.

Huong told me that in cases where remains are found without a positive method of identification in an area where a family lost a member, the family might consult a fortune teller. It may just transpire that the fortune teller will find, miraculously, that the remains are indeed those of the missing son or daughter, so that closure may occur and remains are available to be honoured. Hopefully, the fortune tellers find occasion to be rather more flexible than normal in cases such as these. We would meet a woman whose family found solace in such a solution.

Le Thi Tri did her own bit for the war effort.

"I passed messages. Sometimes I helped with road works, and I took part in combat on occasion. American forces arrested me once and imprisoned me in Hoi An for supporting the Vietcong. They gave me electric shocks, but I told them nothing. They later released me."

She told me that she and her remaining family enjoy freedom and peace. They are pleased that Vietnam is finally united and independent, and are trying to forget the war.

"What did you fight for?"

"We fought for peaceful living." It seemed a self—contradictory sort of statement, but the meaning was clear enough.

I came to understand it better as the journey progressed. They wanted an end to intervention in their country by foreigners and were prepared to pay the price to free future generations after 1,000 years of meddling by outsiders. They had suffered invaders for 2,000 years and were constantly falling back on a long and inspirational history of armed resistance. This capacity to keep fighting despite the pain of their wounds sets these Viet apart from other nations.

Before leaving, we had to decide on what might be an appropriate gift, but nothing had leapt out at us. Even Huong was stumped, so we had something of a crisis on our hands. The home is well appointed and the family did not seem to lack for anything, so Huong asked Tri what she thought might please Ma Thu.

"A picture of peace."

We thanked Tri and bade her farewell. By now Mother Thu was fast asleep. On the way back to our hotel I tried to imagine what a picture of peace might look like. I visualised a swarm of white doves, which seemed rather unexciting, and I had not come across anything like that in Vietnam to date. Huong, however, seemed quite unperturbed.

That evening we visited a few galleries in Hoi An, where Huong unearthed an embroidered picture of a peaceful rural scene—beautifully sewn, complete with white doves flying overhead, water buffalo, and a water hole—all signs of peace, she told me. It was not a picture I would normally purchase, but I have always taken peace for granted, and have been spared bereavement. We decided this was indeed a suitable gift, and after having it reframed, Huong delivered it the next day while I was documenting the interview. The family was delighted.

The interview with Ma Thu had pointed out the extreme hardship and difficulty of the struggle of the Viet people. They had won the promise of elections to unify the country by 1956. Instead of her being able to live in peace with the rest of her family, there came a new foe with fresh forces of far greater numbers. Over time, the newcomers had far more and deadlier weapons at their disposal, and a much greater appetite for the lives of people of all ages, genders and political persuasions.

I visited Ma Thu once again in September 2004. I needed to confirm a few dates in the time line I had drawn, and I also had a small presentation to make that meant a great deal to me. I had missed the old woman and her family, and I would have visited them anyway if I could, since I had returned to Vietnam to check a few facts.

I was delighted to see the grand old woman in excellent shape. She wore a fine blue silk suit with a traditional pattern on it, and she seemed years younger.

In renewing our acquaintanceship, we held hands. As her eyesight is poor and she relies a lot on feel, she immediately moved her hand up my forearm and exclaimed how fat I was. There was quite a gathering in the house, and everyone was delighted to see the old woman in such lively form, for she had been poorly when I met her for the first time the year before.

In confirming identities of all those gathered in the home, we discovered that there were five generations of Ma's family present, since her great grand-daughter had just produced a baby.

As we chatted with Tri, I kept an eye on her mother who had grown weary and was taking a rest. A grand-daughter, or sometimes a great grand-daughter would lie beside her on the bed, quietly talking to her, with the old woman chortling away happily. She is much loved by her family and revels in their company. I have never seen such a display of love and affection. The scene explained volumes about the role of children and family among the peasants of Vietnam. It also emphasised the great tragedy of the war.

"You lost nine brothers, your husband and two daughters to war over twenty-nine years. Ho Chi Minh died in 1969, six years before the end of the war. Did victory ever seem out of sight—did you ever think about giving up?"

"No. Ho left a letter for us before he died, calling on us all to support the war, so we had to continue."

There was another person present during most of this visit. As I was sitting next to Mother Thu a young woman entered the house and proceeded to photograph us. She was a journalist working for a local army magazine, had heard of my visit and wanted to write an article about my journey. The interviewer became the interviewee for a while as we discussed the project and the Hero Mothers.

I presented Ma and her daughter with a large blown up photograph of the pair of them, mounted on a backing board, to ensure the family can enjoy it for years to come. I had also purchased a milky white opal pendant for Tri and a fire opal for Ma Thu, knowing I will probably not see them again. The older woman's opal was not a random purchase: a great fire had raged within her for thirty awful years, even if the coals are banked now.

The old woman's eyesight was poor, so she rubbed her pendant carefully with her thumb, tracing out the shape as Huong described it to her. Huong explained also that it was an Australian stone, and that its miners live underground, like the people at Vinh Moc further up the coast did for a substantial part of the war. This pleased the old woman no end and they lost no time in donning their gifts so that I could take a photograph to the merchant who sold me the pendants in Perth.

In his shop are numerous souvenirs and citations from the US Navy, big spenders when calling in at Fremantle during Australian visits. Five years later, after several trips past his shop I still have not been able to enter the premises to show him my photographs: the family is a bit special to me and they have had far too much contact with members of the US armed forces.

In 2011, during a short visit to Hanoi, I was informed that Nguyen Thi Thu had passed away.

9. Dinh Thi Que

Christmas 2003 was two days away, but writing up the notes from our visit with Ma Thu had temporarily nudged aside any threatening outbreak of Yuletide spirit as far as I was concerned. Nevertheless, the Vietnamese are serious and dedicated celebrants and in Hoi An they were feverishly preparing for some substantial festivities. Their own Tet celebrations were about a month away, and they seemed intent on using the intervening period as a sort of practice run. Red, the colour of good luck, was everywhere as shopkeepers made final adjustments to their elaborate displays of stock. Extravagant bottles of cognac appeared in the most unlikely stalls in the hopes of promoting a bumper trading season.

We arose early the next day for our interview with Ma Que in Nhi Dinh village, Dien Phuoc Community. The terrain around her place was much the same as we had found around Mother Thu's village, since the two homes were only about ten kilometres apart. Dinh Thi Que lived in an ageing, but well-built brick and tile dwelling in a quiet hamlet. The house was painted a pale blue and could use a total paint job anytime, but was otherwise well maintained.

Despite a deeply wrinkled brow, she was quite spry, clearly younger than the Mothers we had seen to date. Her posture was slightly hunched and she had an intent gaze, along with an air of wariness. She had probably grown up dealing with French and Japanese patrols before having to handle the ARVN and the Americans. A wrong answer at the wrong time could cost a Mother and her family dearly; beatings came easily, torture was routine, and execution or murder sometimes resulted, without all the messy complications of legal proceedings. Perhaps this was why none of the old women were intimidated by me, although they were certainly unaccustomed to dealing with Western men. I simply posed no threat—I was a lightweight compare to others they had dealt with.

I recalled reading that anyone found in possession of Vietminh documents was liable to be executed immediately by the French who did not always consider trials necessary, so the Mothers had lived, fought and raised families during very dangerous times. Words had to be carefully measured before being handed out to strangers.

The old woman led us into her house and seated us in small chairs around a low table. Huong completed introductions as somebody poured our first cups of green tea for the day. At my prompting Ma Que began to talk.

She was born in Ha Nong village, Quang Nam Province, in 1928. It was about two kilometres from where she now lives. Her parents had a small farm but times were hard so sometimes they worked for others to earn a little extra money. She was the sixth child of seven in the family.

Inevitably, as was the traditional role of daughters in peasant families, she had home duties. Heavy responsibility came to her early as her father died when she was six years old, and her mother passed away nine years later. Three of her five brothers died of illness, as did her only sister. At fifteen she had lost six members of her family.

Ma Que told me that the family did not suffer until the arrival of the Japanese in the early 1940s. The Japanese arrested her and forced her to work for them.

"Sometimes they beat me. I tried to escape, but they punished me more."

Looking at her fine features I figured she would have been an attractive girl of perhaps fourteen to seventeen years of age so this must have been a very difficult period for her.

Some time after her release she married Le Van Tram, a farmer, in 1945. The relief felt when the Japanese left later that year lasted until French soldiers killed one of her brothers in 1948. He was taken to his home village and shot. She was not forthcoming about the circumstances leading to his death and I chose not to pursue the issue. Perhaps he had been caught on Vietminh business and the French felt the need to convey some special message to the villagers; their delivery could at times be a little clumsy.

Her family decimated, things were finally looking up as she bore a first, healthy son.

Her husband Tram was a Youth Volunteer during the French occupation. They had five sons and three daughters, but two of their daughters died when they were very young. After the American soldiers came, Tram volunteered for military service once again. He died in action against the Americans in 1967. She volunteered no further information about his death, and I left it at that.

"Tell me about your children," I asked her.

"Our eldest son, Le Van Thanh, was born in 1947. He went to school for three years, but he was very clever and could decode messages. He was the General Secretary of the Communist Party in Dien Ban. He was killed by American soldiers about six kilometres away in 1973."

"Were you able to retrieve his body?"

"No. We were afraid of an ambush. The Americans buried him. He was married, and had a son who now lives in Dac Lac with his mother."

My ears pricked up immediately—Thanh's widow would normally live with her mother-in-law. Something unusual might have happened, and I filed it away for follow up later. I would hear an extraordinary love story during my return visit in August 2004.

"My second son, Le Huu, was the Vice Director of the local Youth Volunteer organization. He served as a messenger, but he was attacked by American forces as he was going to a meeting in 1970. He was shot, and tried to escape by swimming across a river, but he died on the riverbank. His body was burnt, and we could not recover it."

She was pleased to receive his belt recently, but she did not show it to me and I did not want to intrude by asking to see it.

"My third son, Le Van Thanh, became a messenger at the age of thirteen. He often used to cover thirty to forty kilometres on foot, but he died at a demonstration at a nearby US base in 1969."

Details were a bit sketchy, but it appeared the demonstration lasted about five days and was finally broken up with aircraft and helicopter fire. Ma Que was allowed to view his body and clearly remembered that his skull was split in two, with damage to his arms, legs, and other parts of his body.

Her remaining daughter fell victim to Agent Orange water pollution after the chemical was sprayed into rivers. She survived the war and now works as a housekeeper in Saigon. Ma told me she still has problems, and no teeth. The old woman recalled emerging from a tunnel in her garden after an aerial attack and noticing a liquid on their vegetables, but they had no way of knowing of the catastrophic effects of the chemical.

"Did you ever doubt that the war would end? As your personal losses increased was the outcome ever in doubt?"

"No, I knew we would win." She said it so emphatically that there was no point in asking further questions on the topic. I never found a Mother, or indeed a family member who questioned Ho's belief that victory would be theirs. If they had any doubts they did not share them with me. General Vo Nguyen Giap, whom I met later, emphasised that he felt the same confidence.

"How do you feel about the war now?"

"I have forgiven the French and the Americans. The Communist Party has helped us find freedom and a better way of life."

I had already resolved never, ever to ask any Mother if she felt it was worth it. It would be cruel, with the answer not worth the grief the question might provoke.

Dinh Thi Que

She has two sons who supported the Vietcong but who survived the war and who have provided her with three grandsons and two granddaughters. One of her sons lives with her with his family, and her other son lives nearby. There are youngsters about and laughter is no stranger to the household. Ma Que is clearly much more fortunate than many others, although I struggle with the terminology. That is what she would have told me, had I asked. Her happiness was obvious.

A daughter-in-law and granddaughter were sometimes present during the interview, staying in the background but constantly watching over her. She is seldom alone. When I asked if I could photograph the three women together, her daughter-in-law quickly rushed off to change her clothing. The granddaughter was shy, perhaps because she sensed the visit was all about Ma, or perhaps because at hamlet level they do not encounter many westerners.

Foreign occupation or intervention cost Ma Que a brother, her husband and three sons, and left her daughter with ongoing health problems. Of the eighteen members of her combined families, that is the parental family and later her own, five lived to a ripe old age. Eight died of natural causes, revealing one of the main reasons for having many children, and five were victims of war.

She endured the peck on the forehead I gave her with good humour, and we made our farewells. We strolled back to our hire car for the return trip to Hoi An, having in two days been welcomed into the homes of two Mothers in the district with an average age of ninety-three years who had lost seventeen family members to war. It had happened within an exceptionally good stone's throw of idyllic Hoi An, the town that seemed to have escaped the ravages of war.

A second interview with Ma Que was one of the main reasons for my return to Vietnam in 2004. She looked frail this time, the only Mother who had not grown noticeably younger since the first interview, and it emerged that she was not well.

She told me she had been beaten between the ages of about fifteen and forty-two years and the cumulative effects cause her pain in her old age. My favourite love story sort of popped out after I asked why her son's widow lived in Dalat, and not with her—this had caught my attention during our first interview a year earlier and was one of my main reasons for this second visit.

The South Vietnamese forces arrested her whole family in 1970. Her daughter-in-law and her three-year-old child were part of the group. The women were being beaten at a prison in Dien Ban run by the South Vietnamese when one of the officers suddenly claimed that Ma's daughter-in-law was his wife. This astonishing claim saw them released from prison, and the officer helped the younger woman and her child escape to Dac Lac Province, which at that time was evidently a far safer place. She was widowed in 1973 and some years later married her rescuer. They have two children.

I wanted to understand why this southern officer had taken such a risk, but I was only partly successful. The women had been beaten regularly and the young officer had tired of seeing it happen. Huong and I thought the young woman must have been very attractive, or presented an appealing sight with her young child. Perhaps it came about as the result of a few seconds of humanity in an inhumane place and time. Whatever, love had surfaced in a very hard place.

I wonder at the thought processes of a regime that would beat a mother accompanied by her three year old daughter. The beatings were presumably not administered in the youngster's presence, but I can only imagine the effect on a child of having her mother return after such a beating. What on earth was a child doing in such an establishment? If it was meant to intimidate them it failed miserably—it is small wonder that children in the first year of their teens would want to join in the affray.

Ma introduced us to her daughter who suffered mild Agent Orange effects. The younger woman told me smilingly that she is able to hold down a job as a cleaner at a school. I had read of the dilemma facing mothers in some of the more remote mountain areas that were subjected to chemical spraying: a minority had suspicions about the spray, but no food alternatives. They could feed contaminated food to their children or watch them starve.

Mother Que insisted on walking us outside and waiting with us until we secured a taxi. We waved goodbye to a gracious woman. As she posed for a few photographs, I noticed that walking now seems to cause her discomfort. She still has to fight a war of sorts; it is as well she has great courage.

10. The road to My Lai

Washington realised by the early 1960s that the South Vietnamese military were no match for the highly committed opposition forces. The US had, after all, been providing military assistance, material and training through MACV (Military Assistance Commission Vietnam) for years and witnessed at first hand the result of clashes with the enemy.

The South would need substantial support to win what was shaping up as an unwinnable civil war that had been heavily promoted by Washington. This would lead to a US Army in Vietnam of over a half million men at the peak of American involvement.

Washington decided that a Vietcong attack on an American airbase in Pleiku in 1965 justified sending in ground troops to help the Southerners—the US aircraft needed better protection. It appears from some accounts that Washington was shocked and outraged that the aircraft that sowed destruction in the South should be attacked. The US Marines arrived later that year on the beaches at Danang, storming in off landing craft. Opportunities for good, aggressive photo shoots disappeared when they found groups of smiling young women waiting to greet them with welcoming messages painted on signs, and floral garlands which they placed around their necks. It was enough to make a hard-bitten drill sergeant scream.

It did not take long for the death toll to start mounting, for the Marines had been allocated one of the toughest territories on the planet. Central Vietnam was known in earlier times as Annam, a Chinese appellation meaning Pacified South. That name was most offensive to the inhabitants since they had a well-earned reputation for both their toughness and their rebellious ways. Both Ho Chi Minh and Giap were from Annam, as were other revolutionaries. So it was in the best Annamite tradition that the locals fought back hard, replacing floral offerings with wreaths.

US land mines were dug up at night and laid elsewhere, causing major problems for the Americans. Even empty ration packs and other metal containers discarded by US soldiers were converted into deadly booby traps, and patrols were ambushed relentlessly. The provinces of Quang Nam, which contained hard fought territory like the place the Americans called Dodge City, and neighbouring Quang Ngai, became very tough territory for all who lived there. And, of course, for those who visited with combat on their minds.

Fifty kilometres south of Hoi An is the tourist attraction of My Son, the major site of the Champa Kingdom that was established around the 4th century C.E. Most of the structures were destroyed during the American War, but it is well worth a visit nonetheless. A further twenty kilometres south lies the town of Chu Lai, site of another massive American base built as efforts to gain control of Quang Ngai Province intensified.

Neil Sheehan, in his Pullitzer Prize-winning non-fiction, *A Bright Shining Lie*, mentions exploits of Johnathon Schell, then a twenty-four-year-old writer from The New Yorker, who had spent several weeks observing the operations of Task Force Oregon, most of the time from the rear seat of the spotter plane that controlled the air strikes.

Sheehan himself had observed five hamlets on the coast in which hundreds had perished under bombs and naval gunfire, but found Schell had additional observations[6]:

Where I had learned that at least ten other hamlets had been flattened as thoroughly as the five along the coast and a further twenty-five heavily damaged, Schell discovered that fully 70 per cent of the estimated 450 hamlets in Quang Ngai had been destroyed. Except for a narrow strip of hamlets along Route 1, which was patrolled after a fashion, the destruction was proceeding apace. Day after day from the back of the spotter plane Schell watched the latest smashing and burning in bombings and shellings and rocket runs by the helicopter gunships and in the meandering progress of flames and smoke from houses set afire by American infantry. He tallied up the previous destruction from the traces of the houses and, going to the military maps, carefully checked his estimates with the L-19 pilots, officers of Task Force Oregon, members of the CORDS team in Quang Ngai, and several local Saigon officials.

Many of the communities lived in "free fire" zones. Sheehan described those zones as he wrote about the earlier destruction in another area[7]:

Rollen Anthis had devised the free-bombing zone system in 1962 as yet another way to generate targets and keep his pilots busy. The corps and divisional commanders and the province chiefs were encouraged to delineate specific zones of guerilla dominance in which anything that moved could be killed and anything that stood could be levelled. (The zones were also called "free-strike zones" and "free-fire zones," because they were open to unrestricted artillery and mortar fire and strafing by helicopter machine gunners once they had been marked for free bombing.) By the summer of 1965 the system was being exploited to achieve a measure of destruction Anthis had probably not imagined, expanding constantly as more and more Viet Cong-held regions were marked off with red lines on the maps. Anthis had usually contented himself with sparsely populated areas. Now, as in Cu Chi, well-populated sections were among those being condemned.

Many peasants chose to stay rather than leave their ancestors behind by moving to the appalling refugee camps. Some moved underground to escape the death that stalked them on the surface.

In one province 85,000 fled their homes because of this destruction, giving Washington the opportunity to describe them as "refugees from Communism"[8].

A little further south, off the main road near the city of Quang Ngai is a group of hamlets collectively known as Son My. It was here that Charlie Company, a unit of the American Division's 11th Light Infantry Brigade, murdered over 500 villagers, mostly women, children and old men, during a few hours of madness on 16 March 1968. It would become infamous as the My Lai massacre.

My third visit to the Memorial was part of my motorcycle trip as I sought to learn about the country without the distraction of a coach load of fellow tourists. I will visit My Lai on any future trip to Vietnam as it conveys to me the tragedy, the barbarity and the futility of the Vietnam War. It is a special place—understated, quiet and graceful, dignified yet somehow most eloquent in its silence.

It is only a couple of hours by Minsk from the homes of Nguyen Thi Thu and Dinh Thi Que, and tourist coaches pass nearby as they travel north to Hoi An or south to Nha Trang. Not many seem to stop by—tourists want to reach their destinations in daylight to begin sightseeing, so most coaches travel around here in the hours of darkness. The Memorial is located in a grassy park on the site of one of the hamlets that was destroyed. Hamlet life progresses quietly beyond the boundaries of the park, with only the occasional sound of a pump or a motor scooter in the distance to be heard. It requires little imagination to step back a couple of centuries in most of rural Vietnam.

Visitors wander about the lawns, reading plaques on raised mounds of grass marking the former location of houses. The plaques show the death toll within each household—eleven here, nine next door. Looking north past the perimeter of the Memorial grounds it is easy to see the flat terrain where soldiers used the ubiquitous Zippo cigarette lighters to burn down houses and pursued whatever villagers appeared before dealing with them in shameful fashion. It was impossible to reconcile the picture that my imagination was painting with the peaceful rural image, so I entered the Museum building in search of enlightenment. There, in full colour, was displayed the truth and reality of My Lai.

A museum guide noticed my concern at the graphic photographs on the wall and explained they were taken by US Army photographer Ron Haeberle. He used his own camera loaded with colour film, and that gave him the copyright to the photographs. The Museum, she explained quietly, had bought the rights to display the images.

My reference of choice for the massacre is the excellent *Four Hours in My Lai*. The story of events of that day makes for tough reading, for there was nothing accidental about what happened there. It was not a question of a soldier snapping under the pressure of enemy fire. There were no enemy soldiers in My Lai, and at no stage was there any return fire as the men of Charlie Company went about the slaughter. By lunchtime, some had become Double Aces, the honorific bestowed upon those who have killed the woman they raped.

My Lai Memorial

People had been scalped, dismembered, mutilated, shot, bayoneted, knifed. Babies had been shot, an old man dumped down a well with a grenade lobbed in after him. A grassy ditch that runs along the western boundary of the park looked a little different in Haeberle's photograph on a wall in the Museum: in the picture it held over a hundred corpses. The photography was superb—there could be no confusion about what was on view. Many faces were recognisable, even if bodies were destroyed. I could only wonder that someone who had such a graphic view of the action had made no attempt to report it, and has, indeed, made a good living from the poisoned fruits of his camera.

For all this, and the cover up that followed, junior officer Lieutenant William Calley spent a few days in prison for the 109 murders of which he was convicted. His immediate superior officer, Captain Ernest Medina, was even more leniently dealt with, being acquitted of over 100 murders, and finding employment in a company owned by F Lee Bailey, his high profile defence lawyer. The difficulties involved in seeking justice in such a situation were perhaps best highlighted by the chilling words of Judge Robert Elliot in the civil district court that overturned Calley's conviction[9]:

Keep in mind that war is war and it is not at all unusual for innocent civilians to be numbered among its victims. It has been so throughout recorded history. It was so when Joshua took Jericho in ancient Biblical times. "And they utterly destroyed all that was in the city, both man and woman, young and old . . . with the edge of the sword" (Joshua 6:21).

Now Joshua did not have charges brought against him for the slaughter of the civilian population of Jericho. But then "the Lord was with Joshua" we are told.

The judicial implication seems to be that the Lord was with William Calley, a view that might surprise the Great Being. The good Judge went on to make a number of observations about Sherman not being charged for devastating the South during the US Civil War. If this seems a little strange, it appears to be consistent with some of the legal findings in the Agent Orange lawsuits.

Surprisingly, there was a real American hero at My Lai. Hugh Clowers Thompson, Jr, a reconnaissance helicopter pilot during the carnage, landed his machine and had an altercation with Calley. Some time later he landed his helicopter once more, between a number of escaping villagers and pursuing US soldiers, and instructed his gunner, Larry Colburn to open fire on any soldiers who gunned down villagers. He radioed for help and helicopters arrived to evacuate the escapees[10].

Thompson discussed some of the events at My Lai with a chaplain friend, who in turn discussed it with his superior. Those worthy churchmen took it no further, and the Army nevertheless decided against charging the chaplains with failing to ensure that the allegations were reported and investigated. Court-martialling men of the cloth was thought to be bad for the morale of the Corps of Chaplains.

The Americal Division was a crap unit, poorly led, with morale and discipline problems. Rather than open it up to scrutiny, to determine perhaps how such a poor outfit ever made it to Vietnam and how a specimen like Calley became an officer, the military sought to cover up the whole disgraceful episode.

Interest in the trial gradually faded[11]:

An overseas observer noticed that after Christmas 1970, with the honorable exception of the Washington Post, journalists were not reporting the nightmarish quality that had begun to infect the court proceedings. Thus the American public never understood the full horror of My Lai—the rapes, tortures and mutilations that were committed. Among the evidence passed by the public was the account given by Gonzalez and McBreen of how Roschevitz, in the 2nd Platoon, had forced a group of women to strip and then executed them by firing a special flechette round from his grenade launcher after they refused to have sex with him. Few outside the courtroom ever heard the appalling story of how Conti had tried to force a woman to perform oral sex on him by holding a gun to the head of her child until Calley came along and told him to pull up his pants and get on with the war.

A flechette is a dart-like projectile that does much greater damage than a normal bullet.

A newspaper article a few years ago mentioned a My Lai Anniversary, possibly the 30th, held with Thompson as guest of honour. The villagers expressed their disappointment that the participating soldiers had not attended, as they were ready to forgive them. Even as I moved around the grounds of the Memorial I was very conscious that I was of the same vintage as some of the participants in the massacre, but I rated not a second glance.

Son My is now a serene but very disturbing place. It poses many questions about the definition of war crimes, the willingness of the Americans to prosecute their own war criminals as they do those of other nations, and the integrity of their judicial process that should be used to uphold standards of conduct. Surely a soldier who places the tip of the barrel of his rifle inside a young woman's genital region and pulls the trigger should expect to be required to answer a few questions. His senior officers should be asked even more.

A few years after my first visit to My Lai, I learnt about Tiger Force, the reconnaissance platoon of 1st Battalion 327th Infantry, a unit of the 101st Airborne, through a remarkable book[12]. The Force had killed an unknown number of civilians, thought to number a few hundred, in Quang Ngai and Quang Tin (Quang Nam) Provinces, with some of the crimes occurring not far from Son My, in 1967. As had been the case at My Lai, some good men refused to participate.

Unlike My Lai, some members of Tiger Force reported the atrocities to their superior officers at base. One soldier even reported incidents to the chaplain, who was of the view that these things happen during times of war, demonstrating a heavenly tolerance to atrocities that must be the result of having God on one's side. The chaplains seem to have been remarkably consistent in Vietnam.

The unit was supposed to ensure the removal of peasants from their land, and their relocation to the fortified villages, so that their crops could be eradicated by Agent Orange spraying. The idea was to deprive the Vietcong of food and other support. Angered at the repeated return of the peasants, Tiger Force commenced a programme of murder. At times there was an element of "sport" to proceedings as peasants were used for target practice. The catalogue of killing is as bestial as that at My Lai, but took place over several months.

No charges were ever laid. Sam Ybarra, one of the proud possessors of a necklace of human ears as well as a collection of gold teeth he had kicked out of the mouths of his victims, would never have to face a prosecutor. Nor would he ever be held accountable for slitting the throat of an infant, among other victims, as he died several years after the end of the war[13].

> It didn't take long before the enemy fire ceased. The Tigers moved closer and, with some of the line company soldiers, began searching the huts. Kerrigan stood outside the doorway of one hooch while Ybarra bolted inside. In the corner was the lifeless body of a young mother shredded by bullets. Next to her was an infant, still alive and crying. Shortly after Ybarra ran into the hut, the crying stopped.

> Kerrigan inched closer to the doorway, then peeked inside. Ybarra was kneeling over the infant's body, a knife in his hand and the baby's severed head on the ground.

No member of Tiger Force was charged with any offense.

The Tiger Force murders ceased about three months before the nearby My Lai massacres. It makes one wonder if My Lai would have happened had the crimes of Tiger Force been properly and publicly dealt with at the time.

The senior investigator handed in the detailed fifty-five page report of his three-year investigation and expected to be involved in the case at least until the hearing. Instead, he was transferred to South Korea.

The authors of *Tiger Force* won the Pullitzer Prize for investigative reporting in 2004.

I returned to Son My in 2004 and struck up a conversation with a group of European backpackers who had visited the museum in Saigon a few days before. There they had learnt of the extensive use of napalm, and its effects, for the first time, as well as other aspects of the war, and they were appalled at Haeberle's photographs.

"I don't see that the Americans in Vietnam were any better than the Nazis," said the distressed young German girl before the subdued group made its way back to their coach.

Five years later I was enjoying a café latte in Ashgrove, Brisbane, when a newspaper article caught my eye. On page 12 of the *Weekend Australian* of May 9-10 2009 under the headline "Ex-GI faces death for murder-rape" appeared the following:

A US federal jury will determine whether former soldier Steven Dale Green should be executed for raping an Iraqi teenager and executing the girl and her family, court officials said yesterday.

Green was found guilty on all 17 criminal counts, which included rape and premeditated murder.

The penalty phase of the trial opens on Monday.

Three other soldiers were given life sentences for the March 2006 atrocity, which was devised over whisky and a game of cards at a traffic check point in Mahmudiyah, south of Baghdad.

While Green confessed to the slayings when army investigators were called to the scene the next day, the involvement of US soldiers did not come to light until stress counsellors talked to the squad several months later.

His lawyer said the verdict was not a surprise because "we never denied his involvement in this case."

"The goal in this case has always been to save our client's life," Darren Wolff said.

Lead prosecutor Maria Ford told jurors during closing argument that the gruelling conditions and tragic losses suffered by Green's unit in no way excused his actions.

"The evidence suggests the defendant was acting purposefully and intentionally with full knowledge of what he was doing," Ms Ford said.

She said Green and the other soldiers changed their clothes and disguised their appearance to throw suspicion on insurgents. They also burned the body of the 14-year-old girl, Abeer al-Jnabi, and their clothes, she said.

"This was a planned, premeditated crime which was carried out in cold blood," Ms Ford told the jurors. But Green's other defence lawyer told the jury that stresses of war had left the soldier a broken man in a strange world.

Lawyer Scott Wendelsdorf blamed the crime on a lack of leadership at Traffic Checkpoint 2, where Green served with the other soldiers involved in the crimes. He said Green had been diagnosed with Combat Operational Stress Disorder before the attack, and claimed former soldiers took advantage of Green's mental condition to carry out the crimes.

AFP AP

There were few young village men at My Lai on that fateful day. Men of fighting age were away on Vietcong duty. Physical pain and suffering was inflicted on old men, children, and of course once again on the women. Perhaps witnessing the unspeakable cruelties inflicted upon their loved ones may have been the cause of the greatest pain of all.

While their menfolk were away waging war, the Mothers were home fulfilling their various duties. That greatly increased their vulnerability: they suffered when their husbands hurt; in the villages they were the first port of call for visiting hostile patrols and they and their young children were available for acts of revenge by the scum of enemy occupying forces.

It should not have surprised anybody that they would fight back, although the ferocity and commitment of the fight would have shocked any foe.

11. Nguyen Thi Huong

The city of Hue is almost equidistant between those twin wartime hot spots of Danang, to the south, and the Demilitarized Zone (DMZ) about 100 kilometres to the north. That, and of course being on the "Street without Joy" ensured that Hue itself would be the location of a substantial military base.

The appellation "Street without Joy" was a French one. It referred to the coastal road from south of Qui Nhon to around Quang Tri, where Vietminh and later Vietcong fighters gave the French military and the Americans who succeeded them little respite—neither military force was able to subdue the locals. Ironically, Bernard Fall, author of the superb book *Street without Joy*, was killed while covering the activities of a US patrol in 1967 on the Street, not far from Hue on Highway 1. He was a mere forty years old at the time.

This old city was greatly damaged during the French-Vietminh struggle as well as the American war that followed, and was practically destroyed during the savage fighting of the 1968 Tet Offensive. The Citadel in Hue is a substantial walled area that was the home of the last Emperor, Bao Dai, of the Nguyen Dynasty, whose reign ended in 1954. It was an earlier member of this dynasty, Nguyen Anh, later to become Emperor Gia Long in 1802, who requested help from the French and thus provided them with the pretext to become directly involved in Vietnam. Gia Long was also miserly about the rights of women, and is not remembered fondly.

Huong and I travelled from Hoi An by tourist bus, a leisurely five-hour trip through some beautiful country. The bus followed the old road up the Hai Van (Sea Cloud) Pass a few miles north of Danang. It was no great surprise when the bus stopped at the very active markets situated at the summit, which were overlooked by some old French bunkers that had probably been modified by the US Marines, for this had been Marine territory during the war, and they had been kept very busy indeed.

We booked into the Thai Binh 2 hotel around lunchtime on Christmas day. It was the same hotel I had previously stayed at, and the receptionists who had tried to help me find Hero Mothers during my ill-fated earlier attempt were delighted to see me legally engaged on my mission. I arranged a room with a balcony for Huong that afforded her a view of parts of the Citadel, thinking that would be a special treat for her in recognition of sterling service to date. It was much later that I discovered she normally travelled with media types with expense accounts that afforded her vastly superior accommodation. She never mentioned it, and it was only by chance that I came to realise she was uncomplainingly slumming it with me.

We set off an hour later to meet two representatives of the local Women's Union who had agreed to accompany us to our first local interview that afternoon. The Union represents the interests of not only the Hero Mothers but any women who encounter problems and need help; the war has ensured that there are many who require assistance on occasion. None of the Hero Mothers was Christian, so we had no difficulty in meeting them over the Christmas period or on Sundays, and officials were equally accommodating.

The women purchased a few small gifts for Ma Huong. It was the thoughtfulness and the courtesy that counted, not the value of the contents. Each place had its little specialties, so we purchased a Hue favourite, rice cakes. The gifts invariably led to laughter and happy small talk that overcame the sort of hump that might otherwise arise from injecting a westerner into a closely-knit social circle.

Nguyen Thi Huong lived in a double storied house on a busy street in the centre of the city. One step from the pavement carried us into the house through varnished, shining double doors. The front room was spacious, set up for visitors with beautifully tiled floors and gleaming furniture. There was an air of martial discipline about the place with everything ship-shape and ready for inspection.

The old woman was expecting us and opened the door for us. She was petite, dressed in a sort of gold brocade two piece suit, similar to the traditional ao dai. I saw a striking and strong face, a lived-in one that had seen hard times, topped by thinning grey hair that receded a little. She looked every inch the battler, a real fighter and an altogether formidable senior citizen who smiled readily when she found the time. She was all hustle and bustle, with a no-nonsense air about her.

She seemed a little mystified at the purpose of my visit, so she had some questions of her own that she directed at Huong. I felt thoroughly inspected by the end of a lengthy indirect interrogation. Huong the Younger was clearly representing me most capably for I found Ma Huong's attitude towards me soften dramatically after introductions had been completed.

One of the Women's Union delegates, Ngo Thi Thanh Thuy, had told us Ma was a fish sauce maker of note, but I did not realize the scale of her operation. She was no enthusiastic amateur whiling away the hours with the occasional stir of a little pot, for we had no sooner sat down than callers started dropping by for plastic bags of her secret sauce. The gourmets walked off with larger jars. A younger woman on the premises dealt with customers for the duration of the interview.

The old woman was quick to let me know she had won a gold medal for her sauce, but that was no surprise since any judge with basic survival instincts would not award her anything less than gold. Tea was taken and we commenced our interview.

She was born in a nearby village in 1926, the fifth child of four sons and four daughters. Without education in a poor family, she found employment at twelve years of age as a housekeeper. She worked for a rich merchant family and travelled up and down the coast with her employers.

Life under the French was tolerable, although it was difficult to move about during that period because there were so many of them around. Later, when the Japanese arrived, her family moved away from the city. The Mothers' concept of hardship was vastly different from mine so I have no doubt that times were tough. The relocation to the countryside to avoid the Japanese was a clear indicator that they had experienced difficult times as the peasants moved most reluctantly, often at the wrong end of a gun barrel.

She married Che Cong Giai in 1946 at the age of twenty years. It was an arranged marriage—he was a farmer and her parents thought he would be a good husband for her, so they discussed it with the parents of the young man. They were local farmers also, and were happy with the proposed match.

"Our parents suggested that we should marry and we did," she told me.

It was a typically clever way of resolving a potential problem. She had limited opportunities to meet a future husband from her village due to her travels with her employers. If she married a man from a different town or province, she would go with him. It would be far better for the family to find a local man of good character from a family known to them all. It also meant of course that the prospective groom had been observed for pretty much all his life—there was little chance of unpleasant surprises.

The parents of the bridegroom would enjoy similar benefits. One of the requirements for a bride was that she display respect for her mother-in-law. If that became a problem, it could probably be resolved by walking down the road to discuss matters with her parents. Little deals could be struck that might not otherwise be possible.

"Giai was a year older than me. He was not only handsome, but kind as well, so I was very happy with him. After our wedding we fell in love," she said.

Several of the Mothers married in this manner and this procedure apparently in no way diminished the strength of the marriage. They all described their husbands as handsome and kind. Parental selection of marriage partners was very much a part of that culture at that time, and parents no doubt selected a marriage partner who appealed to them as well. That would immediately overcome the perennial hurdle of a husband or wife who failed to win the approval of the in-laws.

They became farmers and supported Ho's Revolution. She was a political activist, advising people to embrace the cause. The strong French presence in Hue was required not only because this was the seat of the Emperor, but because this was rebellious territory. The Emperor had to be held in check, but while he tried to please the French, his people planned to rid their country of their foreign oppressors.

Her eldest brother died in Nghe An Province in 1945, the year before she married, while fighting the French. His wife and daughter died from contaminated food supplied by the Japanese. Her youngest brother went missing in action near Hue during the American War.

Her husband answered the call to arms and died in action against the French in 1953. She knows little about his death, for the sad reality is that many men and women, boys and girls simply disappeared. The resources to find reasons and explanations were not available to their families. There was not necessarily a comforting report of their passing. Later, during the American War, whole military units were wiped out, or vapourised if they were on the receiving end of a B52 bombing run—so there were no survivors to record such details.

Che Cong Viet was her only son, born in 1947. His education ceased when he left secondary school to become a member of the Communist Party. He had some security responsibilities but he died in action against US forces nearby while preparing for the Tet offensive of 1968. Comrades from his unit buried him.

Her only daughter, Che Thi Hai, was born in 1949. One day American forces arrested Ma Huong in front of her daughter, who was ten years old. While they were tying her up in spite of this, Hai was terrified and ran away. She somehow fell and died. The soldiers took Ma Huong away and imprisoned her. Family friends buried Hai while Ma Huong was incarcerated.

Sometimes, almost hidden amongst the major horrors of the war, the small inhumanities really hit home. It seems Hai had tried to escape by running across a bridge, and had lost her footing. I was loath to interrupt Ma's train of thought at that point, and did not return to it. There was also a chronological discrepancy: there were no US forces in the country in 1959 other than "advisors" who were there on training and advisory duties. It is unlikely advisors would have arrested Ma—it was probably ARVN personnel. It makes no difference to the old woman and I did not labour the point.

Often, when Mothers were trying to recall dates, they would relate one event to another. For instance, a brother may have died two years after the birth of a son. The birth date might be known and the date of death then arrived at. If the base date was incorrect, so were others. I was not greatly concerned about absolute chronological accuracy.

"Were you involved in the war?" I asked.

"Yes. The Americans beat me once but I revealed nothing."

As I came to know her a little better, I realized that interrogating her would be no easy task—she is even now a strong and very determined woman. I wondered what role she filled, but she clearly did not wish to elaborate on her own involvement during the war years.

"Did you and your family ever think about just giving up? After all, you paid a terrible price over the period 1945-1963, and victory must have seemed distant."

"No, we continued because of the losses. Members of our family died for our country and in search of peace. We had to try to stay alive and try for independence. I once met General Giap to discuss the war when he was travelling along the Ho Chi Minh trail."

Giap would never have made himself available to all and sundry when he travelled along the Trail—that would be a closely-held secret, for fear of attracting heavy bombing from the B52s. He certainly would not discuss the war with everyone he met. I think Ma Huong may have been a bit of a handful to the Americans.

"How did you feel about Ho Chi Minh?"

"He was my father, the most important man. His death was bad news, I cried so much."

There was a break in intensity at this point, as the old woman chatted to Huong, causing great merriment. Huong turned to me, smiling.

"She says you are the first person to hear her whole story. She says also that you asked her more questions than the Communist Party when she applied for membership," she said, laughing.

The old woman looked at me sternly, but I think she meant it kindly. She seemed anxious to return to her kitchen and I took that as a signal that our interview was over.

"Would you like to see how I make the fish sauce?"

"I would be delighted," I told her.

I think this was quite an honour, for she naturally guards the secrets of her award-winning sauce. I was unable to copy her recipe for it is a complex process known only to her and most of the ingredients were something of a mystery to me anyway. There was a huge plastic drum of sauce ready for bottling, with shrimps and all manner of mysterious and exotic ingredients floating about in it. The nose, as a winemaker might say, was complex.

She took advantage of the moment to give it a few quick stirs—she takes quality control very seriously, as befits a winner of gold medals. I could see she was sorely tempted to fill a few bottles as we had made inroads into her production schedule. There was a bucket of charcoal burning nearby, fanned by an old household electric fan. Ma told me that as it was raining outside, she had to use other methods of cooking. I could not work out what the charcoal was used for and was loath to betray my ignorance, but I think she dries shrimps as a side-line.

The old woman runs the entire operation herself with a little manual labour provided by friends and relatives. She rises very early so that she can select the shrimps at market, and she mixes the ingredients. Others are permitted the less critical tasks such as stirring and bagging or bottling. There was of course no electro-magnetic scale or volumetric container: Ma has this uncanny eye and does not need modern technology to make sauce.

The younger woman who had been looking after customers stirred the contents of the drum, and a shy boy of about twelve poked his head around the door to speak to her.

My curiosity was aroused and when we were alone with Ma Huong again we enquired about her assistant.

"My nephew's parents believed in the cause of Southern President Diem, so they travelled south to support him. The nephew remained in Hue, where he later married. He fathered six children and lived in my home with his family. I helped care for him from the day he contracted cancer until the day he died."

Thus she has adopted a family. The widow could not cope on her own so Ma has de facto grandchildren to care for. Looking after them keeps her very active and they have a devoted, loving and caring grandma who will certainly keep them on their toes. Beneath the tough veneer lies a heart the size of a football. So it is that seventy-seven year-old Nguyen Thi Huong, having lost two brothers, her husband, her only son and her only daughter to the foreigners, now has a family for which she works very hard.

The parents-in-law of the widow whose family she is working so hard to help, supported the side responsible for the deaths of her two children, but the young family needed help and Ma Huong is there for them.

When it was time for photographs, she quickly drew on a pink ao dai over her work clothes. I adore the garment, and I think Huong got into the habit of publicising my preference, for most of the Mothers offered to don the garment for photographs. There was laughter as she

Ma Huong in the fish sauce factory

prepared to have her picture taken—I suspect she spends little time in her formal ao dai, and has probably never been photographed by a westerner. She seemed pleased to have her picture taken several times, preened noticeably as she saw the results on my laptop computer, and was delighted to see pictures of the other Hero Mothers we had interviewed to date. She does not travel to many Hero Mother functions.

These Mothers are a proud band, but travel is not easy for them. Air travel is beyond their means, and, in any case, most of them would probably be reluctant to fly. The US lost over 8,000 aircraft during the war, many brought down by little women like Ma Huong, so the appeal of air travel is probably lost on them anyway.

Huong presented the gifts, one of money in this case for there are youngsters to be educated, and we were in turn presented with a bag of fish sauce with instructions to try it forthwith.

The old woman accepted my farewell peck with what sounded like a snort and a smile, and, with a bag of Hue's finest fish sauce in hand, Huong and I bade farewell to yet another remarkable woman.

Later that evening we found a restaurant that knew all about Ma, whose quality sauce has made her a local identity. They prepared a suitable Christmas dinner, and while I found the sauce to be rich and tasty, I was unable to eat the large shrimps in their shells. Huong pronounced it excellent.

We had finished our meal when a group of about six young urchins walked by. A conversation started up and Huong asked me if they could have a little of our left over food, of which there was plenty. Little hands reached out and rice, pork and assorted dishes disappeared into gaping mouths. These kids were starving, and a couple ate until they started choking. Huong told me later that they had possibly never eaten pork before.

I had never seen anything like it before in Vietnam, but noticed that the children were physically under-developed, very poorly dressed, not well cared for. The thirty-year war has wiped out many families and disjointed others; a couple of generations of children have grown up minus a parent, or as orphans. Other relatives or villagers who in the normal scheme of things would help are missing or dead, or trying to come to grips with major problems of their own. Education was interrupted despite the high priority everyone places on it and many are caught in a poverty trap that may take generations to overcome.

My previous smug view of events in Vietnam was by now shot to pieces and I realised I had much further to travel if I was to understand why an impoverished Third World country had been subjected to such severe punishment.

Back in my hotel room, I once again sketched out the picture of the war. These Annamites were emerging as the toughest people I could ever hope to meet but I was starting to have some real problems with the amount of damage done to very good and most likeable people. I was wondering how long it would take the nation to overcome the effects of the trauma that has been visited upon them.

My final thought was a hopeful one: if I enjoyed any sort of success in having my book published, perhaps I could raise funds to get a sort of kids' kitchen going—one great meal a day for the street kids and help with school fees if possible. A dollar goes a long way there and it costs little to help make a big difference. Australia is not without philanthropists, so the dream is alive.

It was a Christmas with a difference, but Jingle Bells had somehow lost its resonance.

I was sifting through my notes at home some months later when that man Giap started preying on my mind. He had been a bit of a shadowy figure as far as I was concerned, just a name attached to military action. Apart from Bernard Fall, who rated him highly, I had not come across him too often my library of American books on the war. Yet he had led his military to victory in the unlikeliest matchup imaginable.

Ma Tuyet had proudly shown me a photograph of her and Giap seated together at a function in Hanoi. He had appeared in a few photographs in the Hero Mothers exhibition in the Army Museum, and attended some of their functions despite his poor health. Ma Huong had mentioned meeting him to discuss the war. I wondered what it was about the man that led to all these villagers entrusting their lives and those of their families to him.

He is a living legend in his country but had happily lived in the shadow of Ho Chi Minh, to whom he was devoted. The French had underestimated Giap, referring to him as the Schoolteacher (and he did indeed teach them many enormous and expensive lessons) and the Americans had not bothered to research him. Robert McNamara had lamented this lapse:[14]

> Our misjudgements of friend and foe alike reflected our profound ignorance of the history, culture and politics of the people in the area, and the personalities and habits of their leaders. We might have made similar misjudgements regarding the Soviets during our frequent confrontations—over Berlin, Cuba, the Middle East, for example—had we not had the advice of Tommy Thompson, Chip Bohlen, and George Kennan. These senior diplomats had spent decades studying the Soviet Union, its people and its leaders, why they behaved as they did, and how they would react to our actions. Their advice proved invaluable in shaping our judgements and decision. No Southeast Asian counterparts existed for senior officials to consult when making decisions on Vietnam.

As outlined in the history summary, such counterparts had existed but had fallen victim to the Cold War mentality in Washington and to McCarthyism. Had they researched Giap properly the US may well have set about the war differently. I used Currey's superb biography[15] as my reference.

Vo Nguyen Giap ("Nguyen the Force Shield") was born in 1911 in Quang Binh province. A brilliant student, he was expelled for leading a student protest at the treatment of a fellow student who had been accused of cheating. He still obtained his history degree from Lycee Albert Sarraut in Hanoi in 1934 and his law degree in 1937.

Giap observed the brutal French reaction to the 1930 uprisings: dozens were beheaded, villages were destroyed, livestock killed and a further 700 dissidents executed without trial. He was imprisoned for his political beliefs and activities in 1930, along with a fifteen-year-old schoolgirl, Nguyen Thi Quang Thai. In 1939, the year the Communist party was banned in France and in French colonies, they were married.

His wife bore him a baby in early January 1940 but she and her activist sister fled to Vinh while Giap and Ho were in China. The French captured his political activist sister-in-law, Minh Khai, who would not talk under torture. She was executed by firing squad in 1941. Her husband had already died in prison.

Quang Thai knew the French were looking for her, so she found someone to care for her baby shortly before they arrested her in Vinh in May 1941. She was jailed in the prison that later gained infamy as the Hanoi Hilton and was subjected to torture there. Apparently afraid of weakening under torture, she committed suicide by swallowing soft belt material, which caused her to choke to death, although US reports state she was hanged by her thumbs and beaten to death. Giap was in China at the time and it would be three years before he would hear from a colleague of the fate of his wife.

The French arrested Giap's father in 1947. He was a nationalist, but not a communist. At the age of seventy, he was tortured and dragged behind a car until he agreed to appeal by radio for his son to lay down his arms. The old man was then released but died later that year. Currey describes the French approach to interrogation on occasions[16]:

French treatment of Giap's family was not uncommon or unusual. Their police and Vietnamese jailers were willing to use any method to persuade prisoners to talk, including forced ingestion of water, electrical shocks, pulling fingernails, and other brutal measures. With female captives they occasionally used a variety of electric shock methods that drove many women literally mad. Jailers used eels—nasty, hard-biting creatures known for their strength and tenacity—and inserted them into the throat or vagina of women. Placed in those soft, wet areas, the eels tried to swim and bite their way to freedom. The torturers watched as their victims were bitten and electrically shocked by the sea creatures. After a time, they removed the eel and continued their questioning. Resistance was sometimes magnificent. One dying woman wanted to be sure she did not speak, and allegedly bit off her tongue and spat it at her interrogator.

In 1944, the first squad of Giap's army possessed two revolvers, seventeen rifles, fourteen flintlocks, and one light machine gun. For the next few years they had to play a cat and mouse game of considerable savagery. French retribution was swift: anyone found in possession of Vietminh literature could be executed on the spot. Heads and amputated arms and legs of cadres or sympathizers were prominently displayed in town markets as a deterrent to peasants desirous of joining the Vietminh.

The Vietminh were as ruthless, and executions numerous. Perhaps the brutal French repressive measures left them with no choice but to match their opponents in the terror stakes. There was a significant death toll among moneylenders, landlords, members of opposing political factions, turncoats and spies, French sympathizers, and stubborn native Roman Catholic priests and nuns. Villagers were sometimes trapped as visits from brutal French were followed by calls from the savage Vietminh.

Giap initially had little to work with by way of military talent and had to husband his resources carefully in order to replace military leaders lost. He was intolerant of weakness and those who would not, or could not admit to failings and faults, and work to improve were re-educated or shot as a last resort.

In mid-September 2004, to my utter amazement, Giap agreed to meet me at his comfortable home in a leafy suburb of Hanoi. I presented him with an album of enlarged photographs I had taken of some of his French battle sites. He looked at Tu Vu, near Hoa Binh, where French forces were overwhelmed. He smiled slightly at a picture of the Mang Yang Pass, in the Central Highlands near where French Mobile Group 100 was destroyed, sending more shivers up French spines in their air-conditioned headquarters in Saigon. He was a little surprised, I think, to see a photo of Muong Khuoa in Laos. I'd had to travel 100km down a couple of rivers in Laos by speedboat to visit that remote village.

Dien Bien Phu pleased him. It had been a huge victory, and probably won independence for his country, but he had lost perhaps 10,000 men during the battle, many from around the Cao Bang and Pac Bo areas.

Giap and Ho had started the war from a cave on the border with China, where the French could not surprise them. It is hallowed ground today.

"I visited the cave at Pac Bo," I said. "It seems a very unlikely place from which to plan liberation of your country. How could you have expected to succeed?"

"Ho said to me the people of Vietnam are strong enough to resist the French." I waited for more, but he had answered my question. He spoke to me of Ho's determination to help his country to freedom, the over-riding task he had set himself and his little group of believers.

"Did you ever think you might lose the struggle?"

"No." It was an immediate and final response.

"Ho told me the mountains and rivers of Vietnam belong to the people of Vietnam."

That comment would scream into my consciousness a week later during a marvellous Minsk motorcycle adventure near the Lao border, on my way to Dien Bien Phu. It was a beautiful landscape of mountains and rivers, forests and little hidden hamlets, with children riding on water buffaloes. I wished I could telephone Giap and tell him that I finally understood.

It was time to go. The old genius was pleased with the photo album, and pointed out to me that I had of course visited the battlegrounds in peacetime. I could not adequately express my gratitude that I had never come up against him or his fighters, be they soldiers, porters, women of the Long Haired Army, child messengers and scouts or indeed the Hero Mothers.

Giap raised his own army, although the Chinese assisted with training. He had no phalanx of senior officers from West Point, Sandhurst or St Cyr to draw from, and he had no military training whatsoever, so he had to learn hastily in his cave, in China and on the battlefield. He was matched against eight successive French Generals,

Huong, the author, and Giap looking at Strongpoint
Huguette—Dien Bien Phu

each one of whom was destined to return home unsuccessful, before much the same fate befell a succession of US commanders. He was a superb logistician who was able to keep supplies moving although the enemy controlled the air. And he kept winning.

It is impossible to compare Giap with Western generals of the 20th century. Giap's forces were almost invariably outgunned. He had no significant navy or air force, no large fleet of army helicopters or long range artillery. He was thus unable to deliver white phosphorus, napalm or Agent Orange, had he had any available and had he chosen to use it. He had no fresh waves of soldiers to fly in for single tours of duty.

It was no wonder Robert McNamara regretted not researching Giap and Ho. Giap's trump card, I believe, was the likes of the women I was meeting, and like the French, the Americans had completely overlooked Ho's secret weapon.

12. Nguyen Thi Ha

Boxing Day morning found us outside the brick and tile home of Nguyen Thi Ha. The house was behind a cement paved forecourt, and the old woman enjoyed a view of open, green fields and the occasional cluster of trees. Rebellious black ducks noisily challenged the serenity of the hamlet. It was easy to forgive them—they were living on borrowed time and they knew it. One could hardly deny them an opportunity to play up a little.

Ma Ha was tiny, slightly stooped, wearing a blue trouser suit with a brownish jersey to keep out the damp chill. She had a receding hairline with her thinning hair pulled back tightly in a bun. The old woman welcomed us with a wavering smile and led us into her home.

Upon entering the house, something seemed different from the homes of the other Mothers we had visited. There was a gloom about the place that I initially attributed to the rainy and overcast conditions, but that was not it. The interior of the house was in need of a lot of maintenance, but that really was not it either. There was an air of sadness, a sense of loss in the house. I realized later that Ma had perhaps lived there only in body for some years and no amount of sprucing up would relieve the atmosphere. Perhaps the house simply reflected the residual effect of years of loneliness and grief.

She was on her own, but relaxed as Huong handled the introductions. We were sipping tea within minutes, and the old woman and I exchanged smiles and nods before she told us her story.

Ma Ha was born in a nearby village in 1928 to farmer parents, the oldest of seven children, having three brothers and three sisters.

"As the eldest child, I had to help around the house. My brothers went to school, and my sisters went to primary school." Education was not a priority for daughters, but it seemed that no matter what the birth order of the Mothers—eldest, second eldest, youngest—conditions somehow conspired to deny them schooling. Those were terrible times, though, and with children contributing to the war effort from any early age many of them were experienced combatants by the time they should have been graduating from high school. Education was largely put on hold for thirty years, something that has made recovery difficult for Vietnam.

Her eldest brother died young of natural causes, while her second brother married before the war and joined the army in 1964.

"He moved south to support the war effort, but spent four or five years in Con Dau prison after troops from the army of the south captured him. He survived the war and returned home, but he has some problems in his head. He fathered seven children."

The problems in his head were no surprise in view of the treatment of prisoners in hellish Con Dau, located on an island south of Saigon. Con Dau featured in so much material I read that I felt compelled to visit it two years later. The next chapter has been devoted to that wretched place.

"My youngest brother graduated from secondary school. He joined the army towards the end of the war, due to his youth, and is now the Vice Director of the Army Bureau. He is married with five children."

Her four sisters actively supported the revolution and all survived the war.

About a week later, as I was reviewing all my interview notes, I was surprised to realise that all six children who reached adulthood had survived the war, a stunning achievement, but at the time of the interview this did not register with me. Ma supported the revolution as well.

She experienced no major problems with the French, but the Japanese arrested her once. They released her after questioning.

"A few years after my release, my parents selected a husband for me, and I married at nineteen, in 1947."

"How did you feel about your parents selecting your husband?"

"I had no time to meet young men because of my duties, but I was happy with my parents' choice. My husband was from the same village, a farmer two years older than me. He joined the Revolution in 1952 to fight the French. Then he was needed in the north to help prepare for the battle at Dien Bien Phu."

The French occupied Dien Bien Phu in late 1953, but the Vietminh won the final battle in mid-1954. The place was not on the radar in 1952, so her husband must have been sent there on other duties initially, which is quite feasible since there was no shortage of military activity in the north during that period.

"Not long before he left, I gave birth to our only son, Ng Van Bui, in June 1952. Of course, I had to raise him on my own, as I did not see my husband, hear from him or hear news of him for twenty-five years. He never saw his son again. While he was away I resisted the French and the Americans. During the US war I hid Vietcong fighters in a tunnel in the garden behind the house."

"It would have been a disaster if the Americans found them."

"Yes, but when US forces came, Bui would sometimes be playing at the camouflaged entrance to the tunnel to distract them."

It was risky stuff. The tunnels almost invariably started off vertically, before setting off horizontally in their chosen direction. Entry would probably have been via a small wooden trapdoor, covered with sand and leaves, invisible except to the closest inspection. You would have to tap on the door to find it. Bui probably played directly above it. Harbouring the fighters was very risky, but Bui would have been involved directly in the war from the age of thirteen anyway, and within a few years he would become a teenage soldier with several years of military experience. For the youngster, as for most of his former playmates, this was all par for the course.

Visiting the Mothers really brought home the involvement of family members of all ages in their war. Youngsters would help with little acts of deception, would become messengers, or guides at thirteen, fighters at sixteen. By the time a nineteen-year-old American from Detroit came into contact with his counterpart, the Viet had been in the business for perhaps six to eight years, with fifteen years of contact with enemy soldiers and a lifetime of bitter memories. The family might have two or three decades of such memories, and a family shrine crowded with recent photographs of members of both genders.

There was a huge gap in ability, experience and motivation that no screaming sergeant back in Boot Camp could hope to compensate for. If it can be said that the back streets of the wrong part of Detroit are a tough school, then it must be said that the Central Highlands of Vietnam during the War was the university where you were awarded your masters degree in bad stuff.

"Bui graduated from primary school and helped me before joining the army at fifteen in 1967. His work was secret and I never learnt what he did, but I know he was once a messenger of some sort."

He was Vietcong and they had to use strict security measures. In a community of divided loyalties, if parents knew nothing about their various family members' military roles, nobody could trick, beat or torture information from them that might cost many lives.

"When the French left, they gave their lists of suspected Ho Chi Minh sympathisers and collaborators to the Americans, so soldiers came for me. I managed to get away the first time, but later I was arrested and beaten. I told them lies and I gave them no information, but they released me." She gave us a funny little smile as she recalled the incident, before drawing a breath and continuing.

"Bui was killed in 1975, during the last months of the war, in Aluoi District, about sixty kilometres from Hue during a bombing raid. Soldiers from the north were heading to Saigon for the final assault, and their Vietcong comrades helped them on their journey south. The whole area received much attention from the South Vietnamese forces. Two friends died with him, and other friends buried them in an unknown location."

Tour guides in Hue told me that chemical contamination and unexploded ordnance renders parts of Aluoi District dangerous even today, and refused to lead me there. Unusually, they recommended I stay away, one of only two places in the country to rate such comments. The other is Con Thien Firebase near Quang Tri, where you need the services of a very good guide on account of unexploded ordnance. Con Thien is forbidden territory to tourists, and is best avoided.

I thought we had reached the conclusion of the interview. This one had proved to be relatively straightforward. I scanned my notes to see if I had missed anything. Yes, there was one little detail.

"Ma, your husband went north in 1952, and you told me earlier that he did return. You had no news of him for twenty-five years, but he is not here. What became of him?" I had assumed that since he had returned but was nowhere to be seen, he had probably died of natural causes. She started to talk to Huong. Then her voice changed, and to everyone's dismay tears welled up in her eyes.

She never heard from him after he left in 1952 until he returned in 1977. It was impossible for him to visit her or get messages to her.

"But he did return?"

"Yes—with his new wife and family." This came out reluctantly.

"His new wife?"

"He had another wife with him, and four children. He had taken a new wife in the north and started a new family with her."

There was a stunned silence while we all absorbed this. She was distraught, and it was some time before everyone regained composure. In the end, the old woman restored some sort of order by vigorously defending her husband, realising that her audience was unimpressed by his conduct.

"A woman can wait for twenty-five years, but for men it is different. I loved him, so I told him I understood. He returned to Hanoi with his new family, where he died in 1989."

She had not a harsh word to say about him. I suspect she would have defended him vigorously had any of us attacked him. It was obvious to everyone that she loves him still and will do so until her dying day. A change of topic was called for.

"What kept you going through all those years?"

"I grew to hate the French, the Japanese and the Americans. It was a fight for freedom and peace."

"What about Ho Chi Minh?"

"I honour and love him. He was a Great Father who loved his people and Vietnam. He went away to learn how to organize the revolution to fight for peace and independence."

It was definitely time for farewells. The old Mother seemed quite pleased to have her photograph taken and offered to wear her ao dai. She soon emerged wearing dark blue, proud and very much in control. She has a fabulous face and I was pleased to be able to take a close up photograph of her fine features. Afterwards, she changed back into normal clothing and showed me where the tunnel had been in her back garden, where young Bui would occasionally perform decoy duty, playing a game for the highest possible stakes. There were flowering trees and fruit trees, all well cared for, and a vegetable garden.

She lives alone, a quiet, private person who seems to have withdrawn from society. I think she has lost interest in her surroundings—she would only have to voice the wish to have her home quickly brightened up, to have somebody move in to keep her company. There are friendly and supportive neighbours about, in addition to the dedicated helpers of the Women's Union and the Peoples' Committee. She has relatives around the area, but perhaps she chooses to spend her time with her late husband and their son.

Showing me around her garden seemed to settle the old woman, who was happy to join us for lunch. We all piled into our hire vehicle and headed for the café she recommended. During the course of the meal and all the conversation, she brightened up considerably and the shadow that had seemed to surround her vanished. The women in our group displayed their social skills so that Mother Ha was soon laughing, eating well and enjoying herself.

She put on a brave face when we said our goodbyes after lunch, but I waved farewell to a small, fragile and deeply hurt old woman.

On the way to our next interview, we agreed that coming home after twenty-five years with a new family in tow was the most thoughtless way her husband could have broken the news to her. There would have been few telephones in that area, but he could have written to her in advance. He could have called on her, alone, to discuss the situation, or he could have sent a message. He could certainly have tried to soften the blow.

She had lost their only child and dealt with the loss on her own. He had four more children. Had he been able to visit her earlier, certainly a very hazardous trip but one that some men had done, she could have had more children and perhaps he would have stayed true to her. She would never have considered remarrying or taking up with another man, so he had condemned her to a lonely life. In a country where family is all-important, he had behaved badly and there was nothing to be said in his defence.

It was only after I had downloaded her close up photograph onto my laptop computer that night, and expanded the picture, that I saw the tears in her eyes.

Mother Ha—after one question too many

13. Island of ghosts

Mother Ha's brother survived several years in Con Dau Prison, but, according to her, "has some problems in his head". We would also meet another Mother, Ma Sam, whose half-sister survived a spell there, but died after her release. Con Dau was originally part of the harsh French penal system, and then fell under the control of the Southern government with some input from the USA. Since it had also cropped up in books and articles I had come across, usually in dark and sinister context, I decided it warranted a visit.

I fitted it in at the end of my last trip to Vietnam in 2005. Huong did not accompany me on that occasion as it was not my intention to conduct any interviews. Had I known what I would find there I would certainly have asked her to accompany me so that I could spend an extra day there talking to locals.

Flights to the Con Son islands departed from Saigon at around 7a.m. and you either spent 20 minutes on the island and caught the return flight home or you stayed overnight. I ended up staying for two days. Fellow passengers on the flight were all Vietnamese, mostly elderly men, many of whom bore flowers and wreaths. They were subdued, but as I would find, Con Dau has that effect on one. We would exchange nods at a cemetery later that day or early the next morning.

A group of sixteen small islands with a total population of less than 5,000, the Con Son islands offer good beaches, hiking, fishing and snorkelling in a peaceful and lush setting. Although tourists are not catered for to any great extent at present, good seafood can be available, and there is reasonable accommodation available on Con Dau, the largest of the islands.

Originally named Iles Poulo Condore by the French, the islands can be reached in thirty minutes by air from Saigon, with visitors landing on an airstrip a few metres above sea level. The flight was met by a small bus, and the short drive along a winding road gave tantalizing glimpses of isolated coves and islets jutting out of the ocean. As we neared town, a pair of cylindrical concrete towers appeared above the canopy of surrounding trees.

The driver explained that this is a memorial, the first visible indicator that we had arrived at a destination with a difference. In a country that has deliberately destroyed most of the signs of its 20th century struggles in an effort to move on and look to the future, Con Dau has retained the buildings that hosted the infliction of great misery, and will even show its scars and share its painful memories with visitors.

My overall impression of Con Dau was of an island struggling to come to grips with its dark recent past before it emerges as an attractive and popular tourist destination at some future date. Respect for the dead who remain on the island currently enjoys priority over competing for the tourist dollar. There is a sense of greyness about the small township, though, that extends well beyond the discolouration that has set in among the stones in the high walls that proliferate in this small community.

At first glance, the town itself was unremarkable, but the story gradually unfolded as I explored the side streets and the back roads. The former Governor's residence, or the Island Lords' Mansion, as some publications describe it, is now a museum located across the road from the infamous Wharf 914. This jetty is named for the number of prisoners who died during its construction. A quick walk revealed that it is about 100 metres long, so there was a fatality every ten centimetres, roughly every five inches of its entire length.

The jetty is a pretty basic structure, leaving no clues as to the reasons for the high death toll, but clearly occupational safety and health for the prison labour force was not a preoccupation with the French. By the time I returned to the mainland it was painfully obvious that those who ran the prison system had a very relaxed attitude towards the preservation of lives of those the French, and later the South Vietnamese, were responsible for under the Geneva Convention.

The Museum is modest and muted: most visitors are Vietnamese who have a fair idea of what they will find there. There are the normal exhibits to view, a few publications for sale, and guides whose presence is a prerequisite for admission to the prison buildings. There are a few pictures of prisoners who somehow piloted strange craft across the water to freedom, some 60 kilometres away, but not as many photographs as one would expect of such a long established institution. The French were careful to take their records with them.

Photographs and X-rays in Con Dau museum are disturbing: an elderly man, both arms deliberately broken. X-rays taken after his release indicate massive force was used on his arms, of which one was so seriously deformed as to be of no use to him after release from prison. There are photographs of skeletal inmates in their shackles which, if one overlooks the occasional well-fed US military officers featured in some of the photographs, look very much like Allied prisoners of war freed from their Japanese captors after the end of World War two. A disturbing aspect of this prison is the realization that some of these acts of barbarity were performed, or at least approved, by countries with a record of taking the moral high ground on civil and human rights, of trumpeting long and loud the requirements of the Geneva Convention.

The French built their first prison on the island in 1862, and gradually reinforced it, enlarged it and added a cluster of other buildings to their remote island detention system. They relocated the original inhabitants of the islands, probably a fair indication of the detention and interrogation standards they intended to follow.

The Service Penitentiare ran the prisons, rather than the French military, so Con Dau fell under the control of the same institution that managed such brutal prisons as Devil's Island, which featured in *Papillion*, the classic true escape story. They employed many guards from their colonial territories, and their lack of concern for the welfare of their charges is well documented.

The South Vietnamese took over the prisons in 1954, with the US becoming involved about a decade later. By the time liberation led to the closure of the prison in 1975, some 200,000 prisoners had served time there. Tragically, about one prisoner in ten will remain forever on the island. In Service Penitentiare establishments, the death toll ran high, a tradition that was maintained by South Vietnam. Prisoners died on construction projects, by execution, under torture, of malnutrition and disease, and quite possibly of despair. Some died during riots and escape attempts, and several hundred died at sea during desperate bids for freedom.

France did not expend too much money or energy on the execution process: the pristine beach a few hundred metres from the prison was one of the favourite sites for their firing squads. Expenditure on interment was modest also: no markers were erected, and graves were often so shallow that bones would be exposed during major storms. Headstones were not an optional extra.

About 2,000 bodies have been recovered and re-interred in nearby Hang Duong National Cemetery, the memorial ground laid out after liberation in 1975. The cemetery is grassed, with a small white post before each grave. Perhaps one grave in five has simply a name on the marker; one in ten recorded a birthplace, birth date and date of death, and a few had an image of the deceased. I found myself staring at the faces of men of all ages who had died badly far away from their families for whatever reason, or non-reason, and wished I could learn more about them.

One grave had five markers bearing five names. I found a young man in town who had a little English, and hired him as my guide for the afternoon. He explained that some were buried in mass graves in the forest; some were buried above previously interred bodies. Perhaps that was the case with this group, or perhaps they died together in an accident, escape bid or before a firing squad.

A large, dark granite gravestone stood out, inviting scrutiny. My guide, who was delighted to show a westerner around the place, told me it attracts visitors from the mainland who call to pay homage to the memory of Vo Thi Sau, the first woman to be executed on Con Dau, in 1952. She is revered for her fierce spirit of resistance to the French: at the age of fifteen years, she attempted to assassinate a minor French official in her village. The bid failed and she was captured.

The French wanted to execute her forthwith, but feelings were running so high in the south that they dared not. A fifteen-year-old girl was a little young for the firing squad, even for the Colonial French. Four years later an opportunity arose to ship her secretly to Con Dau, where she was executed on the beach by firing squad three days after arrival. Strolling along the beach at dawn the next morning, I wondered how the members of the firing squad felt about executing the young girl, but of course it was a silly notion: they would have executed anybody without a qualm.

During my first visit to her grave, two bunches of fresh flowers rested on her headstone; the next day there were twelve. She rests in a shady spot, which is just as well for she receives many visitors who spend some time there in contemplation. Vo Thi Sau has taken her place amongst a large number of heroes of the independence movement. It came as no great surprise to find Vo Thi Sau School near the centre of town as I strolled about the next day.

Another elaborate grave came into sight, and my guide explained that it contained the body of a man honoured because of his strong heart. It seemed unusual in a country where strong hearts were the order of the day, but the guide explained that the man continued his protests and remonstrations about cruel treatment of his fellow prisoners with prison authorities even as he was succumbing to their harsh treatment.

As we walked amongst the graves, occasional visitors from the mainland arrived, armed with incense and flowers. I wished Huong could have been there so that we could record some of their stories, for they certainly would have had something to tell. The island is not readily accessible with relatively expensive and infrequent flights. Some visitors seek graves of relatives, friends, or fellow inmates from the distant past. But it takes a good deal of luck to find one as the cemetery only holds about ten per cent of the dead, and most of the graves are unmarked. One visitor explained that finding a grave was a bonus—the main purpose of his trip was to respect a fellow former prisoner and no grave visit was necessary. His friend would know he had called.

Vietnam is a country of constant contrasts, with a population that has learnt to live with a terrible, violent recent history in scenarios that sometimes seem absurd to an outsider. The town of Con Dau is a case in point. The French built on prized real estate—some of their prison buildings are within a couple of hundred metres of the beautiful foreshore, tucked in behind the buildings with magnificent ocean views that housed the prison officers and the Island Lords.

Within 500 metres or so of Prison 1 is the former Guesthouse where honoured visitors stayed. The eminent composer Camille Saint Saens spent a month there in 1895 finishing an opera. He could have heard the firing squads at work on the beach nearby, but executions were probably suspended for the duration of his stay. One wonders at the ability of a composer to create beautiful music in such an unhappy place. He surely could not have thought he was working in the surrounds of a resort as he arranged symphony and harmony in the midst of abject misery.

Resting place of Vo Thi Sau

A stroll about at night revealed a number of karaoke establishments where the current residents participated or watched from the comfort of easy chairs as they enjoyed a cool drink. There were also a few places where citizens could enjoy large screen television entertainment. The favourite programme at the time was a serial involving a truly evil looking man in a sort of samurai costume who created havoc with a large sword and magic spells. Locals maintained he had a heart of gold and was on the side of sweetness and light, and indeed, he laid waste vast numbers of villains who seemed to have Chinese features, thus underwriting his popularity for all time. I had some concerns about the ultimate fate of women he captured during his campaigns, but I kept my reservations to myself. Perhaps he was liberating, rather than capturing them—the plot was a little complicated for a newcomer to grasp readily.

A morning visit to Prison 1, also known at different times as Lao 1 and Camp Phu Hai, restored a little reality. A cell measuring ten paces by eight held 80 to 100 shackled prisoners who slept on a raised concrete platform with one ankle shackled directly to the common bar that ran the length of the room. This permitted them little movement, but their accommodation was easily the best in the Con Dau prison system.

I asked my guide how they were expected to use the toilet in the corner, but he pointed to a small wooden box that once contained sand, and, of course, human excreta—this was a portable toilet, to be passed to whomever might need it. It was not a large container, so passing it around and using it in the dark would have been a tricky, painful task for people tightly shackled by the ankle. And, of course, its capacity seemed woefully inadequate. That, of course, would not have concerned the constructors of Wharf 914.

It gets cold on the island, and the weather on occasions turns foul, but prisoners were not issued with blankets or bedding so they slept on concrete in such clothes as they possessed. It seems all prisoners other than common criminals were deemed to be political prisoners. This was significant since political prisoners were shackled; common criminals were not, as they were considered less dangerous.

An adjoining building looks like a hospitality centre, with a large bar counter and concrete troughs. This was the Club, built for the enjoyment of officers and visitors. Drinking a beer at the end of the day next to the wretched, overcrowded cells was part of the island routine, it seems.

Prison 2, also known as Lao 2 and Camp Phu Son was built in 1916. It had fourteen small cells for solitary confinement, and a dark cell, from which my guide told me prisoners would sometimes emerge permanently blind.

Some distance away was Prison 3, alias Camp Phu To, and adjoining it was Auxiliary Camp 3, or Camp Phu Tuong. These prisons contained the infamous Tiger Cages, small cells topped with steel grilles. Warders could mount stairs to the level above, from where they could and did pour powdered lime onto the shackled prisoners below, followed by "dirty water." This caused a variety of health problems, including permanent damage to eyes. The short shackles, which seem impossibly small, ensured that prisoners could not sidestep the dirty water any more than they could avoid being assaulted from above with bamboo poles.

Nearby were the "solariums" as the jailers called them, with a classic light humorous touch. These were cells with high walls, open to the elements. There were no raised concrete areas to sleep on, and no drains, so inmates would have to sleep on the floor at ground level during the wet season. Those who have experienced a rainy season in Vietnam will know what that would entail.

Exposure to extreme elements, coupled with an inadequate diet, ensured that these cells took a high toll of their inmates. According to the guide, that was the general idea. Actually, it had to be. These were also places of torture; there was certainly nothing to indicate that survival of inmates was of any concern to the jailers.

The remains of the Ma Thien Lanh Bridge can be found a couple of kilometres along a jungle walk. Nobody seemed to know why the bridge was built, since no roads approach it and it does not seem to be en route to any particular place. Perhaps it was simply a project to keep prisoners busy. It certainly appears to have served that purpose since it claimed a further 356 lives.

A choice section of forest right by the beach will surely never be developed—too many bones lie there; old and decaying stone buildings will remain on prime land near the centre of town. In time, tourists on scuba diving packages may feast on superb seafood within a stone's throw of Prison 1 largely unaware of the tortured and bloody past of this little piece of Vietnam.

Con Dau was a total failure for the jailers; the atrocities here only strengthened the resolve of the people, for the prison accommodated a fair percentage of future leaders of Vietnam. The brutal prison became practically a rite of passage for them, as had the prison at Son La in the far North. They used their prison terms as an opportunity to seek new talent, recruit new Party members, and the prisons were a fertile recruiting ground for revolutionaries. The jailers never understood the bonding effect that being shackled to a common bar has on people.

Reconstruction—shackled female prisoners—the Communist
menace—in a Tiger cage

Vietnam was a dreadful arena for prisoners' rights. The French prisoners of war suffered terribly after the fall of Dien Bien Phu. It must be said that the French were keen sponsors of torture for the preceding two decades at least, and failed to set any sort of standards of decency for the treatment of prisoners. Both North and South Vietnam were careless in treatment of prisoners, to put it mildly, and the US dirtied its hands with the rest of them.

Con Dau was an equal opportunity prison. Women were treated as badly as the men, although that is generally true of the both the French and American wars. Those that survived would return home, some badly damaged, others highly motivated by what they had seen to continue the fight, to mobilise the family unit to oust their tormentors.

14. Le Thi Meo

We were a little down as we approached the well-constructed brick and tile house on the outskirts of Hue city. The interview with Mother Ha had shaken us all.

Ma Meo had lived in her birthplace, Luoi Nong fishing village, Hue Province, for seventy-seven years. Worn out by hard lives and tired of fishing, she and her husband had accepted the house offered to them by the Peoples' Committee seven years earlier and moved for the first time since their wedding day.

The first thing we noticed was the two magnificent front doors that were a stand-out feature of her home. They were of dark wood with delicate inlays, beautifully crafted. My first impression upon entering her house was of warmth, friendliness and light. In pride of place was the little shrine, complete with all the certificates and a picture of the ubiquitous Ho Chi Minh keeping a watchful eye on the family.

Ma Meo was animated and lively, with crinkly eyes and a wide, natural smile. Her face was well worn, but I had to keep reminding myself she was eighty-three years old. Beside her was an elderly man in an olive green military style jacket and baggy grey tracksuit trousers. He turned out to be her husband, Truong Trang.

Trang left nothing to chance, seating himself just around the corner from us during the interview. The day belonged to Ma Meo but he would remain within earshot throughout the afternoon. Between Trang and a young family friend who would keep an eye on her from a distance, the old woman was looked after like the family treasure she clearly is.

She seemed pleased to receive guests, and tea was on the table before we could dispense with the formalities. This was a particularly sociable woman, very much at ease with an unusual visitor. She would not faze easily but as I had noticed before, the Mothers acquired many skills in dealing with foreign military forces on their doorsteps and do not frighten easily.

Trang was fiercely protective of his wife—he was mostly out of sight but would occasionally peer around the corner to observe proceedings, taking care not to distract anybody. I had the opportunity to observe him over the next six hours and found his devotion fascinating. He is obviously still besotted with his wife, and very proud of her. She is hardly unaware of his feelings, and I suspect she constantly reminds him of how lucky he is. This is a household that enjoys robust humour, for there was constant byplay between the various family members and friends who gathered during the course of our visit.

There was a younger man in police uniform about also. I was unsure of him, for I had developed reservations about policemen ever since watching an officer near Pleiku ride off on my Minka motorcycle after confiscating it, without so much as a backward glance. This young officer had a ready smile though, and a monstrous sense of humour, and we would have good times later. He turned out to be Vo Quang Vinh, a family friend.

Tea was taken and the interview was soon underway.

Ma Meo was born in 1920 in a fishing village on the Luoi Nong River, not far from her new house. Her parents were struggling fishermen, living in the poorest village in the whole district. There were not many fish. She was the second child, and had one brother and three sisters.

Schooling was out of the question, so she became a fisherwoman when she grew up. Her only brother, Le Van Quy, born in 1918, was a member of the Peoples Committee of the Communist Party, and a keen supporter of the revolution. The French arrested him several times, but he somehow survived and moved to Hanoi after the victory at Dien Bien Phu in 1954. There was no news of him until his return in 1975 after the end of the war.

We had already learnt that twenty-year silences were not that rare under the difficult conditions at the time. Quy had died only about three months before our visit.

Just then, there was a great deal of chatter and laughter. Vinh, the young police officer, was teasing her about her recent expedition to the local markets with her money shrewdly concealed in a pocket in the bottom of several layers of clothes she had been wearing. He had decided we should hear the story.

An urchin had somehow managed to steal the money. I think it was speculation about how he may have done so that caused the merriment—Huong never did get around to giving me a full translation. I suspect it got a little bawdy. She lost 600,000 Dong, about US$40, a very considerable sum of money in that area. Ma certainly missed the money, but did not seem to begrudge the urchin his success. Once the merriment had died down I returned to my questions.

Her parents decided Trang, who was from the same village, was husband material, and the young couple married in 1940, when she was twenty years old. He was also a fisherman, and after they married they fished together from a small bamboo boat.

"Did you have any problems with the French or Japanese?"

"We had no problems with the Japanese, but I remember Japanese soldiers throwing away any food they found in our houses. I think they wanted us to starve. Trang sometimes worked for them for between one and two kilos of rice for two days work."

It seemed pointless that the Japanese would pay such a pittance and then destroy the fruits of the labour anyway, but it was probably a way of ensuring a steady supply of willing, hungry workers. It was quite efficient, really, in a casual and genocidal sort of way. It was also no doubt an intimidatory gesture, a bit like cuffing the labourers during roll call at the rubber plantations. Ma was anxious to tell me more.

"When the French returned after the War, we supported the Revolution. Once we had two fighters stay with us. During the day they had to stay on the boat, and at night they would come out to fight. One of them was from Quang Nam Province, and he promised to buy me some clothes there when he visited again."

That was the province of Hoi An, home of very fine tailors. That would have excited a young woman, even in tough times.

"Did he bring you clothing?"

"No. The French killed him before he went back. He was buried between our village and the market. I lied about knowing him, but I used to cry when I passed his grave on my way to the market. I could not let the French see me cry—I had to control myself."

The family divided its loyalties during the war. Ma and Trang supported Ho Chi Minh, while her sisters married men who supported Diem.

"My village supported Ho Chi Minh, perhaps ninety-eight per cent," she told me proudly.

"It must have been difficult, risking betrayal to the Americans."

"No. We lived together but kept many secrets. We always hoped to convert the others to support Ho Chi Minh. But the Diem supporters moved away. My sisters moved to Quang Tri, Danang, and Saigon and I did not see them for many years."

"What is your relationship with your sisters like now?"

"We are close. The war is over and we must all get a better life."

The couple had four sons and three daughters, one of whom was a Diem supporter, or perhaps married to a Diem supporter. One daughter is today a farmer, one a nurse, another works in a factory. They all have families, and, not surprisingly, they all live nearby and she sees them often.

"My first son was Truong Van Bong. He was born in 1941. We could not afford proper schooling but he went to school at night two or three times a week. He became a fisherman also, and joined the local district force. He was good with boats, and had local knowledge, so he was useful to the Vietcong. At night he ferried Vietcong across the river, and then he would fish during the day. He married when he was twenty, and had one son.'

'Our village was the base of a Vietcong unit, so one day in 1966 US forces attacked. Bong stayed to help people escape. He was the last to leave, but one of two to die. Trang and I had been away, living on our boat, and we only heard what had happened when we returned. We buried him near the village where his own family still lives."

His widow never remarried, and Ma Meo and her family see her regularly.

The Americans found the villages frustrating. Patrols invariably found no young men there, often a sign that they were fighting for the Vietcong until they returned at night for food and rest. The Vietcong even controlled some of the Strategic Hamlets, forcing the guards to let them in at night for food and rest before slipping away in the early hours of the next morning to carry out the day's fighting.

"My second son, Truong Van Chua, was born in 1943. He attended primary school and then found work as a clerk with a local company. He worked for the Revolution by night doing secret work but US forces captured him. When I visited him in prison, they arrested me also. I was released later but Chua had to wait until the Vietcong entered Hue during the Tet offensive of 1968 to be freed. He then changed his name so that he could continue his work, which had to do with messages, I think. He was killed not long after when Hue was retaken by the ARVN with US support, and he is buried in Hue."

"How did you learn of his death?"

"I knew he had died when his regular messages stopped. I received confirmation some time later."

Ma Meo's third son, Truong Van Ngot, was born in 1945.

"Ngot worked as a clerk for the People's Committee, making identification papers. He had to move to a forest base in a dangerous area, but later the Chief of the Army Bureau wanted him to move to a safer place. But Ngot had lost two brothers, a cousin and a brother-in-law to the enemy and his mother's village had been burnt down twice, so he wanted to stay and fight. He refused to move and was in a tunnel with two Bureau chiefs when it was rocketed. The chiefs died in the attack and he sustained a broken arm. Ngot was taken prisoner but as he was uncooperative he was flown to another base in the highlands. There has been no further news of him since his disappearance in 1968, the year his brother Chua died."

Ma Meo's fourth son survived the war. Truong Van Chin, whom I was to meet later, was born in 1953. He is a police officer, based nearby. The young police officer in attendance, Vo Quang Vinh, is a colleague and close friend. I suspect Chin delegated his young colleague to look after Ma Meo during the interview.

"Were there occasions when you doubted the outcome of the war? You lost a brother during the French war in the 1950s, a son in 1966, and two more sons in 1968, which was probably the worst year of the war. At that time you had just one son left with no end in sight. Did you ever think the war would never end, or that it might be lost?" I was fascinated at how they had all kept going during such terrible times.

"No. I always knew we would win. Even with no food, we must try and try so much against the enemy, and we must win in the end."

"Ho Chi Minh was alive when your sons died, but he died the next year. How did that affect your thinking?"

"I did not hear of his death until later. When I learnt of it I knew we must continue and must win in the end. Now we all have a better life. Thanks to the government and the Communist Party everybody has a better life. Although I lost three sons, I have a son left, and now I have grandchildren and a big family. I am much more fortunate than many other Mothers."

I was thinking about her definition of good fortune when she surprised me again.

"Would you like to stay for dinner?"

"I would love to. Perhaps we could take you to dinner, and save you cooking."

"No, they will cook," she said, vaguely, "the young policeman is a very good cook, so he will help. My family will join us."

I was delighted, and told her so.

She was happy for me to take a few photographs, and posed in a beautiful black ao dai, with gold embroidery. I knew this had to be her finest outfit and she looked stunning. I told her so and there was loud laughter. I should have known better; this would take her a while to live down.

Vinh, the young police officer, discarded his uniform jacket, rolled up his sleeves and headed for the kitchen. Women flew off to buy fresh vegetables. Husband Trang kept a quiet eye on proceedings but he would have severed his right arm rather than interfere: whatever Ma decided was just fine by him—there was a rare chemistry between the two that revealed itself throughout the evening.

Ma's surviving son, Truong Van Chin the police officer, arrived with his wife and children. He was a solid, good looking man, but was wary of me. I expected as much: he had lost three brothers to westerners of my vintage, who had probably also shot at him on a few occasions. Chin had probably had men like me in his gun sights from time to time. He would thaw as the meal progressed.

Suddenly there seemed to be a lot of bodies around the place. Youngsters spread bamboo mats on the floor, and set out plates. Vinh produced cans of beer as seating arrangements were worked out and in no time at all superb food was laid out. Ma sat cross-legged on the bamboo matting, with husband Trang on her right. I sat on his right side, with Vinh on my right. Huong sat opposite me.

Vinh was the most talkative, full of humour and curiosity, and we maintained a lively discussion throughout the meal. Ma was strangely subdued, and I wondered if the presence of a westerner of Vietnam War vintage caused problems for her. As far as I could see, she just sat back and enjoyed the family occasion. Husband Trang had little to say—he kept an eye on his treasure and her enjoyment ensured his.

It was my turn to be questioned by everybody. Vinh, in particular, had many questions to ask. Perhaps he had not met many westerners, for I suddenly found myself in the role of oracle, sounding board and representative of western views.

"What do you think of the US wars in Afghanistan and Iraq? Has the United States learnt anything from the Vietnam War?" asked Vinh. The question was unexpected, and caught me totally unprepared. I was tempted to try to sidestep the issue, but everyone had been most forthright in answering all my questions so I felt I owed Vinh an honest response.

Ma Meo and family—chef extraordinaire Vinh is on the right,
Ho Chi Minh peers down

"I lack expert knowledge of those wars, but I think the US deserves credit for keeping civilian casualties surprisingly low in Afghanistan and Iraq after the appalling loss of life in Vietnam." This now seems to me to be a strange statement: what I meant was that at least the butchery of Vietnam had not been visited upon the Iraqi civilians, but I did not want to get too deeply into that.

In 2003 that invasion was still a recent event; President Bush had with his customary humility claimed victory and Rumsfeld was of the opinion that only a little tidying up remained. Iraq had not yet descended into the quagmire it has since proved to be, but I now suspect that my companions knew much better than I what was to follow. I pointed out to him that Vietnam was not the first country to suffer considerable civilian casualties at the hands of the Allies or the US.

This seemed to surprise them, so I told them about the million German and Japanese civilians who died during deliberate bombing of Cologne, Dresden, Hamburg, Tokyo, Hiroshima, Nagasaki and other cities during World War 2. I told them that as an Australian I was concerned at the pretext that led to the second invasion of Iraq, those elusive weapons of mass destruction.

"Why did Australia follow the Americans again, after Vietnam and Afghanistan?" I had been dreading this question. It has troubled me for years.

"I think our government received faulty or incomplete intelligence. Perhaps the intelligence was good, but poorly interpreted." I think they accepted that. I had by now developed a strong sense of shame at what had been done to Vietnam and the Vietnamese, but I was not able to discuss that over a family dinner gathering with children present in a household that had lost so heavily. Looking around at the other guests, it was obvious that they felt I had not fully answered the question, but I was not comfortable with Iraq as a topic so I returned to Vietnam War issues.

"The American tendency to depose leaders without proper consideration of the consequences worries me. The lessons of history seem to elude Washington. They authorised the removal of Southern President Diem without planning for a suitable successor, resulting in a long line of ineffectual leaders in South Vietnam. Afghanistan had its problems also, and now Saddam has been deposed, but the country is not yet governed properly. The US has lost many more soldiers since claiming victory than they did during the war, if one can call what happened in Iraq a war. It is beginning to look a bit like Vietnam." At that stage the US death toll was about one thousand; it seems a long time ago. I had no idea what the Iraqi civilian casualties were.

I was saved by the bell in the end, for time had flown and our Women's Union representative, Thuy, was overdue at home. Huong presented our gifts, and a small basket of food items, to smiles all round and we bade our farewells to a charming and hospitable family. It had been a long day, and a lovely dinner, but as always my hosts had given me a great deal to reflect upon.

Things were a little different when we returned at the end of August 2004. I wanted to see the family again, and I wondered also if Ma Meo was happy in her new home. Moving is just so foreign to the old peasants, something to be attempted as a last resort.

Young Vinh the police officer could not join us as his wife was at that moment in labour with their first child. Ma's son, Truong Van Chin, who had been wary of me at our first meeting, was in Quang Tri on a police training course.

This time it was we who extended the meal invitation and Ma accepted. A group of about eight of us drove to the restaurant of her choice, in nearby Hue city. Husband Tang chose not to join us—it seems he is something of a homebody, so as the only adult male I was heavily outnumbered.

Halfway to Hue, Ma Meo pointed to a clump of trees a couple of miles away: that was her old fishing village. Things have improved there of late—fishing technology has evidently overcome some of the earlier problems that led to poor catches. I detected an air of wistfulness.

The restaurant was excellent, and we sat outside at a long communal table. Ma had no teeth, so great care was taken in selecting the dishes for the evening.

"Would you like something to drink?"

"I would like a Tiger beer," she replied, to my utter astonishment. She was the first Vietnamese woman I saw drinking beer in about five months of travelling around the country. It was soon evident that she is quite partial to a glass of ale, although I wondered if she would have ordered a beer if Trang had accompanied us.

As soon as her glass was half empty she reached over, clinked glasses with me and uttered a toast. The contents of her glass then disappeared in one great swallow—a truly impressive performance. She sat back and waited for me to follow suit but I wanted to keep a clear head and delayed my turn for a while.

"I think you spend too much time in dubious nightclubs," I told her, and she laughed. The net result, of course, was that she ran out of beer early and would not accept another, so we shared what was left of mine. In return, she dished up an overgenerous portion of a particularly tasty fish dish for me. I think she was a little embarrassed.

On the way home afterwards she again indicated where her fishing village was.

"Do you miss the village, Ma?"

"Yes."

"Do you and Trang still go fishing?"

"No. Too old." I am really not sure about that. I suspect that if a house became available in Luoi Nong fishing village, and a small fishing boat happened to surface, Ma and Trang would be out of the city.

Huong and I had a good chuckle on the way back to the hotel. The old woman had thoroughly enjoyed the dinner, and had been good fun. We concluded that perhaps the absence of the men in her life for the duration of the meal had eased her inhibitions a little. She had certainly enjoyed being the centre of attention.

15. Cave Man Dreaming

One name kept cropping up during interviews with the Mothers; one face peered down from a wall in every house we visited: Ho Chi Minh of the wispy white beard, thinning grey hair and piercing eyes. Photographs often showed a reedy thin man wearing baggy short pants and sandals made from recycled car tyres and tubes. Sometimes he leaned on a walking stick, a man of uncertain health with an air of frailty about him, although once his revolution was under way he proved to be something of an intellectual bulldozer.

A few of the Mothers had expressed their grief at his passing as though he were a member of their families; his people followed him a fair way down the path to extinction. He possessed extraordinary clarity of vision and the gift of simplicity in his writings and speeches, and he never talked down to the vast majority of uneducated among his followers. When they experienced setbacks, he spoke of the need to improve; when they were victorious, he warned against overconfidence and reminded everyone of the long road to victory.

He was an inspirational figure to his people and, needing to know more about the man, I used as my standard reference the superb biography of Ho Chi Minh by distinguished historian William J Duiker. It is absurd to address Ho's role in a few pages, but a very brief look at aspects of his life give some indication about the character of the man Washington (White House and Pentagon) had to deal with. Any errors that follow are of course mine.

Ho was born Nguyen Tat Thanh (Nguyen who will be victorious) in 1890, near the city of Vinh, about 200km north of what would become the Demilitarised Zone after the French War. This is in the northern reaches of Central Vietnam, the former Annam. He arrived in the world in rebellious territory less than 20km from the city that would represent the start of the Ho Chi Minh Trail some seventy years hence, a city that Michael Maclear noted would have two intact buildings by war's end.

His father was a dedicated nationalist who held the equivalent of a Doctorate of Philosophy from Hue and resented the arrival of the French in his country. He had joined a revolutionary movement and when that was unsuccessful, moved back to the family plot of land in the village.

Ho attended the Quoc Hoc, the prestigious school in Hue that became a hotbed of Vietnamese resistance to all outside influences. His military chief, Giap, would attend the same school, as would Diem, later to become President of South Vietnam. Ho left the school around 1910 without a diploma after standing up for a student unfairly expelled by the authorities. He received no further formal education—stories about his brilliant academic career, his medical degree and other qualifications are incorrect.

He was a committed Nationalist, desperate to secure freedom for his country. Since Vietnam had been in a political vacuum during the French occupation, Ho felt the need to learn about forms of government, and his solution was to visit the outside world where he might find enlightenment from great nations. When he found a job in the kitchen of a French ocean liner, Ho changed his name so as to not besmirch the family name with his lowly position. He was to change his name dozens of times over the next thirty years in order to escape imprisonment or execution.

Thanh, or Ho, worked in the kitchen of the Savoy Hotel in London where Escoffier, the great French chef, was in charge. Escoffier liked him and promoted him to the pastry division. His spell at the Savoy apparently left him with a taste for good food, which must have haunted him later as he spent years on the run, living rough.

He is thought to have worked in the steel industry in the USA during World War 1 despite the dangers involved in crossing the Atlantic. He moved to France in 1917, where he became a photo retoucher in Paris, and was active in the Vietnamese community there. Whilst living in Paris he also met many Frenchmen who would rise to positions of political power in the 1950s. Ho bought a suit and tried to present an independence petition to the US delegation at Versailles in 1919 when the Peace Conference was in progress. Disillusionment with Western politics and politicians set in, but his main ambition never wavered. A free and united Vietnam was his ultimate goal.

As a founding member of the French Communist Party he visited Russia before moving to China in 1924 under the name Nguyen Ai Quoc. There he was once more active within the Vietnamese exile community, some of whose members were trained to organise disruptive and destabilising activities in their home country.

It was in Canton that Nguyen Ai Quoc married a Chinese woman, Tang Tuyet Minh[17], a marriage that reportedly produced a daughter. The Hero Mothers I interviewed would no doubt have been shocked at even a suggestion that Ho had married, for he seems to have acquired a special aura, that of an ascetic who lived a life of self-denial so that he could devote his life to his country and his people. I certainly would not like to convey to Ma Huong that Ho had taken a Chinese bride. Ho appears to have been quite unconventional in his relationships with women, due perhaps in part to a life spent largely on the run.

Marital status notwithstanding, Ho decided to move to Thailand. He travelled via Hong Kong, Shanghai, Vladivostok and other places to Paris in 1927, journeying to Thailand through Europe the next year. In 1929 he was sentenced to death *in absentia* by the French in Vietnam, and had to travel about with extreme caution as the reach of the French Surete was considerable. He moved about the region extensively and it was in Hong Kong in 1930 that he met a dark and attractive activist, Nguyen Thi Minh Khai, who had been sent there as his assistant[18]. They would become romantically involved, and possibly marry, before Minh Khai would marry another before being tortured and executed by a French firing squad. Minh Khai was the sister of Giap's wife, who suicided after torture by the French rather than risk betraying her husband.

Ho Chi Minh appeared to like women. Having separated from his Chinese wife, and later from Minh Khai, there are suggestions that he was assigned a "temporary wife" sometime later in Russia, and that he fathered a daughter in that country[19]. In 1965, at age 75 and in failing health, Ho requested an unusual favour of an old Communist Chinese friend: a young woman from China as a companion[20]. He was perhaps too much the father figure in his own country to find a suitable local candidate without sparking a major outcry. His request was quietly shelved.

He was arrested in Hong Kong in 1931, claiming to be Chinese journalist Song Man Cho, and faced extradition proceedings that would see him return to Vietnam where his death sentence awaited him. A great deal of legal work saw this go all the way to the Privy Council where Sir Stafford Cripps represented the government of Hong Kong. Complex dealings eventually resulted in Ho travelling to China in 1934, and then on to Russia during a dangerous period: Stalin's purges led to the execution of many of his friends and associates.

During that decade as he moved between Russia and China, Ho also saw at first hand the traumas of famine in the Ukraine in 1932 that saw 5-7,000,000 die as the result of collectivisation of farmland. He observed the relatively highly-mechanised Japanese military machine bogged down on poor roads in China. It was a fate that would befall the French 20 years hence in Vietnam as they pursued the Vietminh around the North.

Ho finally returned to Vietnam in 1941 after a 30-year absence, adopting the name Ho Chi Minh (He who enlightens) for the first time. Practically a stranger in his own country and with the death sentence still hanging over him, personal security was a pressing issue. He and a few trusted colleagues set up headquarters in a cave at Pac Bo on the Chinese border in order to liberate and unite his country. The location of the cave afforded them the option of walking into China if ever the French attacked their base or threatened to capture the wily patriot.

Ho's genius was perhaps best displayed in his complicated juggling of relationships with more powerful nations. In the early years he did his best to cultivate the USA in the hope they would prevent the return of the French to Indochina after World War 2. When the French did return, Ho cultivated the Chinese, who provided a great deal of support, and the Russians, also a source of massive amounts of aid that included the missiles that helped protect northern cities. Relations between his two great benefactors were at times stormy, and required careful management. In the meantime, he had to cope with dissension within his own country as the war progressed and escalated and there were differing views as to how best to bring the war to a successful conclusion.

The background of this college dropout could hardly have been more different to that of any of his contemporaries in the White House. Ho had been down the road less travelled; he knew his way down the dark and dingy back streets, while John F Kennedy led a privileged and sheltered life. Ho had been a labourer in the USA and baked pies in London, whereas Johnson did not know where Vietnam was when he was so suddenly called into office after Kennedy's assassination. Ho had observed the great purges in Russia, while Nixon's travel had been with entourages on political voyages. Ho died in 1969, six years before the prized unification of his country, but he remains a father figure to a vast number of his people, particularly the older generations, revered almost to the point of worship. He would not see Nixon disgraced by impeachment, the year after his Vice President Spiro Agnew vacated office, also in disgrace.

Today one can visit the cave: the table where the future of Vietnam was mapped out is still in place. Nearby is a serene pool that Ho named Lenin Pool, one he fished at occasionally. According to a guide his form as an angler was unremarkable.

16. Duong Thi Sam

Back in Hue, Huong had a couple more interviews lined up, so we rose early to ensure we would be able to board an evening flight to Saigon. We called in at the home of Ngo Thi Than Thuy, the Women's Union representative who had by now adopted us. We had a little time on our hands, and enjoyed tea with her family before setting off to meet Duong Thi Sam.

When we arrived at the turnoff to her hamlet, there was some concern among the villagers about damage our hire vehicle might cause in the narrow laneway, so we strolled the last few hundred meters to her home. Money is very tight in the Central Highlands, and there was no point risking something as disastrous as running over someone's duck, or colliding with a pig. It was a pleasant walk as her surrounds were particularly picturesque.

There were a few small lakes about, with fish farming one of the main hamlet activities. The place abounded with ducks, chickens, dogs and groups of children. The atmosphere was vibrant and happy, and it seemed an ideal place in which to raise children. Then I realised that this was true of every village we had visited. That nagging wonder at how things had got so out of shape for the peasants of Vietnam was reinforced once more as I tried to imagine military mayhem breaking out in such a delightful setting.

We passed haystacks taller than a house, built in toadstool shape. They were truly impressive, and seeing my fascination with the structures, one of the women with us volunteered that the stacks had often concealed Vietcong fighters. It was not clear to me how one hides fighters in haystacks but I was gaining some understanding of how frustrating it must have been to patrol the villages.

Ma Sam was waiting for us, smartly attired in a blue and white polka dot trouser suit, with a maroon cardigan to keep out the morning chill. She was elfin, sprightly and alert, and seemed pleased to have a group of visitors. She looked like a relative youngster, with young eyes and smile lines around her mouth accentuated by attractive, prominent cheekbones.

Tea was served within minutes and after Huong had dealt with introductions, the old woman seemed keen to get into it.

"I was born in a nearby village in 1931, and I was the oldest of five children. I had two brothers and two sisters. My parents were poor farmers, but my father made farm implements at home to earn more money." This made her easily the youngest of all the Mothers we interviewed.

I started to draw a crude family tree, as I always did in an effort to account for all family members. Huong and I also used the time to gauge initial reaction to our presence in case we needed to change pace or prolong small talk to set somebody at ease. The Mothers sometimes wandered into side conversations that were always fun, and sometimes led to interesting places. Suddenly there were peals of laughter from the women, and Huong was having trouble keeping a straight face while everyone else doubled up with laughter.

Convolutions in the family tree were responsible for the mirth, as Ma's father had an unusual way of achieving that delicate balance between connubial bliss and production of a son and heir. And, I suspect, physical gratification.

Ma Sam's mother had health problems, so she produced only one daughter. Since her wifely duty required that she bear her husband sons, she, as a good wife, suggested to her husband that he take a second wife who might produce the desired results. This he did in 1951, a year before Ma Sam's mother died. This second wife produced two sons and a daughter. Ma Sam had, by this stage, already married and produced a son. This son was born in the same year as her father's second wife's daughter. In a fairly staid community this would certainly have fired up the chatter around the well—Ma Sam's father had become a father and a grandfather in the same year.

I had barely finished sketching detour lines on the family tree when there were more laughing fits. This time it took everyone a little longer to recover.

"Before he took a second wife, my father had a woman friend. He hoped that she might bear him a son. She lived with us secretly, but she bore him a daughter. This was unsatisfactory from Father's point of view, so the woman friend returned with her daughter, to her parents' home."

Father had simply loved women, I thought, trying to imagine how one would conceal a woman friend from neighbours in such a tight little community. The man's treatment of the young woman seemed brutal, but there was barely a raised eyebrow in the house so it seems that either this was acceptable conduct at that time or the women had given up on the man. The relationship was evidently to proceed subject to performance and the woman had not produced a son.

Times have changed and the women present during the interview clearly would have had something to say to Father, had he been around.

"I think I might have to write a separate book about your father's relationships with women," I told the old woman, and we had a chuckle about his arrangements that led to more laughter and head shaking. Ma Sam was pretty relaxed by now—she had been nervous about our reaction to her father's unusual ways, I think.

"How did you feel about your father's unusual approach to producing a son?" I asked her.

"Since my mother loved him, she suggested he take a second wife. My mother did not mind, so I did not mind." She seemed a little bemused about the woman friend, but perhaps she was merely a little embarrassed. We moved on.

She began to support the Revolution in 1945 at age fourteen years. She served as a messenger, and then joined the Long Haired Army, cooking, nursing or helping in any other way she could until 1954. There was lots of fighting and shooting in the area, and her family moved several times. Her half brothers and sisters survived the war because they were too young to be involved.

"Do you know what happened to the daughter born to your father's lady friend?"

"She supported the Revolution, but she died quite young. She spent time in Con Dao prison after US forces arrested her in 1974, but died some time after her release." There was a chronological problem with this. The US forces left Vietnam in 1973 and could not have arrested her. She would actually have been arrested by the ARVN, or Army of the Republic of Vietnam, as the South Vietnamese forces were known.

"Please tell me about your husband."

"I married when I was twenty years old in 1951. My husband was from the same village and was three years older. This was not an arranged marriage—we met and fell in love. He also supported the Revolution and joined the local defence unit."

The family had survived the French occupation unscathed, so I asked her about her children.

"I had a son, Tran Hung Ngu in 1952. The French knew we supported Ho Chi Minh, so we had to move about to avoid imprisonment. Then, in 1954, my husband moved north to assist in the war effort. I heard no further news of him until 1975 or 1976. Life was difficult for Ngu and me because my name was on the lists of supporters of the Revolution that the French had handed over to the Americans. We were both arrested in 1965 when he was only thirteen. After we were released from the American base at Hue, I found domestic work in the city. Ngu was able to attend school for the first time, but he started supporting the Revolution as a messenger. He was returning to his Vietcong forest base when a US bombing raid killed him in a tunnel."

"Were you able to recover his body?"

"Friends buried him, and we recovered his body after the war. He now lies in a nearby military cemetery."

It seemed that Ma's story was relatively straightforward, her father's relationships with women notwithstanding. There was just the one question that needed to be finalized. She had said that there had been no news of her husband until 1975 or 1976.

"What was the eventual news of your husband?"

"He came to visit me. He explained that during his long absence he had been unable to visit me or contact me. I understood that; it was simply too dangerous and there was too much to be done. He met and married another woman, who bore him two sons and two daughters."

She had of course waited for him. She had seen him off on his mission with a toddler in her arms. During his absence, she had raised the child, later losing the young man to the war, grieving alone. Ma Sam remained calm and dignified throughout the interview. We were all a bit aghast at the implications of what she told us, but, like Ma Ha, she calmly defended her man.

"He came alone to visit me and to explain everything to me. I understood how such a thing could happen. He also came to stay with me for a few months to care for me when I received news of the death of Ngu. He visited me once more, and brought his second wife with him".

Somewhere in there was some chronology that needed to be straightened out. Perhaps she only learnt of the death of her son after the war—that was not unusual. She was toughing it out and there was no point in harassing her for details. It was time to move on. I had noticed framed photographs of father and son, the two men in her life on the little family shrine in her main room: it was obvious to us all that she loves her husband still.

"I travelled to Hanoi for his funeral. I feel he is still my husband."

She has long since reconciled herself with those distant events, and while she has bitter memories about foreigners sometimes, she looks to the future. US soldiers burnt down her previous two houses, but she built the house she now lives in. After 1975, she was a cook at a restaurant in Hue city owned by the Peoples' Committee. Left unsaid was the tough time she would have had from 1975 to 1994 before the Hero Mother financial support first became available. She lives by herself, an unusual existence for an elderly female villager. This probably illustrates why the loss of an only child qualifies someone for Hero Mother status and thus assistance with accommodation and finance.

Ma was happy to pose for a few photographs, and changed into an elegant, dark red ao dai for more formal photographs. It was lunchtime and she readily accepted our lunch invitation. Somebody recommended an eatery in a nearby town that laid on excellent food, where she ate well, was good company and seemed quite cheerful

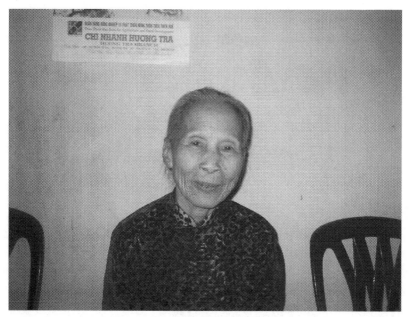

Ma Sam

She was serene as she waved us on our way, but to me she was a forlorn, sad figure. The women with me saw her a little differently, I think, but unlike them I have never been exposed to the aftermath of war.

On the way back to Hue we agreed that her husband had the decency to return alone to tell her the news. She had not suddenly met his new wife and replacement family at her front door after such a long absence. If he later visited with his new wife, it could only have been at Ma's invitation.

17. Nguyen Thi Chau

Our final interview in Hue was with Mother Chau, who lives in a former hamlet that is now an outer suburb of Hue city. Somebody always called ahead of our visits to ensure the Hero Mothers would be home when we visited. News of our visit had evidently preceded us as there was a carnival atmosphere about the place, and perhaps twenty people of all ages had gathered around her home.

She was tiny, dressed in a sort of pink brocade top and loose grey trousers. Her welcome was a little subdued and although she seemed physically quite strong, it was obvious from the outset that she was not well. The only Mother who seems to have some demons to deal with, her hooded eyelids were constantly moving about and she regularly cocked her head to one side as she seemed to listen to internal voices. I had no way of knowing if her war experience was the cause. Ma was very old, and I realised that the interview was going to prove very difficult, and that we would certainly not be going the normal distance with Ma Chau.

The centrepiece of her home was, of course, the shrine, easily the most elaborate one we had seen so far. Well-tended, it offered plenty of fresh fruit and flowers to the ancestors, some of whom were portrayed in photographs. The walls held certificates, calendars and calendar pictures. The room felt rather like a communal gathering point focused on a very busy shrine.

Tea was on the table almost as we sat down. Friends and relatives of all ages surrounded us so it was immediately clear that Ma enjoys plenty of support in the village. One woman in particular, a relative of advanced years, never left her side. She was on full alert, and reminded me of pictures I had seen of Red Indian chiefs of old. The woman stood out because she looked fierce with her pronounced cheekbones, prominent nose and piercing eyes. Her long grey ponytail contrasted strongly with the buns and short hairstyles we had seen throughout our other interviews. She was quietly watchful, but became more involved when we needed help, with Ma Chau struggling mightily with memory and chronology.

After introductions and formalities had been dealt with, it was time for Ma Chau to enjoy the first of many chewing gums. A young woman had been watching her anxiously and quickly obliged; she immediately set about preparing the next chew. A whitish paste, rather like freshly harvested rubber, would be cubed and wrapped in a fresh leaf, awaiting consumption. With a heavy frown, Ma turned her attention to us and the interview commenced.

It took a bit of a communal effort and perhaps five minutes to establish that she was born in 1918. We gathered the rest of our information with help from the officials present, her relatives and available documents.

She was the eldest child, with three brothers and a sister. Poverty had again proved to be a family problem. Her three brothers all supported the Revolution. The fate of one brother is unknown, but the other two survived the war. One has since died and the other now lives in Hanoi. Ng Thi Thua, her sister, supported the war performing duties as a guard. She had some primary school education, largely attended underground due to heavy military action in the area. She died around 1999.

Ma Chau married in 1944 at the age of twenty-six years. This was quite a late marriage, but perhaps the arrival on the scene of the Japanese caused major social disruption. The parents arranged the marriage but she was happy with the choice. Unusually, her father-in-law had a big farm that employed many workers, and he had several wives.

Ng Van Hap, her husband, was born in 1915 or 1916. He had schooling at home, where he learnt Chinese. Like her, he supported the Revolution, and like the husbands of Mothers Ha and Sam, he went north in the early 1950s to support the war effort. Unlike them, he returned home after the victory at Dien Bien Phu in 1954. In 1963 he joined the military to fight in the American War, heading south to assist in that theatre. There was no American War in 1963, but there

Ma Chau at the family shrine

were US advisors in Vietnam and there was clearly going to be US involvement in Vietnam.

Following her arrest in 1964 for supporting the Revolution, Ma was released after revealing nothing. Husband Hap was based in Quang Binh Province, just north of the seventeenth parallel where he was the Chief of a Division of the Air Force, with responsibilities for anti-aircraft defence. It was a very dangerous area and he was shot dead near Quang Tri in 1966, during a training trip.

Nguyen Van Minh, their only son, was born in 1948. He was the Vice Director of Hung Tra Post Office, the village in which we were conducting our interview, but joined the army in 1966 upon learning of the death of his father. He had duties as a guide and later had some sort of signals role. Minh was killed in a forest at Khe Dien while acting as a guide. He had never married.

Nguyen Thi Tam, their daughter, was born in 1950. She, too, was angered at the death of her father, and joined the army with her brother in 1966. She had secret duties, the nature of which Ma never learnt. She was the General Secretary of the Communist Party in Hung Tra village. When Tam was shot dead in Con Son, near Hue city, in 1972, Ma Chau had lost her whole family to the war.

The standard of living was low during the period of French and US occupation, she told us.

"We wonder why they came," she said, probably in reference to the Americans, the most recent foreign arrivals. The French had arrived before her birth.

"Anyway, they have gone", she muttered, more to herself than to Huong.

The old woman seemed exhausted, but when I wanted to take a few photographs she obligingly changed into a stunning, deep blue ao dai, and impatiently posed for a few photographs outside, among the fruit trees. She was looking troubled again as we handed our gifts to the woman of the striking features.

We bade our farewells, and, surprisingly, I was pleased to be heading back to Hue. There had been something particularly sad about the interview, a sense that the open, inviting appearance of the place somehow belied the utter devastation that lay within. At least Ma Chau was surrounded by people who loved her and cared for her.

We had several hours to spare before our evening flight to Saigon, leaving us an opportunity to see a little of Hue, a city with enormous connection to the war.

Hue is home to the Quoc Hoc, the prestigious National Academy founded by decree of the emperor at the end of the 19th century. Alumni of the Academy include General Vo Nguyen Giap, Ho Chi Minh and President Diem himself. One of the earlier revolutionary heroes, Phan Boi Chau, was under house arrest in Hue for many years under the French, and inspired many of the rebellious students at the Academy.

Hue was the last Emperor's capital of Vietnam. It was also the home city of Ngo Dinh Diem, the only Catholic President of the South, who had sort of deposed the last Emperor. The city was also the scene of a barbaric war crime when the Vietcong murdered perhaps four thousand civilians after taking the city in the Tet Offensive in early 1968, although the extent of the killing is disputed even amongst Western historians. The invaders took advantage of the opportunity to settle personal scores.

"Be sure to write about them burying people alive when you write your book", a Viet Khieu, that is a Vietnamese who lives abroad, instructed me. We had met two years before during a skin diving cruise off the coast at Nha Trang. He had a most impressive business card, with finely grained board boldly embossed in several colours. He held a high position in a Canadian government agency, and his family had prospered in their new country. His bitterness caused me to think his family had been victims of the atrocity. Yet, like many who left Vietnam as refugees, his longing for the land of his birth showed in his eyes as we spoke.

The skipper of the dive cruise boat we were on at that time had been extensively "re-educated" after the war, having served with the Americans. I think he had things to tell me, but he would be staying behind as I left for Australia and I was not going to compromise him.

Ngo Dinh Diem was an interesting choice as President of South Vietnam. Catholics were a 10 per cent minority religious group in Vietnam, so he faced difficulties even before he alienated the Buddhists. Diem was not regarded as personally corrupt, but the same could not be said of the family and cronies he surrounded himself with. In the end, his government became dysfunctional.

Washington supported his removal, but probably hoped for a gentler farewell. There was to be no villa in the South of France for Diem—he was murdered by order of several of his Generals who were concerned at his style of government. He was shot in the back of a military vehicle with his brother in 1963, then succeeded by a bewildering array of ineffectual leaders who were no match for Ho Chi Minh and his team to the north.

An English architect I met on a bus on a previous trip told me he could read the story of the trauma of Hue in the design of the buildings. Buildings were erected out of period to replace those destroyed, and were then altered later as they were in turn destroyed, repaired, or replaced. He could pretty well follow the path of the fighting.

The fine Thien Mu Pagoda sits on the banks of the Perfume River, providing serenity and magnificent photo opportunities around dusk each day. The sunset, framed by distant mountains, reflects off the water as sampans slowly ply their trade up and down the river. During my first visit to the country, I had been captivated by the serenity of the pagoda. Young monks had just finished martial arts training towards evening when an old Vietnamese woman detached herself from her family group and shyly approached me.

"You look just like Hemingway," she told me, smiling.

"Madam, I wish I could write like him," I told her, and we laughed, and talked of the serenity of the place before we parted company. She spoke of her love of the country, as did so many others I have met since, regardless of political persuasion or philosophy. I think this fierce, universal love of country is one of the main contributors to that fierce Vietnamese spirit of resistance.

A few minutes later, almost inevitably, I practically stumbled into a famous relic of the war years in the form of an old Austin Westminster circa 1955. It was from this pagoda that the monk Thich Quang Duc travelled to Saigon where his act of self-immolation in protest at President Diem's treatment of Buddhists was captured by a photographer and rocketed around the world. A fellow monk had poured petrol over him as he sat in a lotus position on a street. Another friend had lit the match. Duc uttered not a sound until his body toppled over some ten minutes later. The rusty, rather tired old blue Austin that carried him to his death is on permanent display at the Pagoda.

Madam Ngo Dinh Nhu was married to the brother of President Diem and, like both her husband and her brother-in-law, was not known for her ties to her countrymen and women. Upon hearing of Duc's self-immolation she described it as a "barbecue". The significance of the act itself apparently evaded her.

Huong showed me around the large grey Notre Dame Cathedral that the Americans apparently built for President Diem, whose brother was once the Bishop of Hue. Perhaps I had spent too much time around the Hero Mothers; perhaps too many sad stories had crept into my head, but it looked like just so much cement to me. Hue is a fine city, but it was not a time for sightseeing.

18. Satan's rainbow

I had spent considerable time interviewing the Hero Mothers, but it took some time for me to realise the war in Vietnam created several strains of heroic mothers. Those who are recognised as Hero Mothers are the most readily identifiable, but they are actually in the minority. Meeting them during my journey led to interviews with a couple of other mothers from a far larger group of heroes who are still fighting a war that will last longer than the remaining days of their lives, or indeed the lives of their children. The fact that it is a war they cannot possibly win does not deter them.

Agent Orange is perhaps the greatest horror of the war that saw the Geneva Convention pulped, squeezed and sprayed over large tracts of Vietnam. It was one of about fifteen herbicides used in Vietnam. It was named after the orange coloured band that identified the contents of drums, some other defoliants being Agents Blue, Green, White, Orange 11, and Pink. Agent Orange was the only spray that contained dioxins, the component that continues to spread fresh misery throughout the country. It has also ruined young lives and old in the USA and Australia, albeit on a relatively miniscule scale, although that would be of no comfort to the families affected.

Mother Que had recalled finding a liquid on the vegetables in her garden after an aerial attack, and we had met her daughter, who fell victim to Agent Orange. That story, together with the refusal of guides in Hue to accompany me to Aluoi because of chemical contamination in that district, prompted me to learn a little more about the problems associated with the chemical. This in turn led me a year later, during my fourth and penultimate visit to Vietnam in 2004 to an unusual institution in Hanoi and some inspirational people of all ages.

It started off in Tu Lien, a suburb some thirty minutes from central Hanoi.

The strains of a vaguely familiar tune took me by surprise, given the place Huong and I were visiting at the time. I had to severely test my memory to recognise the song.

"You put your left foot out . . ." It was of course the Hokey Pokey song. The reason for my surprise was that we were visiting the Friendship Village, run by the Vietnam Veterans Association. It is an Agent Orange treatment centre, a village financed by private foreign subscription. Sadly, but almost inevitably, Australia does not contribute.

We felt compelled to investigate the source of such obvious merriment, so with our guide's permission we entered an extraordinarily cheerful classroom. An enthusiastic young Western teacher was running her class through the words of the song she had written on the blackboard. She was demonstrating in lively fashion the appropriate body movements. Near her was a beautiful young woman in a wheelchair whose left foot, like her right, will not be going anywhere or doing anything for the rest of her life. Eyes shining, laughing, she happily pumped her arms in the air. She glanced at us, smiled broadly for a nanosecond, and returned her eyes to the blackboard. It was my first sighting of a true rock queen; the picture is imprinted on my mind and I hope it never recedes. If it does, I have the image captured in a photograph.

Huong had met the young woman before; she is 24 year-old Giang, a sort of honorary second in command of musical theatre and cheerleading I think, whose legs functioned normally until they started troubling her at 15. They are useless now, but the glow in her face suggested she had just won an Olympic gold medal.

We did not want to intrude any further, so we left them to it, but I spoke to the teacher by telephone a few days later. She turned out to be a Scot—a young geology student from Edinburgh who had completed a couple of months of voluntary work in India, and was enjoying a couple of months of teaching in Vietnam before resuming her studies. Song was a great teaching medium in a musical nation and the response to her classes had been overwhelming.

The village emphasizes education and vocational training for the youngsters, promoting self—esteem as well as the prospect of a degree of independence. They know they are loved, and leave with a sense of hope of a better future. We passed through a sewing room where parkas or anoraks are made, along with a variety of other goods. After visiting the artificial flower production area, we strolled through the award-winning vegetable garden to the continuing strains of the Hokey Pokey.

In another building we met a friendly group of male war veterans from Thanh Hoa who are experiencing health problems. They would stay at the village for a few weeks to undergo medical programmes, before rotating out to allow another group to receive treatment. The common denominator for all these men was their passage during the war along the Ho Chi Minh trail: Agent Orange returned to haunt them forty years later. One man survived three B52 bomb attacks only to be struck down by a chemical all these years later. He shook his head, smiling wryly in disbelief at his bad luck.

The Hokey Pokey in progress—Cheerleader Giang in the wheelchair

They were a very sociable group and there was the stream of banter and laughter that one associates with a group of ex-servicemen who have faced danger together. They were concerned about their health, and some have friends and family members who have themselves been touched by that wretched chemical. One of the tragedies of Agent

Orange is the feelings of guilt you detect in the old men that they have contaminated their loved ones. They feel guilty because the Americans used the spray to combat them—the spray was used to deny them forest cover as they moved about, and they took home the contamination that would ruin their family lives.

We entered what looked like a double hospital ward, and found a stunning young woman in animated conversation with her mother. This was thirty-year-old Huong, sister of Giang the rocker, who was afflicted by dioxins at birth. She sits upright on her bed, in a position that somehow seems unnatural. That may be because she has only a pair of miniature winglets where her legs should be, and sits on them. The sisters are in the village courtesy of a German newspaper that collected funds that will allow them permanent residency. Their mother is concerned about them and visits as often as possible. Mother and daughters are very close, and there is strong rapport between them, but the mother has some distance to travel and has the rest of the family to care for. It is an unnatural arrangement for a close-knit family.

I didn't meet the American war veteran who works at the village because he was away at the time. Suel Jones was a US Marine based near Quang Tri during the war, in an area that was heavily sprayed with Agent Orange. Some time after he returned to the US, his partner miscarried, due he believes to Agent Orange issues. He spends half his year helping in Vietnam. The village relies on foreign funding, and particularly needs money and specialist know-how to help make their guests as self-sufficient as possible, and raise their quality of life. There is simply not the money available for the government to be able to assist all victims as much as it would like.

The Vice Director who met us as we arrived at the Village was himself a war veteran, and he enjoyed the assistance of a physiotherapist from Germany. She was sent by a German organisation to pass on her special skills in working with physically handicapped people to physiotherapists from all over the country, who in turn pass their knowledge on to others.

"What is your most urgent requirement here at the moment?" I asked her when we were alone.

"I'm not sure my answer would be the same as the Vice Director's," she told me, "but we need physiotherapists experienced in dealing with physically challenged patients. There is a great shortage of such skills in this country."

We learned of surgical teams that move about the country, performing surgery to correct problems like severely deformed limbs. The benefits are sometimes only cosmetic, such as the straightening of hideously deformed limbs, but it is important for victims to know that they are loved, that they are important, that people care about them.

That evening, back in my hotel room, I reshuffled my dreams list: the children's kitchen in Hue now ranked second to a mobile surgical unit with a rotating team of Australian surgeons regularly achieving miracles, and passing on their skills to some of the less experienced local doctors. Five years later I have made no progress in this direction, but the passion is very much alive and publication of this book will energise me to knock on the doors that really matter: those of philanthropists, and those that lead to the White House in Washington, DC and Parliament House, Canberra.

A few days later we visited the family of Nhu Van Phuc, a 52 year-old war veteran who lives with his wife and three children in central Hanoi, within a couple of hundred metres of the Army Museum. At the time of our visit, he was on duty as a factory guard, but his wife Nguyen Thi Tu welcomed us at the door of their modest apartment. We stepped into the main room of their house, where I met a profoundly stricken Agent Orange victim for the first time.

Eldest son Phong was in his normal place, a wooden cot in a corner of the front room of the house. It was in a well-lit spot, close to a window, and he would be able to hear people talking outside as they passed the home, or even glimpse passers-by occasionally. The 21-year-old was excited to see us—he was upright in his cot, leaning in a corner before moving about and making loud grunting noises.

He was severely deformed. Both legs were withered, but his right leg was at least functional. He spent most of his time sitting in his cot, or wedged upright in the corner from where he could see his mother. His hair was short and there were numerous cuts on his scalp where he had hurt himself with his favourite toy, a short plastic comb. Taking away his comb upsets him a great deal.

Phong has simian features, and is an intimidating presence to newcomers. Communication with him is impossible although he sometimes repeats lines he memorises from a few television shows, and repeats names he recalls from family conversation. He could leave his cot by himself if he chooses to, but has not so far felt the urge. Weather changes upset him, and that was evidently what caused him to play so fiercely with his comb.

During our interview with his mother, he would call out names, laugh and make a lot of barking noises. His mood seemed to vary from relative happiness to anger, and the mood swings were sudden and disturbing.

Tu told us that she has known her husband all her life. The couple grew up in the same commune, in a small village in Ha Nam Province. She was a friend of his sister; they became friends and fell in love, but were separated when Phuc joined the army in 1975, the year the Northerners won their war against the South. He was based in Tay Ninh in the south of Vietnam, an exit point for the Ho Chi Minh trail. It was also an area of concentrated Vietcong numbers, so Agent Orange had been used liberally in the area for some years before. Phuc took two weeks leave in 1982 and travelled north where the young couple married.

He remained in the south until 1987, spending time also in Cambodia, but visited Tu annually. In the meantime, however, she was pregnant with a honeymoon baby she would have to raise on her own until her husband's return from the south. His military wage was always very small, and until his return Tu raised Phong on her own, breeding pigs and chickens to provide for the family.

A month after Phong was born in 1983, Tu saw a doctor who diagnosed a brain problem. The baby's left hand was inactive also, and he spent three months in hospital. Then followed stints in a children's hospital and treatment with Chinese medicine and acupuncture.

Before the birth in 1989 of Tung, her second son, Tu fell pregnant twice, but miscarried. Like so many families, the young couple didn't know about the effects of Agent Orange—they thought they were being punished for some sins in the past, wrongdoings that may even have been committed by previous generations.

Tung was now 17 years old and appeared quite normal but is not without his own problems. He has no appetite and is physically weak. Despite some blood and skin ailments, he attends school, but is lethargic and tires easily, possibly because of his stomach disorder. His parents face a dilemma as they love their son and do not want to send him to a village that will care for him, even if one could be found. In the meantime, the artistic young man dreams of a career as a telecommunications engineer.

The third son is 12 year-old Thang, who has liver trouble; he stresses easily, and requires gentle treatment. He is not sporty, although he is a keen follower of football. The youngster lacks some sort of control mechanism—when he does go out to play he continues until someone persuades him to stop; the same thing happens when he is on a computer. He dreams of a career as an art teacher, although his artistic talent does not yet match that of his brother Tung.

It is a tough situation for Tu. Her husband lacks patience with his three sons, so she has the responsibility of raising the family. This is one of the traditional woman's roles, but it is far more difficult for her since there is no respite care available, no visiting carers or nurses, and she does not know what it means to have a day to herself, or even a very brief holiday away. She worries about who will look after her children when she is no longer around.

Tu is an attractive woman who looks younger than her forty-seven years, despite all the difficulties she deals with every day of her life. As we talked with her, Phong was in the background making noises but she maintained her natural dignity as the woman of the house even as she kept an eye on her son.

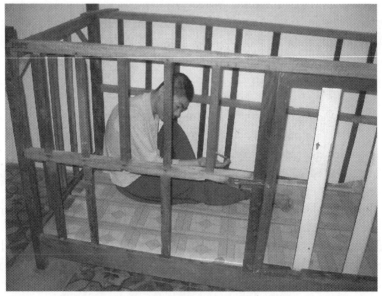

Phong at 21 years of age

At the end of the interview we left a remarkable but weary mother to her demanding routine of family care. Phong called out to us as we left, but only he and his Maker know what he said.

Our next visit was to the To family, who lived in a village thirty minutes from Hanoi. The dioxins had skipped a generation in their case, and had targeted only one very junior member of the family, as was indicated by the small wheelchair parked near the front entrance to the house.

To Tien Hoa is the 55-year-old grandfather in this household. A war veteran, he works now in furthering the interests of the elderly in his community. Over cups of tea, he told of how he joined the army in 1968, the worst year for both sides in terms of casualties. He volunteered, applying in writing five times before being accepted. He was refused at first because he already had a brother serving in the army.

As had emerged during interviews with the Hero Mothers, the war machine grew hungrier as the conflict progressed. 1968 was the year of Khe Sanh and the Tet Offensive disasters, so normal recruitment criteria were abandoned. The only sons of families were allowed to join up, and families like that of Mother Thu in Dien Ban were allowed to contribute any number of children.

Hoa was sent south with his military unit to Quang Tri, a real hot spot, arriving there partly by way of the Ho Chi Minh Trail. The young soldiers were of course aware of Agent Orange spraying in the area, but they had no idea of the potential consequences. The army issued some protective clothing but it was too heavy to wear continuously. They were issued masks, but these were soaked during river crossings and since that rendered them heavy and uncomfortable, they were mostly abandoned.

He now has an occasional rash, especially if he drinks alcohol, but seems to have otherwise escaped the ravages of the chemical. Hoa married Nguyen Thi Gai in 1973, and they had four children, of whom only the oldest son showed any ill effects, having only four toes on one foot. It appeared as though the family had been spared, but the good fortune was not to last.

The remarkable youngster who normally scurries about in his little wheelchair at high speed interrupted his play to join us. His personality was so strong, the vibes that emanated from his tiny frame so positive, that I hardly noticed that his body seemed to end at the waist.

To Thanh Nam

To Thanh Nam was born in 1997. He has sparkling, piercing eyes to match a powerful presence; what he lacks is legs, but that is barely noticeable after a few minutes, so adept is he at flitting about the place using his arms. He moved from his chair to the arm of his grandfather's in a couple of easy movements. There was a very strong connection between the two, and since Nam's father was out working, it was up to Grandpa Hoa to tell us about the youngster.

When Nam was born, the hospital viewed his deformity as a normal one, that is, not necessarily Agent Orange-related, but the Red Cross visited the family the following year and confirmed that the deformity was due to the chemical. Hoa described his joy at the arrival of his first grandchild, heightened of course because it was a grandson, but now he feels sad. This could have been partly because the old man feels responsible because he was the one who contacted the chemical. There is nothing anyone can say to relieve the sorrow of these old warriors.

The youngster attends a normal school, and is very intelligent, something that became obvious after a few minutes in his company. He has not yet decided on a career but possesses that marvellous attitude common to all the victims we saw that he is not really handicapped in any way, just a little challenged. Sadly, Nam is going to need all that fabulous fighting spirit that is so generously distributed throughout the country, as he makes his way through life.

Grandfather Hoa told us some of his friends have problems within their families too. There was a lot of spraying around Quang Tri, he said. Within two days of spraying, the trees were defoliated, at which stage napalm was often dropped to complete the destructive cycle. A guide in the area had told me that tigers and other animals had inhabited the area before the war, but those who survived the heavy bombing had moved towards Laos as their forest environment disappeared. Thirty years later they have not returned and I could not establish the ultimate fate of the animals. Indochina was not a good address for them for the period 1965-75, and I have no idea what effect Agent Orange may have had on them. It could not have been beneficial.

I mentioned to Hoa a recently declassified report I had read about a secret American operation known as Project Pink Rose that began in 1965. The Joint Chiefs of Staff received a recommendation from the Commander in Chief Pacific "to develop a capability to destroy by fire large areas of forest and jungle growth in Southeast Asia".

A test operation was documented at Chu Phong Mountain near Pleiku when 15 B52s dropped incendiaries on a defoliated area. The results indicated that this technique might work, but nobody divulged that burning dioxins significantly increases their toxicity. So, not only were cancer—causing chemicals introduced into the war, but their toxicity was increased by the burning process. The programme was terminated in 1967, but Hoa recalled being aware that it was still operational a year later. He may have been commenting on something that occurred the year before, passed on to him by other veterans of the day.

Nam's father was able to obtain permission to have three children, despite a government policy limiting families to two, since his oldest son was handicapped. Nam's two siblings have no Agent Orange problems at this stage, but the family will not rest easy for at least another generation.

There were a number of framed certificates on the wall, and Hoa modestly told me about his commendation from his army days. His mortar unit had enjoyed success against US tanks on Highway 9 near Lang Vei, not far from Quang Tri, and near a military airport in Aluoi in the A Shau Valley, destroying ten tanks. His face grew animated as I asked him to draw pictures of the action so that I could grasp what had happened, and for a few minutes the old soldier took a break from Agent Orange as he recalled past glory.

By the time we left, it was clear that he would happily exchange the awards for his grandson's health, but unfortunately the gods of this particular war followed very different rules and no such deals will be countenanced.

In an effort to help me come to grips with the scale of the problem, Huong arranged a meeting in July 2005 with Dr Tran Duc Phan and Mac Thi Hoa, Director and Deputy Director respectively of the Agent Orange Victims Fund of the Vietnam Red Cross Society. They confirmed that there are about two million Agent Orange victims living in Vietnam at present. The number keeps changing as people die, to be replaced by new victims. I was handed a copy of *Agent Orange in the Vietnam War—History and Consequences,* by Prof Le Cao Dai, M.D. of the Vietnam Red Cross Society.

It is a well-compiled book, a superb introduction to a very complex issue about which so much has been spoken and written, with so much yet to be agreed on. A passage in the introduction by Prof Nguyen Trong Nhan seems to convey the unique attitude of many Vietnamese to the war in general:

> Without question, the scientists of Viet Nam and many countries, including the United States, must continue to co-operate in long-term research to understand more clearly the damage caused by Agent Orange. It is also true that our long term interest is to let the past stay in the past. Yet as human beings, we cannot in good conscience forget. We must take action now, not delay any longer, for the sake of those who have been hurt by Agent Orange.

A US Veteran website[21] is helpful. American Vietnam veterans had common cause for years with Vietnamese Agent Orange victims: their claims for assistance and recognition were also disputed. On page 2 of their November 1990 web page they address the origins of Agent Orange:

> Agent Orange had its genesis as a defoliant in an obscure laboratory at the University of Chicago during World War 2. Working on experimental plant growth at the time, Professor EJ Kraus, chairman of the school's botany department, discovered that he could regulate the growth of plants through the infusion of various hormones. Among the discoveries he made was that certain broadleaf vegetation could be killed by causing the plants to experience sudden, uncontrolled growth. It was similar to giving the plants cancer by introducing specific chemicals. In some instances deterioration of the vegetation was noticed within 24-48 hours of the introduction of the chemicals.

There was no use for the chemical during World War 2 but:

> Army scientists found that by mixing 2,4-D and 2,4,5-trichlorophenoxyacetic acid (2,4,5T) and spraying it on plants, there would be an almost immediate negative effect on the foliage. What they didn't realize, or chose to ignore, was that 2,4,5-T contained dioxin, a useless by-product of herbicide production. It would be twenty more years until concern was raised about dioxin, a chemical the Environmental Protection Agency (EPA) would later call "one of the most perplexing and potentially dangerous known to man."

The Veterans' website states that the makers and Air Force personnel were aware of the dangers of Agent Orange. It quotes Dr James Clary, an Air Force scientist in Vietnam who helped write the history of Operation Ranch Hand. Clary says the Air Force knew Agent Orange was far more hazardous to the health of humans than anyone would admit at the time:

> "When we (military scientists) initiated the herbicide programme in the 1960s," Clary wrote in a 1988 letter to a Member of Congress investigating Agent Orange, "we were aware of the potential for damage due to dioxin contamination in the herbicide. We were even aware that the military formulation had a dioxin concentration higher than the 'civilian' version, due to the lower cost and speed of manufacture.

However, because the material was to be used on the 'enemy,' none of us were overly concerned. We never considered a scenario in which our own personnel would become contaminated with the herbicide. And, if we had, we would have expected our own government to give assistance to veterans so contaminated."

It appears that nobody seriously considered the consequences for the Vietnamese who lived in the areas that received the twelve million gallons of Agent Orange. They were, after all, the enemy. The test case against manufacturers of the chemical (Dow, Monsanto, Diamond Shamrock Corporation, Hercules Inc, T-H Agricultural & Nutrition Co and Thompson Chemicals Corporation all manufactured the product) was dismissed by a New York District Judge in March 2005. An article in "The Australian" newspaper of 12 March 2005 caught my attention:

US District Judge Jack Weinstein rejected the case in New York yesterday, saying he did not agree that the defoliant and similar herbicides used in the Vietnam war should be considered poisons banned under the international rules of war.

The article went on to suggest another problem with the case:

Judge Weinstein found the plaintiffs could not prove Agent Orange had caused their illnesses, citing a lack of large scale research.

US Veterans' claims were settled in 1984. Under the terms of the settlement, the veterans who claimed exposure to Agent Orange would receive $180 million from the chemical companies. But those companies did not have to accept blame for any injuries that occurred as a result of Agent Orange. The US government was not a party to the litigation.

"This resolution is a compassionate, expedient and productive means of meeting the needs of the people involved," said David Buzzelli, vice president of government and public affairs for Dow Chemical.

So it seems that whilst American and Australian Vietnam Veterans and their dependants are entitled to Agent Orange benefits, inadequate as they probably are, the Vietnamese who lived under the spray or who spent a lot more time passing through those areas have failed to find justice in the United States. The article closed with an item that enraged me.

"We've said all along that any issues regarding wartime activities should be resolved by the US and Vietnamese governments," said Dow Chemical spokesman Scot Wheeler. "We believe defoliants saved lives by protecting allied forces from enemy ambush and did not create adverse health effects."

I attempted to contact Mr Wheeler to point out to him that there is no record of Agent Orange saving Vietnamese lives, and to suggest that Vietnamese lives surely have some value. I also proposed to offer to escort selected chemical company personnel to Agent Orange treatment facilities so that they could explain their views to youngsters like Giang. I received an email from a Dow administrator asking for a copy of the article, and I duly forwarded it to her. A week later I was unable to contact her—her address no longer functioned. Dow had declined my invitation, and Mr Wheeler was not inclined or allowed to discuss the article with me.

In the meantime, babies continue to arrive with birth defects. Possible health problems associated with Agent Orange run to two pages. It includes an appalling list of cancers, diseases of the nervous systems and skin diseases.

Some of the men who brought Agent Orange back to their families seem to be in denial, as though unwilling to accept their role in the tragedy, even though it is not of their making. That leaves most of the burden to be borne by that centre piece of the Vietnamese family: the Mother.

The Vietnam War is still being fought and it is the mothers like Nguyen Thi Tu who are in the front line. Tragically, while her parents fought a thirty-year war that deserved to end in lasting peace, hers will be a lifelong struggle where even the smallest victories will be great ones. There can be no decisive Dien Bien Phu victory for her family. She knows that, but she will fight while she breathes.

An American perspective of sorts on the use of herbicides revealed itself to me in late 2007, after I had been working for a few months in Providence, Rhode Island in the USA. I returned to my comfortable apartment within easy walking distance of Brown University to find the lawn liberally sprinkled with neat little signs mounted on spikes.

I waited for the man in the chemical mask to put away his spray equipment, and then asked him about the signs.

"I've sprayed herbicide on the grass to keep the weeds out. We are required by law to put those signs out. There are a lot of dogs around and we can't have them getting sick."

Protecting New England dogs from poisonous chemicals!

19. Dinh Thi Chuy

The house of the last Hero Mother we would interview was in Saigon, but proved to be the most elusive of all the Mothers' homes. On a hot and humid New Year's Eve, we found ourselves in a very busy, chaotic part of the city, searching for a street amidst a lot of roadwork and property development, earthmoving equipment and construction detritus. We eventually turned onto a bumpy, narrow dirt road and stopped outside a smart new house that seemed rather out of place amongst such ordinary surroundings. This was certainly the most opulent dwelling we had visited to date.

Numerous large bonsai-style plants in massive pots on display in the front yard advertised a side-line run by Ma Chuy's entrepreneurial son. Near this display were tables, chairs and umbrellas, part of the outdoor café that was clearly the major business enterprise. It was great location: there was high traffic volume close by but the café provided a haven for stressed travelers wishing to escape the noise and bustle. When the developer's wreckage is removed, this will be a delightful setting.

A relatively corpulent, self-composed woman, dressed in a smart maroon trouser suit strode out to meet us. She wore a little gold jewellery, the first we had seen amongst the Mothers. We shed our shoes and followed her into a bright and airy main room with many windows and great natural light. The old woman arranged for her daughter-in-law to provide fresh tea, and then sat on her high-backed formal chair, slipping easily between the lotus position that comes so naturally to the old peasant women and a knees-under-chin posture. She was relaxed and after our normal introductions, she was happy to tell us her story.

"I was born in Ha Tay Province in 1922."

This interested me immediately. She was born in Ma It's territory, but she was a long way from her birthplace. This was unusual, and I wondered where the interview might take us.

"I was the fifth of seven children, with one brother and five sisters. My parents were poor farmers who owned their own rice paddy, but they also undertook outside work to earn a little more money. My brother studied Chinese and classical Vietnamese, but none of my sisters went to school. In 1943, I heard of work on the rubber plantations in the south, so I signed a contract."

She had undertaken the same journey as Ma It, but travelled about forty years later, when conditions were hopefully, but not necessarily better. She had journeyed at the age of twenty-one years, whereas Ma It had been only fifteen. Ma Chuy had undertaken her journey at an age where most young women were already married and starting their own families. I was surprised also that she had travelled during the time of the starvation and the Japanese occupation. She had been one brave young woman.

"While we were waiting for the ship to take us to Saigon, I met the man I would marry. His name was Nguyen Van Moc and he was a farmer from Nam Dinh. He was going to work at the same plantation. It was true love, and we travelled together to a new life."

"Were conditions on the plantation as you were told they would be?" I asked her.

"No. Conditions were hard. We had to sign a three-year contract. There were no holidays during that period, and we had to remain on the plantation the whole time. The plantation was guarded, and we worked six days a week, from five o'clock in the morning until five o'clock in the evening. Sundays were our free days, although you could not leave the plantation. If you tried to escape you would be beaten or sent to prison."

The plantation was a closed society. The young couple married in the plantation canteen, as many did—there were no opportunities to meet outsiders for three years. There was a small hospital on site and a company-owned market satisfied most of their material needs. Her supervisor was Vietnamese; they administered the beatings while the French overseers stayed away. French and other foreign senior managers attended to more serious disciplinary matters. Not a great deal had changed in the forty years since Ma It's time on the plantations.

Ma Chuy had her first baby there. She had to work until the seventh month of her pregnancy, and returned to the trees when her baby was two months old. There was nobody to help look after her baby, so she had to take it with her to the plantations every day. But something in the rubber trees was harmful to the baby and it died a few months later.

Ma Chuy with son Luong

I had been watching her face intently, and it softened slightly as she told us about her baby. I thought to myself, well, it's been sixty years and she's had plenty of time to come to grips with it, but even with everything else that's happened in her life, it still hurts. She's a Hero Mother, so Christ knows where we'll end up before the day is over. How the French played with the lives of the peasants! She was ready to continue.

"The Japanese came to the plantation in 1945. They had some problems with the French. There was a labour dispute, and then a big strike. Then there was a revolt, and a lot of damage to the plantation. We had no more work and we were a long way from home. Without enough money to return to our families in the north, we moved to the forests in Long An Province."

Again, I thought, what a terrible predicament for the young couple. They had worked very hard under dreadful conditions for perhaps two years and had not the money to return home. Family is so important to them, and to be reduced to living in a forest in the distant south must have taxed their strength terribly. Long An is to the west of Saigon, on the Cambodian border. There they met a kindly couple who suggested they might do better at Cu Chi, a little closer to the city. They moved, and friendly people in Cu Chi helped them build a house. They did whatever work they could find and raised five sons and a daughter. They decided their family would support Ho Chi Minh.

"Nguyen Van Kim was my oldest son. He was born in 1948, and went to primary school. He left school at thirteen to become a Youth Volunteer, and served as a messenger. When he was fifteen years old he decided to follow the General of a division, working in the Army Bureau; at seventeen he survived a tunnel bombing attack that killed the General. He then joined a special army division fighting in Saigon where US forces shot him, and he died three days later in December 1966. Friends buried him but I don't know where he lies. He was eighteen years old when he died, and he had not married."

I should have been used to this by now, but I never became hardened to what turned out to be a typical biography. It seemed that an average young school kid could be expected to become a volunteer messenger at thirteen, a soldier at sixteen, and as a five-year war veteran quite possibly a casualty of war at eighteen. They missed the precious normal teen years, rushing instead through years of fire and fear, dying before even knowing a girlfriend. They were preceded often by brothers and sisters, parents, uncles and aunts.

"My second son, Nguyen Van Dinh, was born in 1950. He became a Youth Volunteer at fourteen and later moved to Saigon to serve as a messenger. He died in a bombing raid in the Cu Chi area in 1969. Locals buried him, but I don't know where he is. He died when he was nineteen years old, and he was not married either.'

'Nguyen Van Chinh was my third son, born in 1952. He was a Vietcong messenger at fifteen, but he was wounded by rocket fire in 1968. He survived the war but had problems with his legs until he died in 1982. Chin married and had two sons and a daughter."

Here was a war veteran invalided at sixteen years of age. I was interested that Ma's first three sons had started their military service at ages thirteen, fourteen and fifteen. I meant to ask her if that was in some way significant, but by the end of the interview I passed on the question.

"My fourth son was Nguyen Van Luong, born in 1954. Like his three brothers he served as a messenger, working out of Saigon. He was wounded by rocket fire and lost an eye, but survived the war. He married and has one daughter, but hopes for another child next year. With help from the People's Committee, he built this house that we now share."

I was to meet him minutes later, a pleasant and articulate man who wears dark glasses that almost conceal his bad eye. A man who had lost three brothers, had another invalided out as a teenager, and had himself lost an eye. Oh, yes, and who was trying for a second baby at fifty years of age. I had come across yet another veteran who makes light of his injuries, is possessed of a ready smile and who considers himself fortunate despite a pretty terrible war.

Ma still had some more to tell me.

"Nguyen Van Sang was my youngest boy, born in 1956. He joined an entertainment division. They used to visit troops to raise morale. He was killed during an artillery attack in Cu Chi in 1973 when he was seventeen. Some friends buried him, but I don't know where he lies."

I wanted to ask her if he had perhaps hoped for a future as an entertainer, when the war ended, but they probably never really expected the war to end. How could they, after twenty-seven years? It struck me as being a cruel question so I stifled it.

Her husband Moc died of natural causes in 1957, so she had not only raised a large family on her own, but had mourned the annihilation of her family alone.

"Supporters of Diem identified me to the authorities and I was arrested in 1969. I spent five years in Thu Duc prison, Saigon. I was beaten sometimes, but I told them nothing," she said. "I received news of the deaths of two of my sons from friends who came to visit me in prison. I would cry at night, when I was alone, because I had to be strong. I am fine now, although weather changes cause problems for my old prison injuries."

"Cu Chi was a dangerous and treacherous area. There was the added risk of being informed on by neighbours. How do you feel about those sympathetic to the south? How do you feel about foreigners who were involved in the war?" I asked her.

"It was a long time ago."

She had produced a son roughly every two years and lost one every three years. She had been imprisoned and beaten. Thinking back to the story of Ma Gom I wonder if any family in Cu Chi survived the war intact. Ma Chuy lost sons aged seventeen, eighteen and nineteen. Another had died at thirty, probably because of war damage. She considers herself lucky, because she has a son left who only lost one eye, and a daughter who carries no physical injuries.

I had mixed feelings on the trip back to our hotel. My awareness of the massive destruction wrought upon Vietnam had of course increased with each interview, but although I had a great deal to learn before I could complete the journey I realised that there was no way of avoiding a permanent feeling of utter revulsion at what had been perpetrated by countries that have made no effort whatsoever to redress great wrongs. As far as Hero Mothers were concerned my journey was over, for as I wrote up my notes that evening I understood that I could not have handled any more interviews.

20. Those Viet women

I had interviewed eleven amazing old women of staggering strength and durability. The French and the Americans were shocked to find that even as the toll of the conflict kept mounting and the scale of the war escalated, the peasants nevertheless kept stepping up to the plate. The Vietnamese women once more carried their share of the load throughout one of the longest wars in history. Some reputable historians believe they carried more than their share.

Women had helped the war effort by providing food, accommodation, first aid, and intelligence. They had stood behind their men as they set off for war; they had raised their children and stood behind them as they followed that same deadly path; when called upon they had acted as spies, messengers, booby trap makers and placers, construction workers, porters and guides, road and bridge builders. When the going got even tougher, as it often did, they took up arms as formidable anti-aircraft gunners, infantry soldiers, mortar women, or pretty much anything else anyone could dream up. And they did it bloody well.

My tiny sample of eleven Hero Mothers was an average eighty-five years of age, and had lost an average five immediate family members to the war. They had grown up in poverty, been burdened with heavy responsibility at an early age, and were denied any formal education. Perhaps they had simply not understood they were well on the way to extinction.

This had not been a normal, five-year twentieth century type of war, but a conflict that grandmother passed on to daughter as a sort of macabre inheritance, knowing that the baton might well end up in the hand of a grand-daughter. The war might well have been lost if the women had wavered and I wanted to find the key to their resilience.

The Women's Museum in Hanoi is well worth a visit. It tells of the prominent role of women in the history of Vietnam. To the consternation and great cost of enemy forces, troubled times had brought out the very best in them for two millennia. It was difficult to understand what aroused such ferocity and exposed such leadership skills in the gentle, diminutive gender and I cast about for somebody who could explain things to me. There had to be much more to this than sheer guts and what seemed to be a natural talent for fighting at the fiercest level.

Professor Le Van Lan had previously told me about the starvation of 1944-5, already covered in a separate chapter. When Huong contacted him once more on my behalf, he had run out of hours in his days, but generously agreed to see me over breakfast one Saturday morning. We collected him at his home in the heart of the Old City in Hanoi and strolled to his regular breakfast café, run by the third generation of the family that has provided him with his first meal of the day for fifty years.

"What sets Vietnamese women apart from those in other countries—what makes tiny women race around fighting wars on elephants? They have since updated their technology, and have done it rather well, but do they ever give up?" I asked him.

"It is simply a matter of maintaining a tradition," he said. "The women do what comes naturally, what they have always done." He made it sound as if it was all just some sort of feminine routine, and strangely enough, he seems to be right.

"The storyboards in the Women's Museum show some pretty strong stuff. I mean, the two Trung sisters waged war on the Chinese in AD40. That is a serious course of action," I said. "I understand the Chinese had executed Trung Trac's husband, but her reaction seems a bit extreme by any standards. Declaring war on China is no light undertaking, nor is waging the war from the lead elephant."

Trung Trac, an angry widow after the execution of her husband by the Chinese, and her younger sister, Trung Nhi, rebelled. The sisters developed their martial skills, trained up 36 women as Generals (one of whom happened to be their mother) and formed an army of 80,000. They gave the Chinese a torrid time and even set up their own state. The sisters were finally defeated, after they had overrun 65 fortresses.

They chose suicide before submission, and threw themselves into a river and drowned.

Then there was Lady Trieu, who led an uprising against the Chinese in the third century. She started her military career at 20, and was defeated three years later. She, too, chose suicide rather than become a prisoner. No doubt she would have anticipated an unpleasant end, and the Chinese would probably not have disappointed her, for she must have sorely troubled them.

The Chinese expected women to be rather more subdued, but those of their troublesome Southern neighbour did not always embrace the respect for authority that Confucianism demanded. Leading an uprising against the Chinese when barely out of one's teenage years seems a little rash. To do so in a society where women were expected to be seen and not heard and to somehow raise an army in a male dominated society and campaign successfully for three years seems downright ridiculous.

During my first visit to the Women's Museum I had come across a history exhibit I could not locate on subsequent visits. The troublesome Lady Trieu was said to be 9ft tall with 3ft breasts that she used to hoick over each shoulder as she charged into battle on her elephant. In a nation where the women struggle to nudge 5ft and are not famous for their awesome chests, she must have been a rare sight indeed. Whatever, the Chinese did not take her lightly.

It is not difficult to imagine the reluctance of a Chinese commander, brought to account before his Emperor, to admit to yet another defeat by a force led by a young and diminutive female member of a tiny neighbouring state. Survival would require inflation of the dimensions of this remarkable woman, along with an imaginative description of the course of the battle. Surely the Emperor would have heard of unfavourable conditions, outnumbered forces, of numerous near misses and a great deal of bad luck.

Someone else told me of other efforts to besmirch her legend: one account of her final, losing battle suggested she had surrendered after discovering that the Chinese army was unwashed and unkempt. Her victories must rankle with the Chinese for them to suggest that Lady Trieu was defeated by male body odour. What a desperate defence for a military leader of such a major power!

"What about the lady who was sentenced to death by trampling by elephants?" I asked Professor Le Van Lan after our breakfast plates had been removed. I figured that had to be a bedtime story that had grown with time, but I was wrong once again.

Lady Bui Thi Xuan was a fighter during the Tay Son Rebellion which was a contest between the government of the day and the three brothers Nguyen. The Rebellion started in the town of Tay Son in Quang Ngai Province in the Central Highlands in 1765. The three brothers ended up in control of Southern and Central Vietnam, and one of them, Nguyen Hue, heavily defeated a Chinese army of 200,000 at Dong Da, near Hanoi. Tourists can visit what is said to be a Chinese mass burial mound there, and a very substantial hill it is.

Lady Xuan rose to the rank of General and chose to dress in red. After she fell into the hands of the enemy, she was sentenced to death by elephant trampling to ensure that her spirit did not return. A Frenchman who witnessed the execution recorded that her captors placed her in a well and an elephant was produced to carry out the sentence. However, the elephant refused to trample her, and knelt by her instead—it was one of her animals, and had to be replaced by another so that the execution could be completed.

The cruel and unusual punishment did not work. Her spirit returned. It was surely active in the 1960s and 1970s on the Ho Chi Minh trail high in the Truong Son mountains along the Lao border, along with the spirits of the Trung Sisters and Lady Trieu when the B52 bombers came. Somebody certainly inspired the women who laboured, fought and died there and almost everywhere else.

The Women's Museum in Hanoi holds numerous other exhibits, such as a very rusty old scimitar that Mrs Nguyen Thi Chien used to capture a French Lieutenant in 1952. There is a photograph of a temporary bridge used to carry wounded across a river: women are up to their necks in the water, with struts over their shoulders providing the foundations for temporary crosspieces to walk on. It is the ultimate transportable bamboo bridge—a sort of Bailey bridge, Ho Chi Minh Trail style. A few planks, add strong women, and cross the river.

Then there was Ngo Thi Tuyen, a hero from the American War. She was an anti-aircraft gunner at the vital Dragon's Jaw Bridge over the Song (River) Ma. This was near Thanh Hoa, from where materiel or personnel were sent south to Vinh before moving down the Ho Chi Minh Trail. She was a busy lady in early 1965[22]:

On April 3 and 4, 1965, she helped shoot down many U.S. aircraft. On these two days, many planes had been sent to destroy the bridge, and after fulfilling her duty to capture U.S. airmen who parachuted out of their planes, she then helped one of our naval ships anchored in the river, which asked the militia to transport empty cartridges to the bank and in turn to take loaded ammunition to the ship to prepare for the fighting. She volunteered to walk into the river and swim to the ship in the face of the bombs from the U.S. aircraft overhead. She carried ammunition, rice and water to the ship, and stayed on board to clean cartridges until dusk. That night she returned to shore and helped her comrades dig trenches, fill bomb craters, and cook dinner.

On April 4, at 9 a.m., the United States attacked the area fiercely. She volunteered to carry rice for the armies on the battlefield. When trucks arrived, she volunteered to transport shells from them to the artillery, even though she was exhausted and ordered to rest. Two cases were stuck together, and couldn't be separated out (sic) with the implements at hand, and so afraid that a delay would cause problems, she put both cases, weighing 98 kilograms, on her back, walked to the dike at the river bank, and handed them to the armed forces. That night the enemy hammered at the bridge, and under a shower of bombs, she gave orders to keep the boats supplied with bullets and rice—as she dug trenches to shelter the artillery.

On May 26, after the enemy attacked the area, another ship asked for volunteers to bandage the wounded. Tuyen ran into the river, began to swim to the ship, but exhausted, was pushed back by the tide. She rested and tried again, bandaged the wounded soldiers, carrying some on her back to the bank. There she stayed, loading cartridges and serving the battlefield's needs until the last minute. As well, she made sure that food production was kept up, encouraging the farmers who were afraid of the bombs. She mobilised the militia and students to till the fields, and the harvest came in on time and the armed forces had vegetables to eat. For this, she was awarded two first class medals and a Ho Chi Minh Badge of Honour and certificate of merit. On January 1, 1967, she was given the title "Hero of the People's Armed Forces" by the National Assembly and the Government.

The honours awarded her may seem a little quaint, but there was nothing quaint about the exploits of a nineteen-year-old peasant girl, who weighed less than fifty kilograms. Any US Marine, or indeed any soldier anywhere, would be justifiably proud to receive such a citation.

The same source quotes US confirmation of that raid, made by a force of seventy-nine aircraft flown by their most experienced pilots. The F-100s struck first, followed by F-105s. Despite all the regular attention, the bridge stood until a smart bomb destroyed it in 1972.

Folk lore later had it that the Dagon Jaw Bridge stood all that time because of the brave efforts of the teenage girl.

I would once have dismissed the story of Ngo Thi Tuyen as an exaggeration, along with the Trung sisters, but the Hero Mothers have changed forever my view of little women, particularly if they are Vietnamese. Besides, the Vietnamese do not invent history.

Le Van Lan and I then talked about Vo Thi Sau. She was the young woman executed by firing squad on Con Dau Island, as mentioned previously in the chapter "Island of Ghosts". We discussed Hero Mothers like Ma Gom, who grew angry as their family death toll mounted, and simply picked up AK47 assault rifles and joined their parents, husbands and children on the battlefield.

"You mentioned this tradition that Vietnamese women maintain," I said to the professor, "and the results are extraordinary, but I still don't understand what makes your tiny women so fierce and so very brave during bad times. Sure, in the West we had Joan of Arc and Boadicea, and probably a few others, but your country is tiny and seems to churn out women who form a sort of unbreakable backbone," I said.

"Three things make the Viet women so strong. By tradition, they have the authority, and they use it when they must. Their instinct to protect their children is overpowering, rising to the fore in time of danger. It is a national characteristic to make sacrifices for the safety of their children, no matter the cost of such a sacrifice."

He told me of an expression "Ben uot me nam, ben rao con nam." In a house with a leaking roof, containing two beds, if one bed has water dripping through the leaks the mother sleeps in the wet bed, the children in the dry one.

"This is nothing new to the western world," I told him, "we share that value, but we do not have the same fearsome female warrior tradition."

"We have another saying 'Giac den nha dan ba cung danh' which translates roughly as 'when the pirates come, resist them', and that is what they do".

This clearly is taken quite literally. I noted that the expression that Le Van Lan offered set no limits on the degree of resistance, or the period of such resistance, so it is clearly interpreted as total. When the women take something on board they do so wholeheartedly.

"In the past," continued Le Van Lan, "there were attempts by the Chinese to not only subdue the troublesome Vietnamese, but to replace our culture and traditions with those of China. This was particularly so during the Han dynasty, when Vietnam was ruled by the Chinese through local chieftains. They were replaced by Chinese administrators, as further measures were implemented.'

'The population of Vietnam at the time was about 1,000,000, divided roughly equally between the old, those of child producing age, and children. Genders were about equal throughout. The Chinese killed or captured 100,000 men of the middle bracket. That is, they permanently removed almost two thirds of the men who would, in the short term, produce children.'

'Chinese troops and other Chinese men were available to replace the missing men. They knew that with time the Vietnamese women would need love, would want to make love, and would want children. That duly happened, but wherever possible, the mothers raised their children in the traditional Vietnamese manner. The language, culture, history and legends taught the children were those of Vietnam, so that Chinese influence was limited to a single generation at most. There was something of a blood transfusion, but not a cultural one."

It was long-haired resistance, that is, resistance by the women, never half-hearted. I forgot to enquire as to the fate of the 100,000 men the Chinese removed from Vietnam, but they would have been killed, or enslaved, which was probably a fate worse than death. I realised that the Vietnamese, particularly those of the far North, cut their teeth fighting against vastly superior, ruthless armies. This was to be bad news for opponents in the 20th century.

We had conversed well into extra time, and the professor had to hurry home for his next engagement. On our way back, I asked if I could take his picture. He looked about for a suitable backdrop and found a shop that sold a staggering variety of articles made from recycled tyres. His eyes lit up.

"Very Vietnamese. You can take my picture over there," he said, and posed beside piles of mystery items. He is proudly Vietnamese, with what seems to be the national sense of humour.

The rights of the women of Vietnam have fluctuated over the centuries between the constricting tendencies of Confucianism when Chinese influence was high and the more liberated influences of other leaders such as the revered 15th century Emperor Le Loi, one of the great rulers of Vietnam. He not only defeated the Chinese in battle, but passed enlightened laws that extended new rights to women. The Chinese saw women as subservient and largely without rights, whereas Le Loi decreed, among other things, that women could own property, a major breakthrough at the time.

A little research yielded many modern female heroes who served their county in an endless variety of roles. Vo Thi Mho became an officer in an exclusively female guerilla fighting force around Cu Chi in South Vietnam, and her story is one of a very successful killer tempered occasionally with the compassion of a woman, a mother[23].

The daughter of a Vietminh fighter, three of her brothers died in the war against the Americans. She was fifteen when her home was destroyed by bombs in the early hours of a morning, perhaps explaining her imposing combat record as she fought in and around the tunnels at Cu Chi for years.

On one occasion she had three American soldiers relax near her position at the mouth of a tunnel, and had lined them up in the sights of her AK-47. They showed each other photographs and started crying as a young boy with her prepared to open fire but she stopped him. The Americans were allowed to walk away. There was an inquiry into her conduct but she survived the storm. Vo Thi Mho was seventeen years old at the time, a veteran of two years warfare in the tunnels. The boy soldier with her was ten years old.

Truong Nhu Tang, a founder of the NLF, came under treatment from an unusual woman doctor in refuge in the Cambodian jungle[24]. Thuy Ba graduated as a doctor of medicine in Hanoi in 1960 and took six months to move to the South via the Ho Chi Minh Trail. Tang writes that she was the first woman to make the journey that claimed the lives of about half of the travellers in those days. She proceeded to practice medicine in an area subjected to constant B52 bombing raids as the Americans sought to destroy the NLF and Vietcong headquarters.

And so the list goes on. The sad reality is that you can stop in any village north of Saigon and start a conversation with any old woman to discover that she was probably a fighter of some sort, and that she fought on a number of fronts whereas our servicemen usually fought on the battlefield while their wives kept the family on track back home. This is not to suggest that life was easy further south—I did not explore it to the same degree and cannot comment with the same confidence.

Estimates of 1,500,000 women fighting in the regular North Vietnamese forces with 1,000,000 in the militia are unsurprising[25] and while their exploits are not widely publicised in the West they are bound to be discussed around the family dinner table for centuries to come as they join the legendary figures of old in inspiring future generations.

Nor have women always been fairly treated. As recently as 1812 Emperor Gia Long promulgated a set of laws, his "Hoang Viet Laws", some of which represented a giant step backwards for women. He abolished the Tay Son reforms, reverting to Confucian values with a legal code similar to those of the Qing empire in China at the time. The following grounds for a man to divorce his wife, listed on a board in the Women's Museum, illustrates the low esteem in which he held women:

If a wife cannot give birth to a son

If a wife is lustful

If a wife does not attend to the husband's parents

If a wife is gossipy

If a wife commits robbery

If a wife is jealous

If a wife has a fatal illness

In setting out the grounds for divorce the Emperor apparently adopted a flexible approach that would allow males many means of ridding themselves of troublesome or unsatisfactory wives, or of simply acquiring a younger model. There did not seem to be any similar grounds that would allow a wife to divorce her husband. The wife was deemed responsible for the production of sons, probably to ensure that an impotent husband could strut about with ego intact. A lustful wife could be divorced easily, but husbands were not similarly constrained.

There again, the Emperor who drafted the above laws is the one who used French assistance in settling a domestic political problem and lost his own country in the process.

Despite some of the injustices or inequalities, the women have invariably set aside the cooking utensils whenever their country has called to fight like Ghurkhas for as long as necessary.

21. Ngo Thi Tuyen—the Heavy Lifter

On 20 August 2011 I found myself standing at a door numbered 301. That this door was located at the entrance to a house in a busy street in Thanh Hoa City, in the province of the same name was not entirely coincidental. It was an address I should have called at years before.

Ngo Thi Tuyen features in the previous chapter as a leading Vietnamese heroine of the American War. Her feats around the Dragon Jaw Bridge are well documented, but I was keen to meet her so that readers might get an insight into what motivated her at the time, although Karen Gottschang Turner and Phan Thanh Hao did a superb job in their book *Even the Women Must Fight*.

I should mention at the outset that their book is my main source of information about this remarkable woman, and led me to Thanh Hoa. This chapter is not an effort to plagiarise that excellent publication, but simply to record the meeting. There was no question of disputing facts or seeking to somehow improve or expand upon Turner and Hao: nothing new emerged during our interview, nor was it sought.

Having met the Hero Mothers some years earlier I felt the need to see this remarkable woman in order to obtain a sort of closure on the Vietnam journey: my book had a hole in it that only Tuyen would fill. They had written about a somewhat embittered woman who believed she had not been particularly well treated by the authorities and I was anxious to see if her lot had improved. I also wanted to clarify a few matters arising from their book, a real must-read publication for anyone with an interest in the amazing contribution of women to the war.

Huong and I drove from Hanoi along Highway 1 which in parts was in appalling shape, so the trip took 3 hours. The same journey had taken about 2 hours a few years ago when I travelled by Minsk motorcycle. The road had been in superb condition then, possibly because the South East Asia Games were about to commence in Vietnam. Still, I was absurdly pleased we had beaten the Turner/Hao time of 4 hours some years before when the road had once again been in poor shape.

It had been raining, and Highway 1 had several inches of muddy water along some stretches. The road had some deep potholes, so that buses were zigzagging across the highway to save overloading their suspension as well as that of their passengers. It caused minor chaos in parts, but oncoming traffic took evasive action and nobody became too excited. I took perverse pleasure from the dilemma of the Porsche driver who looked unhappy, and was grateful not to be travelling by Minsk.

We had seen the Dragon Jaw Bridge on our way in, and I was surprised at how small it was, considering the bitter fighting it had precipitated and the heavy casualties suffered by both sides. It had, however, been the only bridge heading south in the area at the time and was literally a lifeline for the Communist forces.

The house we stood before was a pleasant, three-storey structure in good condition, so something major had changed in Tuyen's living conditions.

A petite, cheerful woman met us at the door. She had a ready smile and flashing eyes that missed nothing, and seemed too young to have fought 40 years before. She was a bustler, an energetic woman who did not so much walk as attack, although she moved with a measure of discomfort that reflected her old back injury.

Huong explained to her that my journey was incomplete, that I felt it needed a little of her personal story. Tuyen was relaxed as we enjoyed her tea: she had spent time with Westerners before and had been featured in books. She had met Giap, Ho, Le Duc Tho and far more important people than me. She had been interviewed and feted by writers, historians, politicians and journalists. That was obvious as we looked through her massive collection of ceremonial and press photographs.

She was born in 1946. Huong pointed out to her that this was the year of my birth also, but Tuyen gleefully reminded us that in Vietnam birthdate is actually date of conception, so she was older than me. With seniority established, we commenced the interview.

Tuyen was born to farmer parents near the village of NamNam, which is right by the Dragon Jaw Bridge and about 5 kilometres from where she now lives. She had 5 sisters and a brother. The family had little money, so as was the custom at the time, the girls received no education but helped around the house and in the fields.

Her brother joined the army in the war against the French and was killed at Dien Bien Phu in 1954. This encouraged her to join the local militia at 18 years of age in 1963 where she had transport and logistics responsibilities. She joined the Communist Party in 1965 in response to radio calls and public appeals for the populace to help the South.

In the same year, as the US stepped up its involvement in Vietnam substantially, she attended a military course nearby, and it was there she met Bui Xuan Thu and they fell in love. They married later that year but the war was cruel to the young couple. The attacks on the Dragon Jaw Bridge occurred hours after their wedding, and after four days of marriage her husband was sent to Laos where he had a political and advisory role.

They met again in 1967 when Thu had to attend a course in Nghe Anh Province and she was able to travel there and spend two days with him. Tragically, he died during a US bombing attack on his return trip to Laos. Tuyen tried unsuccessfully to find his body after the war.

A visit to the bridge revealed the difficulty of the task facing US airmen trying to attack the bridge—they had to run a gauntlet of anti-aircraft guns mounted on river banks facing them from side on. The bridge also had a hill at each end on which were mounted more guns to give them a hosing on their way through before more gunners gave them a touch-up on the way out. It would not have been the sort of mission a pilot would relish. One would have to attack at low level, so if your aircraft took a fatal hit you would not have the altitude to bail out at sea close to a friendly fleet—if you survived, you would be taken prisoner.

Tuyen posed for a photograph in front of a substantial monument listing too many names. Her strongest memory is not of the air raids of 3 and 4 April 1965, but that of 26 May, because the casualties were so much higher. An entire contingent of 22 young women, recent high school graduates and comrades, died on the river bank. It was a small theatre of war, with local players, so casualties were often friends, schoolmates and acquaintances.

The action on that day lasted from 7am to 4pm without a break. The hardy peasants of NamNam village, of course, were irrepressible as one would expect, and turned out to fire whatever weapons they possessed, as was their normal custom. Part of Tuyen's duty was to recover US pilots who bailed out, to ensure their safety. This was probably because they possessed valuable intelligence that might be lost if the villagers reached them first. She was also a trained anti-aircraft gunner.

The Heavy Lifter at the Dragon Jaw Bridge

The older villagers had been asked to move away from the area so that younger folk could take up the fight, but that plan met with mixed success. Tuyen's parents refused and stayed on to take their chances with the aerial bombing as well as shelling from the US Navy.

We headed off to a nearby restaurant for a most pleasant lunch, with Tuyen ordering her delicious favourite dishes. Shortly afterwards her second husband joined us. He retired as a Colonel, but like his wife he is still actively involved in Veteran's Affairs. His health is not too good, but in an aside he told me his wife is much younger. I believe it was said with considerable pride—an old man's pride at having landed a young wife. They both look at ease with life.

We spoke briefly about the plight of a lack of government recognition for the war veterans who became unmarried mothers in order to have a child to love. Turner mentioned Tuyen's concern for the cause, and while I believe she was not keen to discuss it with a Western male, it is an issue she still feels strongly about.

Tuyen's life has changed dramatically for the better, and it seems Turner and Hao are mainly responsible for that, having added two storeys to the house to give the couple some welcome living space.

Some aspects of her fame do not excite this peasant woman. She does not enjoy making speeches and is not accustomed to dressing formally or wearing high heels; she has received extra education and is active in the community where she serves as a role model, but likes to keep it simple. Even as work is in progress to create parklands where heavy weapons once fired incessantly and hundreds died, she works to ensure that her young comrades, fellow gunners and the NamNam villagers are not forgotten.

As we bade our farewells, she handed me a special gift for my wife: she had recently been to Hue where she purchased one of the conical hats for which the area is famous. It has Hue scenes described in purple wool, and it was obviously a bit special. She is a warm and generous woman, and I have undertaken to call in at number 301 when next I travel Highway 1.

22. First fighters, first blood

Listening to the Hero Mothers helped me gain an understanding of what they had endured. The reasons for their extraordinary perseverance were clear, and it was understandable why they were prepared to fight to the death rather be forced to return to subjugation by any foreign power. I had stopped thinking of them as Communist fighters: they fought on the Communist side, certainly, but not one of them could have explained the meaning of that term to me.

What they did know was that democracy, as represented by the French, and later the Americans, along with their allies the Australians, New Zealanders and Thais had meant exploitation, abuse, oppression and death on a grand scale.

There was more to their motivation than history, tradition and the fierce nationalism that seems to thrive in the Central and Northern regions. The barbarity of the French provided early motivation, and in setting off on one last mission for a different purpose I was to have colonial cruelty inadvertently waved before my disbelieving eyes.

Ma Sam and Ma Ha had farewelled their husbands as they set off to wage war for twenty and twenty-five years respectively. The Mothers had young children to raise and a war effort to support even as they struggled at home alone for all those years. Not for them, along with thousands of others, the long and lasting marriage that was almost a birthright in that society at that time. It was yet another impost of the war on the women. In search of a little male perspective on this long struggle, I had read about the youngsters from the North who had left home in their teens to enlist but I had yet to meet such a fighter.

Back in Perth I read about Giap's reunion with his old fighters from his Pac Bo cave days[26]. The description of the first battle of the war in the obscure Northern village fascinated me. It seemed unbelievable that such a small skirmish could have been the commencement of a struggle that would become the first major defeat for the world's major super-power.

This village suddenly seemed to be the place to visit, but I couldn't find it on the map. In a moment of wild optimism I faxed Huong at the Press Office in Hanoi and presented her with a challenge. It was a long shot, a hopeless task, really, or so I thought. She produced the goods once more and I flew to Hanoi in July 2005 in a state of excitement.

Huong had been able to establish that there were three survivors of the original Tran Hung Dao Platoon, the very first official fighting unit of Giap's peasant soldiers. One old soldier could not be found, another was in very poor health, but Ha Hung Long was willing and able to see us.

Huong and I travelled to the town of Tuyen Quang, a few hours west of Hanoi, both astride Minsks. Tuyen Quang is a substantial city, but finding Long's home was easy, for he is something of an icon around that area. Expecting to meet a frail old man, we were welcomed instead by a fit and hearty eighty-one-year-old who has retained a military bearing, looks at least twenty years younger than his age, and has the same robust sense of humour that we encountered in all the older generation Vietnamese we interviewed.

He had the same easy manner we had enjoyed with the group of old soldiers, the Agent Orange victims from Than Hoa at the Friendship Village. Long cheerfully poured tea throughout the afternoon, while his vivacious wife Phung Thi Luong, popped in occasionally to keep an eye on her man.

He was born in Cao Bang in 1924 into a poor peasant family. Cao Bang is a regional centre, in an area that has seen a lot of action over the past couple of millennia. It is on the main route from China, so the Mongols probably passed through the place on their way south on three occasions, before returning north, defeated, presumably with local forces snapping at their heels. The Chinese had little joy on their excursions also. This tough old town, wheezy and unpretentious, is perhaps twenty kilometres from the Cave at Pac Bo where the whole bloody war started.

When Long was seventeen, he met Pham Van Dong, who would later be Prime Minister of his country for thirty years. Dong had also taken up residence in the cave at Pac Bo, and persuaded the teenager to join their fledgling underground movement in 1941. That cave must have been an exciting, extraordinary place in 1941—there was just so much talent around.

"Did you really walk to the cave and just sign up with Ho and Giap?" I asked him, for it seemed a strange way to start an army, and it had always sounded unlikely to me. I mean, who starts an army like that?

"One day I told my parents I was going to the markets, but I walked to the cave instead to join up with General Giap."

"How did your parents feel about that?"

"They were unhappy at first, but there was nothing they could do. One day, supporters of the French went to their home and arrested my family, but they released them later."

It wasn't too hard to understand the parental anger: falling into the hands of the French was never good news, even for the hardy inhabitants of the far north, and somebody probably received a beating during the interview. Long smiled, but I sensed he was embarrassed.

After a spell at the cave, something about the young peasant must have hinted at potential leadership qualities, since Giap sent him to China where he underwent military training for three years.

"Not long after my return in 1944, Giap decided that we should mount our first attack on the French. The target selected was the French outpost at Khai Phat," he told me.

Giap had apparently decided it was time to test the mettle of the new recruits and check the quality of their training. An attack on a small, remote garrison was ideal for their purpose. The French had behaved obnoxiously there, and had taken as their headquarters the substantial new home of Comrade Lac, a prosperous villager who, by the looks of his title was sympathetic to the communist cause.

Tran Hung Dao had provided the Viet with perhaps their two greatest victories, against no less an opponent than the Mongols who had conquered China, so at a ceremony in the forest about seven kilometres from Khai Phat, the historian-cum-lawyer-cum-General Vo Nguyen Giap swore these first thirty-four men into his army at 5 p.m. on 22 December 1944, as members of the Tran Hung Dao Platoon.

In order to have valuable information about the layout of the village, disposition of the enemy and the daily routine at the base, the Vietminh used a twelve-year-old local lad named Hoang as a spy. According to Long, there was only one French officer present at the village, with the rest of the force made up of Vietnamese troops.

"We were disguised as Vietnamese French soldiers, and so we Vietminh were able to close in on the village. We commenced our attack at 5 p.m. on Christmas Day, 1944. We shot and wounded the armoury guard and cut the garrison's access to weapons, so they surrendered immediately without loss of life. The French officer had been killed during the engagement. We encouraged our prisoners to defect, and later released them."

This is consistent with other accounts of conduct around that time. Their treatment of their fellow Vietnamese, who served as soldiers for the French, and later the Americans, would harden as the war progressed.

This minor encounter was the first involving Ho's official armed forces. As modest an engagement as it was, Khai Phat could be regarded as the first battle of the Vietnam War, and the French officer the first casualty.

"We were pleased with our success, so the next day we successfully attacked the French outpost at nearby Na Ngan village. Once again, the French officer was the only casualty. After efforts to persuade them to join us we again released the Vietnamese serving with the French."

Long had a surprise up his sleeve.

"On 27 or 28 December 1944, our platoon attacked yet another French outpost at Dong Mu, closer to the Chinese border. This time the garrison was ready for us and Comrade Xuan Truong died in action." Truong thus became the first official Vietminh casualty of the war, in an action I had never read about.

"What went wrong for you?" I asked Long

"Dong Mu is near the Chinese border and some Chinese brigands in the area had threatened to attack the French unless they were paid some money. The French were offended at this threat and were waiting for the Chinese attack."

The Chinese insult had stung the French and the Tran Hung Dao Platoon had the misfortune to attack the wrong place at the wrong time.

"I have not come across this before," I protested.

"We were defeated, so Ho did not want it in our history," Long told me. Cunning old Ho was a superb motivator and propagandist and made the most of his victories in order to gain new recruits and support for his movement. Dong Mu never made it into official Vietminh history or folklore as it did not produce a result that could be profitably repeated in villages throughout the country by anxious recruiters and propagandists.

"When did you stop fighting?"

"In 1958. I left the army at the age of thirty-four."

His retirement before the American War and at such a young age surprised me. This was because I had lost track of the length of the war. Long stepped out during a lull in the fighting, during the few quiet years between the French and American Wars, having by then spent half his life in military service. His duties had ranged from irritating the Japanese during their occupation of his country and acquiring their weapons wherever possible, to worrying the French and fighting them in several major battles. He was involved in heavy French defeats along Colonial Route 4 around Cao Bang and Dong Khe, an operation that cost some 6,000 French lives and was the beginning of the end for the French. He was occasionally responsible for the security of Ho Chi Minh when he visited the troops in that area.

He spent time along the Chinese border, since his knowledge of the language made him an ideal liaison officer for dealing with substantial military aid from a neighbour that had turned communist in 1949. Later he was at the landmark battle at Dien Bien Phu where he had transport responsibilities. Dien Bien Phu was perhaps as much a battle of logistics as it was of direct combat, and the defeat of the French in that valley saw their departure from Indochina.

Long entered the steel industry in 1958, and became a director of Brick and Steel Co in Tuyen Quang. He told me he was still a soldier after 1958, since his steel mill produced vital war material. The US targeted Tuyen Quang, and he remembers American bombing raids in the area One raid caused a village to disappear, including a whole family of eleven.

I waited until he was finished and then I said, jokingly, "I'm surprised you found time to start a family."

"I met Luong in Ha Giang Province in 1946. She was a Vietminh activist and we met when we were both on Vietminh assignments."

They somehow found the time to have six sons and a daughter while they waged war on Colonial France.

He is happy in his autumn years, with a modest but comfortable home. He enjoys the respect of his community not just because of his unique place in the history of the war, but because of his successful civilian career, the closeness of his family and the role he plays in his community. This makes him a rich man according to measures of wealth among his peers.

Ha Hung Long

He was surprised to hear that we intended visiting the scene of his first battle. I believe he would have enjoyed accompanying us, but he was to travel to Hanoi the next day and our schedule left us with no flexibility. We were going to be travelling along a rough back road by Minsk, and he would probably have preferred to walk. I believe he could have done it.

Long looked to be in excellent condition. This was an octogenarian who could serve another ten years if required, and I suspected he might enjoy the challenge. He is most impressive, and if he is representative of the quality of those early recruits, it is easy to see how the French struggled against them from the outset. We bade farewell to this remarkable man and his wife and completed preparations for a trip through rough mountain roads to an obscure village.

What set Long apart from the husbands of Ma Sam and Ma Ha was that he had fought in the region where he lived: they had travelled a long way north to fight. His life would have taken a different turn if he had moved down the Ho Chi Minh Trail to fight. Had he survived the journey and the B52 raids, as well as the subsequent fighting there remained the hazard of Agent Orange contamination. Long had been fortunate—if you can thus describe a man who has waged war for seventeen years.

Our interview over, Huong and I set off for Khai Phat, scene of the first military action. We rode through stunning country on the worst roads I have ever encountered. On occasions we travelled through areas that have not seen cars for years, but that served as supply routes for Vietminh campaigns at Na-San and Dien Bien Phu. Human porters would have carried heavy loads. The men pushed bicycles bearing two hundred kilogram loads to the battle-sites, while the women shouldered heavy loads in baskets suspended from either end of long poles. In parts there was little overhead cover: the porters and soldiers would have travelled at night to escape harassment by French aircraft. Our progress was very slow, and mechanical problems, if they had occurred would have been very awkward as we were isolated for hours at a time. It was marvellous—in ideal conditions in peacetime.

Two days later, having spent a day at Ba Be, a magnificent lakeside tourist attraction, we arrived at Khai Phat to visit whatever was left of the original battle scene. The village is well off the tourist track, but we had linked up with the main road from Cao Bang in the north-east, with the good bituminised surface providing welcome relief to our sore joints.

We finally crested a mountain pass from where we viewed a tiny village in the valley below. It was a picture postcard-pretty scene and we had finally reached our destination.

We passed through the village to visit the hilltop forest where Giap had inducted his first platoon. There is a memorial to celebrate the event, and we strolled through the forest to the small pagoda that commemorates the occasion. Among the thirty-four names engraved in granite was that of Ha Hung Long. Cao Bang had provided more than half of the platoon, according to a plaque at the site.

We returned to Khai Phat which remains a small village sixty years after its brief moment of fame. Nestled as it is in the base of a valley, it is bisected by a river. One building stands out from the rest: the former house of Comrade Lac where the battle took place. The good Comrade had operated a business of sorts, although I forgot to enquire about that.

The layout of the building suggested that whatever had been stored there had not been bulky or too heavy. I suspect he was a food merchant, for even today foodstuffs are not easily found in the area. I wonder now how Comrade Lac fared in the first few years after the departure of the French in 1956—the Communists had instituted disastrous, bloody "reforms" as those who had profited from exploiting their fellows found themselves before vengeful village courts. Many personal accounts were settled before Ho eventually restored order.

Lac's house is a relatively substantial building, conspicuous because it has been magnificently restored. The house is now a museum, and consists of two large rooms, each of which has timber mezzanine storage. Decoratively plastered, thick brick walls and a well-constructed tile roof bear testimony to Comrade Lac's business acumen, and the dwelling would clearly have caught the attention of a French officer seeking comfortable accommodation. A curator was present to assist us, and provided us with a further insight into events on that fateful day.

The French officer was at a church service when the attack commenced; it was, after all, Christmas Day. He returned on horseback at the sound of gunfire. When challenged by the Vietminh he immediately raised his hands in surrender, but Vo Van Danh misinterpreted that gesture, thinking he was reaching for a weapon. Danh shot him dead, drawing first blood in the Vietnam War.

A handsome man, possibly in his fifties, gazed at us from a photograph: this was Hoang, who had been the twelve-year-old spy for the Vietminh. He survived the war, but has since passed away.

A tree that seemed to have been severely lopped stood close to the front door. It seemed to sort of cringe, and that made it quite conspicuous. I wondered if it had been there during the battle, and whether it had since died, or had just been unwell. The curator noticed my interest.

"That was the tree he used to hang the heads from," she said to us.

"Heads?" I asked.

"The French officer would sometimes hang the heads of Vietminh or suspects from this tree as a warning. Sometimes he would hang the rest of the bodies outside the front gate, with signs attached warning of the risks of joining the Vietminh." I was aware of the practice, but it was sobering to be at the site of such grisly displays.

The vision of that stump as a Christmas tree just will not go away. It is not just that the tree was used for that purpose, but that the officer had evidently been a God-fearing man who had attended church, and I wondered if he had a family back in Marseille or wherever he came from. Had he mailed off his Christmas gifts early to ensure their arrival in time? Had this devout Frenchman truly entered into the spirit of Christmas with a little frivolity, perhaps?

A few heads on the tree would have added a nice touch to that special day as he rode off to church to demonstrate his piety to his deity. Perhaps he crossed his fingers behind his back during Confession, although his deeds were merely par for the course for those parts and God was probably away at the time, having been conspicuous by his absence from Vietnam for a hundred years. I suspect the village was chosen as the site of the first attack because of the unfortunate conduct of the French officer.

Our presence in the village had stirred up considerable interest. A few children peeped coyly at us as we walked about, and their number grew steadily. They grew bolder, and peered through the windows as we moved about in the museum. I would occasionally make as if to catch one of them and this seemed to cause hysterics, so I made a mental note to have my beard trimmed—something about me seemed to excite them and I have no other distinguishing features.

Huong told me afterwards that they had wanted to know if her visitor was French. It seems I was probably the first westerner in the village since that day in 1944, and I was rather pleased to be able to call myself Australian.

Khai Phat is not the place to announce your Gallic roots with pride, any more than My Lai is the spot to unfurl your US flag and wave it about proudly, even though the locals have long since forgiven the deplorable conduct of all involved.

The house of Comrade Lac. The Christmas tree is in the
background, to the left.

There was quite a large group to wave us off on our return journey.
Our Minsks made hard work of leaving the valley, and I was struck
once more by wonder at the obscurity, the remoteness of the first
battleground of a major and brutal war.

I never did get an answer about the Christmas tree from the
curator—whether it was dead or just unwell. It probably died of
shame.

The French sealed their own fate with conduct like this: the resolve
of a mother upon seeing one of her children dealt with in this way
would be unbreakable. When Ho offered them an opportunity to fight
they grabbed it and they stayed with it: there could be no turning
back.

It was purely coincidental that I had planned a visit to Dien Bien
Phu for one week after my interview with General Giap. At the time
I felt that my fourth visit to Vietnam would be my last, and although
I had been to Dien Bien Phu before, I had not done the trip by
motorcycle. I wanted a sort of grand farewell to a wonderful country
whilst also getting a feel for what it would have felt like for any military
column silly enough to travel to Dien Bien Phu by road.

The short answer was that it would have been suicidal. It was a sixteen-hour trip by bus from Hanoi at the time of my trip, or a fourteen-hour trip by more modern Minsk, a machine I had hired in Hanoi. Mountain roads provided about five hours of delight, but a military column could never have survived the trip through tough country populated by hostile locals. A French column would have expected roadblocks and ambushes at every turn, at the crest of every hill. It would truly have been a journey of hellish attrition.

Along the way, a couple of hours from Hanoi, the road passes through Hoa Binh, site of a demoralising French defeat at Tu Vu on the Song Da (Black River). Two hours later you pass through Na San, a hilltop French military base set up along the lines of Dien Bien Phu, site of a successful French operation. At Na San, however, the French enjoyed the advantage of occupying the high ground. At Dien Phu they were in a basin, at the mercy of an enemy above.

Not long after Na San comes Son La, a tough mountain town. It is a mountain trading centre, not set up for tourism at all. A visit to the old and infamous French prison told of the usual harsh conditions, but most of the prison was missing. It transpired that a US aircraft returning to base in Thailand had jettisoned its bomb-load overhead. It was standard practice at the time and took a heavy toll among villagers in Vietnam and Laos. In Washington it was all written off as collateral damage, inevitable in wartime. When you oppose the USA.

From Son La to Dien Bien Phu is a very pleasant run as long as you are not a French soldier hell-bent on destruction.

The French military machine was in the process of being dismantled by the Vietminh in Vietnam in 1950-1953. The French had enjoyed some success, but faced with an enemy that was prepared to pay a heavy price for ultimate victory they could foresee years of attrition ahead. They were destined to fight in remote parts of the country, travelling about on the few main roads because of their reliance on heavy equipment. That made them vulnerable to ambush. The Vietminh had a nasty habit of ambushing the main French military column, while leaving another ambush party in place for the French rescue squad that would normally race in to assist their beleaguered comrades.

The concept of a major set-piece battle thus had enormous appeal for the French: they would be able to use their artillery and superior training and tactics to good advantage in destroying the Vietminh forces.

They believed the answer was to invest Dien Bien Phu by parachute assault, which they did on 20 November 1953, and set up a fortress before issuing an invitation to Giap to take them on. Unfortunately for the French, Giap accepted.

When you disembark from your airliner at the airport in Dien Bien Phu you step onto the runway, which is not far from the original military landing strip. If you do a 360 degree turn, you will find that there are mountains around you for about 130 degrees. You would wonder how anyone could allow the enemy to occupy that high ground, thus allowing them clear observation of your activities throughout the strongpoint. If you had wondered back in late 1953 when the operation was planned why such a remote and inaccessible place was selected as a battleground, making supply and reinforcement by land impossible, you would have been told that supply by air would be secure. That was perhaps the major French error: they selected the low ground and banked on air supply for logistical support.

Bernard Fall's *Hell in a Small Place* was my reference for my visits to Dien Bien Phu, although I read several other accounts of the siege. Fall's picture of the main French commanders reads like something from a B grade movie.

Colonel Christian Marie Ferdinand de la Croix de Castries, whose family "had served France with the sword since the Crusades"[27] and included a field marshall, a general who had served with Lafayette in America, eight other generals, an admiral and four royal lieutenant-governors, was the Commander. Irresistible to women and frequently sought by irate husbands as a result, he was a daredevil pilot and holder of two world championships for horseback riding. He brought with him a formidable combat record. It was said the strong-points constructed along the extensive perimeter were named after his mistresses: Gabrielle, Beatrice, Dominique, Eliane, Marcelle, Isabelle, Claudine, Huguette and Anne-Marie. Even the drop-zones where the initial parachute landings were made were similarly named: Natasha, Octavie and Simone.

There was nothing feminine about de Castries' senior officers: the hard-bitten Breton Lieutenant Colonel Pierre Langlais had once patrolled the Sahara Desert with a prestigious camel corps and had a formidable fighting record. Then there was tough and well-credentialed

Major Marcel Bigeard who later was accused of torturing prisoners in Algeria but went on to become French Minister for Defence.

There was a clutch of other fierce officers, who could be expected to put up a fine fight, and indeed they did, but they were doomed to defeat before the battle proper began.

When the final battle commenced on 13 March 1954 the Vietminh poured artillery fire onto Beatrice and overran the strongpoint. This brought them even closer to the airstrip which would now be subjected to very accurate fire and anti-aircraft fire. Aircraft were destroyed on the ground: the use of the airfield, the key component of the whole Dien Bien Phu strategy, was lost on the first day. Strong-point Gabrielle fell two days later, and from that date until Dien Bien Phu fell to the Vietminh at 1730 on 7 May 1954 the battle was fought bitterly, day and night, with frequent hand-to-hand combat.

Giap had decided not to follow "human wall" tactics, whereby masses of soldiers simply rushed enemy positions. Instead they dug or tunneled trenches towards the French positions. French aircraft would drop photographs of the changed layouts daily to de Castries, but the French could do nothing about the problem as the enemy positions were soon too close to their own. Bombing the Vietminh would cost too many French lives.

This may have been the precursor to the tactic used later against the Americans of "holding the belt". Superior air power enabled the Americans to pound their enemy with napalm, white phosphorus and other bombs, so the Vietcong or PAVN forces would close in on the Americans until they were not prepared to risk hitting their own men—the effect of napalm on American skin made it an unacceptable risk.

The reasons for the French defeat were numerous and too complex to warrant close examination here, but underestimation of Giap, and French over confidence were major contributors. Logistical support played perhaps the major role in the outcome so that with the help of the likes of Ha Hung Long the Vietminh achieved improbable success and won freedom from France.

It came as no surprise to find that the women played a significant if understated role at Dien Bien Phu[28]:

The hard labour of ordinary women contributed to the demise of French military control of Vietnam at the final battle at Dien Bien Phu in 1954. Of more than 260,000 laborers (sic)—some sources call them conscripts, others volunteers—who hauled supplies, half were women. Men pushed pack bicycles, and women used the shoulder poles.

The French reliance on air support was badly flawed. Once Beatrice and Gabrielle fell, since aircraft could no longer land on the airstrip, supply was made via parachute drops. As the Vietminh steadily reduced the area under French control, supplies would regularly land in Vietminh territory, so that French positions were bombarded with French shells. The Vietminh logistical effort was superb. Their supply line was 600 miles long, and they utilised bicycles that were modified to carry 200 kilograms of supplies, and a fleet of 600 2.5 tonne trucks[29]. That enabled the Vietminh to shell the French far more heavily than they expected, ensuring ultimate victory.

There were many other reasons for the fall of Dien Bien Phu, not the least of which was the courage and commitment of the Vietminh, so ably led by the diminutive man I had met in Hanoi.

The significance of Dien Bien Phu is that it demonstrated Western powers could be defeated, and it became a rallying point for the Communist forces throughout their later campaigns and for nationalists in other French colonies.

The price some of the women paid for their role in the struggle—apart, that is, from revelations during interviews and private research—was made clear to me as I rode through stunning Lai Chau after visiting Dien Bien Phu. A very old woman, aged perhaps eighty years, was trying to pull a massive bamboo cutting across the road. She had back trouble, and was practically bent in half as she struggled. The bamboo was freshly cut, and her anxious manner suggested to me that perhaps she was engaged in some illegal act. When I stopped to offer my assistance she hobbled off as fast as she could.

In her condition she ought to have been living on a pension, receiving medical care, not doing hard manual labour. I would have loved to hear her story, but Lai Chau was once a tough spot for the French who had a military base in the area and I had a feeling the old woman was not kindly disposed to westerners. I rode back an hour later to see if I could find her, without success. But the bamboo had disappeared.

23. Wearing the pain

The one sign of the ferocity of the War that travellers off the beaten track in rural Vietnam are likely to encounter almost wherever they go is the cemeteries that dot the countryside. There are major war cemeteries near Quang Tri, and at Dien Bien Phu, Cao Bang and elsewhere, but it was when riding through idyllic hamlets in remote areas that the clumps of distinctive headstones gave me some idea of what the war meant to the peasants.

Most Australian towns have their war memorial, normally a stone obelisk engraved with the names of those who served, with asterisks against names indicating those who died. Tragic as the asterisks are, they are usually comfortably in the minority. In Vietnam, the village headstones tend to be the dominant memorial, often presiding over an empty grave because of the great numbers of fighters of both genders missing in action.

The ubiquity of those cemeteries disturbed me into trying to gain some idea of the intensity of the war to the peasants in the hamlets, and I finally found a useful comparative insight.

Michael Maclear wrote about Bardstown, Kentucky[30], a small American town that was particularly hard hit by the Vietnam War, having lost fifteen young men from a population of 5,800. On one particularly bad day, four of its young were killed. The agony of such losses left the residents of Bardstown with mixed feelings about the War, about lives lost on national duty.

Chronicled elsewhere were the experiences of peasants in a Vietnamese village in the Red River Delta in North Vietnam. The name of the village did not appear in the article.

In the late nineteenth century three hundred villagers were reported to have been massacred by the French. In 1930, a year of anti-colonial uprisings around the country, more than half the houses of this village were burned, a local leader was beheaded, and 19 villagers were exiled, including some to French Guiana in South America. In 1951, the French bombed the village four times, leaving 30 villagers dead and 78 houses destroyed. American aircraft destroyed the local secondary school and adjacent homes in 1965. In addition to the civilians killed by the bombs, the village sent 360 men to fight in the war. I could find no reference to the number who survived the war.

I had visited a village near Quang Tri in 2003, accompanied by a guide with impeccable Vietcong credentials. I was following in the footsteps of Bernard Fall, looking for a village that had been part of a major, but unsuccessful sweep to round up Vietminh. We stopped off at an impoverished village off the beaten track to obtain directions. My guide's conversation with the locals seemed a little strained, and we departed fairly quickly. I queried my guide about his abbreviated discussions.

"They wanted to know if you were French."

"Why?"

"During the operation you are interested in the French caught no Vietminh and they were very angry. They killed all the villagers they could find". This was an early pointer to the savagery of the entire war.

The death toll of the war is in itself grim, but it is difficult to relate to the thirty-year duration. If one overlooks the first couple of village skirmishes at the end of 1944, the Vietnam War can be said to have commenced in 1945. In US terms the war started from around the time that Truman came into power and finally ended a year into Gerald Ford's term. In Australia, Lyons would have recently become Prime Minister at the start of the struggle, and it would have ended around the time of the dismissal of Gough Whitlam. It must have been an eternity for the people of Vietnam, on either side.

Due to logistical constraints, fighting units of the North as well as Vietcong units in the South tended to be localised. That is, they were made up of soldiers from particular areas. That meant that each military disaster resulted in devastating news being conveyed to anxious hamlets that were no strangers to unwelcome messengers. A B52 bombing raid that caught a convoy at a vulnerable time could devastate a series of villages in a remote corner of the distant north.

A couple of Veterans from North Vietnam told me that the most frightening part of a B52 bombing run was not the damage, which was colossal, but that the bombs arrived unannounced, so when the first one arrived everyone knew there would be miles of devastation. There was no hope of evading it or sheltering from it—you had no time. The bomb-load of a B52 has a devastation area of 1 kilometre by 2 kilometres.

Although some 31 B52s were lost during the war (18 to enemy fire), the losses only started in 1972. Until then, it was an impersonal war for the crews, taking off from their bases in Thailand, Guam and Okinawa, dropping their 30 ton bomb load at 30,000 feet in relative safety and then returning to base. Later, bombing over North Vietnam was far more personal since the North Vietnamese retaliated with surface-to-air missiles and fighter aircraft.

In attempting to establish how such punishment could be absorbed for thirty years it became clear that at least some of the answer lies in the strength of their small village or family groups, and partly in the strength of their tradition. Then there was an ability to bend or improvise where necessary to form a type of shock absorber.

The strength of the village should not be underestimated. A small cluster of houses formed a hamlet, and a group of hamlets formed a village, the basic governmental organisation. The village was the centre of the universe for many of the residents, and formed a community that was as self-sufficient as possible.

There was a structure to the village that had evolved over the centuries and that had been refined until it served their communities well even through turbulent times. Village leaders were elected by heads of households, and exercised autonomous government that rulers tampered with at their peril, for an old saying that "the law of the sovereign gives way before the custom of the village" held true.

The French and the Americans had to deal with this system. In places like Dodge City and other parts of Quang Nam Province, life became almost unbearable for the foreigners. As a family death toll mounted, the remaining members of the family vowed to continue the fight so that those who had died would not have done so in vain. Many youngsters could hardly wait for their turn to fight as had a couple of generations of family before them—sometimes they would be joining those generations.

Mother Gom had been thus motivated in her late forties. The only children of Ma Chau had joined the fight after hearing of their father's death, and had died fighting. It was thus very much a family war, where even the children would contribute from an early age and the military machine was an equal opportunity employer.

This tenacity came partly from the tradition of strong women in times of national strife, and partly from faith and belief in their remarkable leaders. Ho was very much a man of the world, but dressed as a peasant, lived as a peasant, and spoke to them as equals. He promised no miracles and warned of heavy losses in a long struggle; a blood price would have to be paid. He was a father figure, a leader and visionary and they would have followed him anywhere. With his military genius, Giap, he delivered victories that inspired confidence to the extent that the eventual outcome was never in doubt. When you are subjected to very heavy punishment, faith helps get you through the day.

The heavy price tag was always going to be accepted as each level of their society was issued its share of the pain. It had been that way for 2,000 years. Patriotism is very much an attribute of the Vietnamese and you do not have to scratch very hard to find it. It is not some sort of propaganda—it is wholehearted, embedded in their national history. This is the stuff of legends, handed down from one generation to the next. It makes little difference if some of the legends have been exaggerated over the centuries: wide-eyed children will in time pass them on in the remotest villages and they will continue to inspire.

Where a villager lost a family member, the hamlet and village around them was an extended family, so losses turned their society into a very close-knit one. The way the war was fought, and the one-sided distribution of long range weapons and air power prevented Hanoi from sending teams of people to help when a village was pulverized. The community dealt with it. They learned to cope with everything. The more they hurt, the harder they fought.

The French and Americans incurred heavy casualties on occasions through mounting rescue missions to recover lost pilots or soldiers in tough situations—it was an article of faith that they would do so. The Viet did not have the armour, long-range artillery or air power to mount rescue missions, and did not attempt to do so. Any unit that found itself in difficulties was left to its own devices. It was tough stuff, but everyone knew the situation.

And then the war was over. It was time to sort out the wreckage and start the process of reconstruction in a poor, devastated country. Vietnam was, and had been a third world country. How would a mother cope, having lost perhaps an only child, a husband, parents, grand children, siblings? They handled it in some interesting ways.

A mother who had no family of her own left might be lent a family who would move in with her and love her as if she were their own. Probably equally importantly, they would allow her the opportunity to care for them as if they were her own. This new family might be related, such as Ma Gom's granddaughter from Saigon, the young family Ma Huong was looking after in Hue, or the couple living with Ma It in Ha Tay Province. It might be from a friendly family in the village, or strangers in need of a grandmother and some tender loving care. There was no shortage of people in need.

A mother who had lost an only son may also have had a daughter who had married and moved away to live with her husband's family. If the husband's family had other children, family arrangements could be reshuffled so that the daughter and her family could live with mother. Tradition was occasionally over-ridden in the cause of humanity.

There were many Vietnamese survivors of the war who had psychiatric problems. Some of this was due either to after-effects of B-52 bombings that had driven some insane and left others with a variety of problems, or due to the terrifying napalm attacks. Displaced, confused survivors wandered about for years, seeking their homes and families.

The ferocity of the B-52 raids caused massive physical and psychological damage. Truong Nhu Tang survived several such attacks as the Americans sought to destroy his secret base on the Cambodian border. He describes that experience[31]:

> From a kilometre away, the sonic roar of the B-52 explosions tore eardrums, leaving many of the jungle dwellers permanently deaf. From a kilometre, the shock waves knocked their victims senseless. Any hit within a half kilometre would collapse the walls of an unreinforced bunker, burying the people cowering inside. Seen up close, the bomb craters were gigantic—thirty feet across and nearly as deep.

The crater he described was of course caused by a single bomb. Even if it was a one-tonne bomb, it meant that the immediate surrounds would have received another twenty-nine per aircraft. The devastation would have been enormous. He describes his first experiences of attacks[32]:

> The first few times I experienced a B-52 attack it seemed, as I strained to press myself into the bunker floor, that I had been caught in the Apocalypse. The terror was complete. One lost control of bodily functions as the mind screamed incomprehensible orders to get out. On one occasion a Soviet delegation was visiting our ministry when a particularly short-notice warning came through. When it was over, no one had been hurt, but the entire delegation had sustained considerable damage to its dignity—uncontrollable trembling and wet pants the all-too-obvious outward signs of inner convulsions. The visitors could have spared themselves their feeling of embarrassment; each of their hosts was a veteran of the same symptoms.

Sometimes these damaged wanderers became part of a type of adoption process. A mother who had lost her family may have come across a younger man or woman wandering about and each would decide that the other was either a missing family member, or a new member to be welcomed into the fold. Mother now had a son or daughter, and vice versa. Each party would have someone to care for. It mattered not if one party, or both parties, had a few problems.

Huong introduced me to her uncle, Tran Minh Be. He is her uncle, not by birth, but because her grandfather, Do Nhu Ty said so.

Grandfather Ty was in his 50s, single, and a veteran soldier at an army rest camp in North Vietnam in 1955. There he met Be, a young soldier from Hue in Central Vietnam who had been sent north to help with the war effort, as had been the husbands of Ma Ha and Ma Sam. The younger man had lost touch with his family and had no idea as to when the war might end or when he might see his family again.

They were expecting a long war and Ty felt sorry for him, so the bachelor adopted the younger man, who now had a father in the north with whom he could at least keep in touch. When Ty later married, his wife accepted the situation and bore him several children. Uncle Be remains the first son, with all the privileges, duties and responsibilities that go with it; he now has rather a lot of family and an extra home city, something that bemuses him slightly but bothers him not at all. He is a head of one family now and a member of another.

Huong and I dropped in to see him in his family apartment near Hoan Kiem Lake in Hanoi. He lives above the sidewalk hat shop run by his family. It is a good little business, managed enthusiastically and capably by the younger ones. He smiles readily, and admits his is an unusual family arrangement but says it causes him no difficulty.

In 2003 I was fortunate to spend an hour with Phan Thanh Hao, co-author with Karen Gottschang Turner of *Even the Women Must Fight*, at her home in Hanoi. That book had made a great impression on me on a flight from Australia before I commenced my journey. Hao confirmed what Huong had told me, and related a family experience to me.

During the war, a relative died in action but his remains were never found. This troubled the family, who wanted closure, something to bring home to venerate, so they visited the area where he died. The weather was poor so they decided in advance that if sunlight penetrated the area, they would accept that spot as his final resting place.

Some sunlight duly appeared and a little soil was taken home so that rituals could be observed. Hao still has mixed feelings about whether what they did was right or not but they all feel better. It was a matter of doing the best you can under the circumstances.

Hao's book and other sources had taught me that many single women who had actively participated in the war were considered poor marriage material after hostilities ceased. Many of these women spent their best years fighting, labouring or scouting, sometimes in very inhospitable country. Many had contracted diseases such as malaria, had developed back trouble because of hard labour or heavy loads carried, or were wounded.

Some parents warned their sons against marrying these women. Some of the women even warned their lovers off, afraid that they might not be able to discharge their wifely duties. They were afraid of being bad wives, barren perhaps or unable to contribute to the family coffers. A bleak and lonely future quite foreign to Vietnamese culture and tradition seemed to be their reward for their sacrifice.

Becoming a single mother was socially unacceptable. The government now found itself caught in a dilemma: these women had done as much as the men to liberate their country and were to be denied a family of their own. It finally relaxed its views about single parenthood to some extent. A "husband for the night" could be found, so that these single women might have a child to care for and to love, to live with, and to care for them in their old age.

This is not to suggest that there was the happiest possible ending for everybody in some fairy-tale country. There is a great deal of sorrow and suffering still, but these caring and ingenious people did what they could to relieve pain wherever possible. A guide at the Army Museum in Hanoi was pleased to tell a tour group an unusual story with a typical Vietnam twist.

A young man who had survived a B52 bombing raid, but who had been damaged in the process, wandered about for nearly thirty years, looking for familiar surroundings. He knocked on the door of a house in a village he was passing through, and was admitted and welcomed by the wife he had left behind. She had of course waited for him. It is unlikely that his somewhat damaged condition would hinder the future relationship. He had been damaged and she would care for him. It was the story of the War, encapsulated in two paragraphs.

24. Epilogue

The journey ended in 2005 when we returned to Hanoi after visiting sleepy Khai Phat where the fighting had started sixty years before. We had motorcycled back through feisty old Cao Bang, following the route of the French retreat along Colonial Route 4, through small towns like Dong Khe and That Khe where Giap had extracted a heavy price from the forces of the country that had violated his nation and his family.

The mighty Mongols may have passed through this territory on their way to three defeats, two of which were particularly severe. Chinese armies passed through on a number of occasions, with mixed results, and the French had fled to Hanoi as a rabble, several thousand good men the poorer. The water buffalo we met along the way knew nothing of these momentous events; they would not have cared anyway for they are hedonists, concerned with more immediate pleasures such as eating and wallowing about in rivers.

Before returning my rented motorcycle to the ever reliable Mr Cuong, I rode to the Highland Coffee shop at Hoan Kiem Lake, the heart of Hanoi, for a final coffee. They serve a very fine brew from the Central Highlands, in the area around Buon Ma Thuot, not far from where my old Minsk had once been confiscated during an earlier stage of the journey.

Huong's adopted Uncle Be lived two hundred metres away, General Giap perhaps two kilometres, only a decent stone's throw away from where his old friend Ho Chi Minh lies in state. The Army Museum and young Nhu Hong Phong, the 21 year-old, who barks in his wooden cot, were a five minute ride away. It would take twenty minutes to reach Ma Tuyet.

A nearby block of apartments had as a centrepiece a large circular fishpond with its own unusual centrepiece—the remains of the Boeing B52 bomber that had been shot down during a mission: it had nosed in so forcefully that nobody bothered to remove it.

Perhaps a kilometre away was the Hoa Lo Prison Museum, which has passed into legend as the Hanoi Hilton, where American prisoners of war were incarcerated under harsh conditions. US Senator John McCain, a Presidential candidate in the 2009 elections, was a pilot during the Vietnam War and distinguished himself by his courageous conduct in this prison. He was unknowingly following a Vietminh tradition—the French had tortured Vietnamese to an extent that captive American pilots could not have imagined in their worst nightmares, and the guillotine and the firing squads had done brisk business.

The scars left by the greatest foreign policy disaster in US history do not disturb the casual traveller, for they are not visible along the tourist routes. The Vietnamese are in any case not given to displaying their wounds. They have been through all this before, and are too busy looking ahead to be preoccupied with past suffering. All the same, one cannot help mourning that the war came about almost as a malicious conspiracy by the gods, for there were many reasons why there should have been no war at all.

The country could so easily have gained independence in the late 1940s, if Roosevelt had lived longer and had been able to follow his personal preference. If China had not fallen to the Communists in 1949, Vietnam would probably have been a staunch ally of the United States and a bastion of democracy.

Tragically, Vietnam itself had little influence on the course of events. It was, after all, a third world country with no international clout. More importantly, it was a backward Communist country, undeserving of a voice.

A second tragedy is that so little has been made of the truly appalling loss of life. Vietnam lost 500,000 lives during the French War and 2,000,000 as a result of starvation under the Japanese. The American War probably cost over 3,000,000 lives. These disasters translate in relative terms to 69,000,000 lives in the United States today, two thirds of them civilian. One can only speculate at the righteous indignation that would have followed such outrageous carnage had it been inflicted upon the USA or Australia, or indeed any Western country. It happened thirty short years ago and we were part of it, but we have successfully tiptoed away from it all.

Yet the loss of 2,595 lives in New York on 9/11 seems to haunt us all so much more. Events on that terrible day, insignificant in Vietnam War terms, became an immediate international priority, cause for invasion of Afghanistan and Iraq and threats to any countries deemed to be part of an "axis of evil". One must wonder at the remarkable ability of Westerners to absorb others' losses whilst forgiving ourselves our trespasses as we would never forgive others. Lest we forget, we Australians should be aware that we held the school bully's jacket while he beat the crap out of the little kids.

A third tragedy is the very mean manner in which the French and the US forces conducted themselves. The French were aghast at the conduct of the Gestapo in their country, but their own practices were no better. Had the Germans had exclusive use of pesticides and napalm, those righteous and relentless prosecutors of war criminals at Nuremburg would have watched the gallows collapse under the strain of executions. In Vietnam, the US deployed these weapons to save American lives, which made any weaponry acceptable. And they got away with it.

A fourth tragedy is the absence of any meaningful effort at rehabilitation or compensation for the enormous damage and suffering. Lack of funding has made the reconstruction of a severely traumatized nation a slow and painful process, patently unfair to a country that did not start the conflagration. Promised funding to assist the reconstruction process was withheld in what must be one of the great hypocritical gestures of the century. It is particularly disturbing to read some of the material gloating about the financial abyss Vietnam plunged into as China and Russia withdrew their support over time.

The Vietnamese paid a severe penalty for winning the war. The Allies rightly made enormous resources available to help Germany recover from its defeat in World War 2—this after its invasion of many peaceful neighbouring countries, along with the atrocity of the Holocaust and a whole catalogue of other war crimes. Japan received the same benefits despite the appalling civilian death toll from its invasion of China and other countries, the treachery of the attack on Pearl Harbour and numerous acts of barbarity it is still inclined to deny.

The guiding principle seems to be that children and other innocents should not be punished for the deeds of the guilty. There is rather a large number of Vietnamese who will be delighted to hear that. Vietnam invaded nobody, indulged in no genocide and did not invite the USA to send over soldiers to die on Vietnamese soil. Thus, it seems, its credentials for humanitarian aid are inadequate.

President Jimmy Carter was asked about the disbursement of the $3.25 billion in aid secretly promised by Richard Nixon during secret peace talks, but it was the peanut farmer Jimmy Carter who confirmed there would be no payment because both sides had suffered. Indeed.

In order to ensure that recovery would be slow and painful, obstacles were placed in the path of the recovery process. Twenty years after leaving Vietnam, the US ceased opposing foreign aid to Vietnam, and it took twenty-one years to lift the trade embargo. The USA demonstrated that in matters military it is a garrulous winner and an utterly merciless and ungraceful loser.

I recently purchased a copy of "Vietnam at Peace', a superb photographic essay by Philip Jones Griffiths. The foreword by John Pilger makes interesting, but troublesome reading:

Consider the odds. Ho Chi Minh's nationalists had fought for thirty years, first against the French, whose tree-lined boulevards, pink-washed villas and terraces were facades which concealed unrelenting plunder and cruelty; then against the Japanese who, in 1944, starved to death two million Vietnamese in order to feed their own troops; then against the Americans, with whom Ho repeatedly tried to forge an alliance against China; then against the Khmer Rouge, who attacked from the west; then against the Chinese, who attacked from the north. All of them were sent off at immeasurable cost.

And that was not the end of it. Having secretly promised to pay the Vietnamese $3.25 billion as a 'reconstruction grant' in return for their safe passage out, the Americans—Nixon and Kissinger, that is—reneged and not a cent was paid. On April 30, 1975, the last day of the war, the US Treasury froze Vietnam's only hard currency assets: $70 million. Two weeks later, the US Commerce Department classified Vietnam as a 'Category Z' country. This meant, in effect, the suspension of all trade with most of the world that America could bully. American voluntary agencies were denied export licences for humanitarian aid. Revenge was the policy.

Washington's allies joined in. In 1979, Margaret Thatcher persuaded the European Community to halt its regular shipments of milk to Vietnamese children. The health of infants under five so deteriorated following the milk ban that, according to the World Health Organisation, the majority of them were stunted and tens of thousands of the very youngest went progressively blind due to a lack of Vitamin A.

Among Washington's demons, not even Cuba was subjected to such punishment. "We have smashed the country to bits," wrote Telford Taylor, Chief United States Prosecutor at the Nuremberg Trials, "and (we) will not even take the trouble to clean up the blood and rubble."

Two incidents involving Americans in Vietnam linger in my memory. A young officer from a guided missile destroyer told me in a Saigon bar that the great thing about being in the US armed forces was that "when you push that button you know there's going to be a whole lot of hurt at the other end." I wanted to ask him if they had mentioned Vietnam during his officer training at Annapolis or wherever, but managed to refrain.

On another occasion I rang the US Embassy in Hanoi to continue my research into the $3.25 billion promised by Kissinger during secret peace talks but unpaid—this was years before I read Pilger's above foreword. An Information Officer confirmed the money was never paid, but told me that the USA offers more Fulbright scholarships to Vietnamese per capita than to any other nationality in the world.

Elsewhere, I found reference to an annual gift of prosthetic limbs to Vietnam valued at around a million dollars. Perhaps that is a concession to the average one thousand Vietnamese who have died every year since the end of the war from unexploded ordnance lying around the country.

An Australian businessman who sat next to me at a cricket match in Perth confessed he was sick to death of hearing about how the US had supposedly wronged the Vietnamese. It soon emerged he had no idea about events there, for he was a few million war victims short in his estimates of their casualties, but Ponting was batting well and I could not intrude on his enjoyment of the game. Hell, at the end of the day it is our boundaries that count.

A fifth tragedy is that the US has never acknowledged that it was wrong to do what it did in Vietnam, although Robert McNamara has—after a fashion. The war was known at one stage as McNamara's War, after the Secretary of Defence, 1961-68. Still troubled by the war, McNamara made some telling observations many years later. In listing eleven major causes for the US disaster one really stands out; it applies to other interventions since Vietnam and will no doubt apply to interventions yet to follow[33]:

> We did not recognize that neither our people nor our leaders are omniscient. Where our own security is not directly at stake, our judgment of what is in another people's or country's best interest should be put to the test of open discussion in international forums. We do not have the God-given right to shape every nation in our own image or as we choose.

He could perhaps have added that, having put it to the international forum, the response of that forum should be considered and treated with respect, unlike European sentiments about war in Iraq. He observed further:[34]

> Our misjudgements of friend and foe alike reflected our profound ignorance of the history, culture, and politics of the people in the area, and the personalities and habits of their leaders. We might have made similar misunderstandings regarding the Soviets during our frequent confrontations—over Berlin, Cuba, the Middle East, for example—had we not had the advice of Tommy Thompson, Chip Bohlen, and George Kennan. These senior diplomats had spent decades studying the Soviet Union, its people and its leaders, why they behaved as they did and how they would react to our actions. Their advice proved invaluable in shaping our judgements and decisions. No Southeast Asian counterparts existed for senior officials to consult when making decisions on Vietnam.

That was so because the China experts who could have provided expert advice had been destroyed during the McCarthy era, as is mentioned in the Historical Background chapter.

We failed then—as we have since—to recognize the limitations of modern, high-technology military equipment, forces, and doctrine in confronting unconventional, highly motivated people's movements. We failed as well to adapt our military tactics to the task of winning the hearts and minds of people from a totally different culture[35].

The Vietnam War is a stark illustration of what happens when unlimited funds, weaponry and technology are married to men of great education but little wisdom. The lack of wisdom is apparent in the commitment of over half a million men to a struggle in a distant country without even a little basic research; in the firm belief bombing tonnages and civilian damage equals ultimate victory; in the refusal to come to the aid of a poor nation that has been heavily violated. Good eyesight is not the same as clear vision, and tragically it fell to the Vietnamese to foot the bill for the unnecessary demonstration. Power and wisdom should ideally be in balance, but that was not the case.

Perhaps the final tragedy is that many of the lessons of Vietnam have not been learnt, as evidenced by subsequent events in Afghanistan and Iraq.

The Mothers have never heard of Fall, Halberstam, Sheehan and Karnow, authors of some of the better publications about aspects of the war, from whom I learned enough to know that it was time to buy a Minsk and learn more, so that I might better interpret what they were telling me. The Mothers' knowledge of events came from the commissars, the village headmen, neighbours, family, participants, or from personal observation as participants themselves. They have no real idea of the scale of the damage; talk of millions of lives lost is meaningless to them, for their world ends at the village boundary, and one hundred is a huge number in the hamlet. They can, however, count the headstones in the cemeteries.

They are not as clever as some of the power merchants of the Vietnam War are, or were, or were thought to be, or were thought to be for a while; men like McNamara, the Bundy brothers, the Kennedys. None attended Groton, the Boston preparatory school for powerful men of the future, or Harvard or Yale, and that was probably a good thing; had they been so splendidly educated they would have known that they were undertaking an impossible mission and that Ho must fail. They might well have decided against the fight for freedom.

The Vietnamese receive western visitors with the utmost courtesy and generous hospitality. They are happy to share a table over lunch, a beer or a glass of rice wine; a good laugh. I lost track of the number of old men who waved me down in the far north, wanting to share a drink that was forbidden to me: my motorcycle skills are perilously low and alcohol was out of the question while I was on the road. There is no grandstanding, no accusatory moment; hard stories are delivered in matter-of-fact fashion. It is humbling stuff. The old women are even surprised and honoured that a westerner should call to hear their stories. They are too damn modest to take a bow, although they do preen a little when having their photographs taken.

The women live in their hamlets and villages, as comfortable as they can be, for there is nothing anybody can do to reverse what happened. They make the most of what family they have left, or have managed to adopt, and they look to the future. Those who caused the damage have long since been forgiven, even though most Mothers remain mystified as to why all these people came from such distant countries to kill. They wonder about a society that is prepared to roast villagers alive, poison food sources and cause horrendous birth defects even in future generations. They wonder why the destroyers do not return to help. One might say that our demonstration of the qualities of both Christianity and democracy left some a little underwhelmed—they recognise bastardry in its various forms.

Vietnam has seemingly always had heroes to see it through its darkest hours; this most recent struggle has discovered no single hero, but many thousands who deserve to be honoured. There are even Hero Trees, Hero Rivers, Hero Mountains and Hero Caves, natural features that at some stage provided avenues of escape or shelter for fighters. It seems crazy, until you understand that most of the fighters came from obscure hamlets and villages, illiterate and often barefoot, seemingly ill equipped for the task ahead. They were fortified, however, with knowledge of past heroes, of legendary characters and great and often improbable victories that sustained them during troubled times.

They travel about incognito, these old heroes. The ancient woman gathering her heavy load of bamboo, the old bloke selling tyre pressure on the Hanoi street corner, next to his mate who will saw a piece of wood for a fee—they are the ones who won the war.

I was privileged to observe, however briefly, how a society accustomed over millennia to interrupting its timeless, relatively untroubled lifestyle to repel threats to the nation followed a scrawny, charismatic leader down a path of excruciating agony. Perhaps it was a little like the Children's Crusade, except that some of the old followers did return. They were far fewer than they should have been, but they did win a mighty victory.

Trying to put the Vietnam War into some sort of perspective is difficult: what relativity can one use to help readers grasp the scale of an almost forgotten conflict? A country less than half the size of New South Wales (Vietnam is about the size of Italy) was subjected to more than three times the total Allied bombing tonnage during World War 2. If one extracts data for South Vietnam, theoretically friendly territory during the war (and this speaks volumes of the strategy for winning the hearts and minds of the locals) the figures look even worse. Every quarter acre of land (the great Australian dream was once the house on a quarter acre block) would have hosted the arrival of a 250 kilogram bomb. Regardless of where on the block this bomb landed, it would have destroyed any normal domestic structure. Even the Holden would have gone.

It disturbs me that we Australians have walked away from Vietnam, having helped the Americans wreak such massive destruction. It is as though it never really happened. I feel desperately sorry for those who served there and who have been vilified for doing so: one should not be blamed for doing the bidding of the government of one's country, and thus, in theory at least, one's fellow countrymen. However, a bumper sticker I saw on a Vietnam Veteran's car offends me. It reads "When I left we were winning" or words to that effect. My problem with that is merely one of fact: we were never winning and we never were going to. My reasoning is spelt out in the next page.

If there is a defining moment throughout the whole trip for me, something that stands out above all else, it is a simple truth, an utterly disarming statement from Le Thi Gom, the Hero Mother from Cu Chi, she of the heavily scarred legs. I had scanned the rude family tree that had more or less drawn itself during the interview. The chronology that bothered me read:

Brother	1949
Father	1952
Husband	1963
Daughter	1963
Son	1968
Son	1969
Brother	1969
Son (13)	1969

It was the intermingling of the generations that brought me undone, and I had to ask the question.

"What kept you going, Ma?"

"They kept killing my family."

25. Historical background

The Chinese occupied and ruled Vietnam for 1,000 years from about 200 BC. It was an uneasy occupation for them, for their efforts to subjugate the Vietnamese and replace their culture with that of China were opposed and thwarted many times during this period. Vietnamese women were at the forefront of these rebellious forays on several occasions.

In AD40, the Trung sisters drove the Chinese from Vietnam with an army of 80,000 but were defeated by the Chinese three years later. When finally beaten in battle the sisters chose suicide by drowning rather than the humiliation of surrender.

In AD248 Trieu Thi Trinh won more than 30 battles against the Chinese. When finally defeated at 23 years of age, she, too, drowned herself rather than surrender. Other formidable women followed, and a separate chapter, "Those Viet Women", is devoted to them.

The Chinese were defeated in 938 by Ngo Quyen at the battle of Bach-dang River. Shallow-draft boats provoked the Chinese and lured them into a trap, with underwater stakes at low tide wrecking the Chinese fleet, tactics they used centuries later against the Mongols. They reached into their history a thousand years later to become experts at setting baited traps for the French and the Americans.

After conquering China, the Mongols entered Vietnam in 1257. They sacked the capital which the Vietnamese abandoned. The Viet refused to risk decimation in a pitched battle but sapped the strength of the Mongols with a series of minor skirmishes that helped drive them back to China. The tactic of falling away before an enemy and choosing when to fight proved successful as late as in the 1950s against the French, and again in the 1960s against the Americans.

The Mongols returned in 1283 with a great army under Kublai Khan and entered Vietnam against the wishes of Emperor Tran Hung Dao. They were punished for the lack of manners by Emperor Dao who drove the Mongols back to China.

The defeat rankled with the Mongols who returned with an army of 300,000 in 1287. Tran Hung Dao accommodated them once more with a severe thrashing that cost the visitors most of their battle fleet. The tactic of appearing to retreat in order to lure the enemy into a trap once again paid dividends, and the Mongols never returned.

In the 15th century the Chinese once again regained control of Vietnam but their reign ended after ten years, following an uprising led by the revered Le Loi.

Nguyen Hue, also destined to become a national hero, defeated a Chinese army of 200,000 at Dong Da in 1789. Dong Da is now in a suburb on the outskirts of Hanoi where tourists can visit a hill said to be the burial mound of Chinese soldiers. It is a sizeable hill.

There were many other battles, rebellions and uprisings over the centuries that illustrate the willingness of this small country to engage a vastly superior enemy in battle when it chooses and its ability to win. Heroes somehow always appeared to see their country through major crises. Lonely Planet expresses this most aptly[36]:

After Le Loi's victory over the Chinese, Nguyen Trai, a scholar and Le Loi's companion in arms, wrote his famous Great Proclamation (Binh Ngo Dai Cao), extraordinary for the compelling voice it gave to Vietnam's fierce spirit of independence:

'Our people long ago established Vietnam as an independent nation with its own civilization. We have our own mountains and our own rivers, our own customs and traditions, and these are different from those of the foreign country to the north . . . . we have sometimes been weak and sometimes powerful, but at no time have we suffered from a lack of heroes.'

There was no shortage of rebellions, wars and intrigue over the centuries. In 1784 Nguyen Anh, who later ruled as Emperor Gia Long, appealed to the French for help in suppressing the Tayson rebellion of the brothers Nguyen. He obtained French assistance and the rebellion ended in 1799 but, as the French lingered, so their involvement in Indochina commenced. It would last for 170 years.

Saigon fell to the French in 1861, with the rest of the country under their control within the next twenty years. It would take ninety-three years and a number of heroes to oust them. Many of the same heroes would then deal with the Americans.

One such hero, Nguyen Tat Tanh, was born in 1890, and would achieve fame as Ho Chi Minh. He spent thirty years abroad before returning to his country to pursue his goal of national liberation, and would become the father of modern Vietnam. Ho died in 1969, some six years before the unification of the two Vietnams.

There had been a number of nationalist and Communist movements in Vietnam and Ho saw an opportunity to strengthen resistance to the French. In Hong Kong, in 1929 "he assembled different factional leaders at a local football stadium during a match to avoid detection by the British colonial police and persuaded them to close ranks. They labelled the new movement the Indochinese Communist Party"[37].

The Japanese occupied Vietnam in 1940, but left the French to run things under Japanese supervision. France had surrendered to Germany by then, and the Vichy French government was in power, so France and Japan were nominal allies. This did not necessarily sit well with the French in Vietnam but they were compelled to follow instructions.

Ho Chi Minh returned from his lengthy travels in 1941. He based himself in a cave at Pac Bo, not far from Cao Bang, an old war-torn town close to the northern Chinese border. It is only about 200 km from Hanoi as the crow flies, but the crow spends little time airborne around here. Access to the area is difficult as there are mountain ranges, rivers and ravines to be navigated, and there is only a single good road through the region.

This was in the heart of Ho's Bac Viet, the north where he was revered. Ho assembled his team and they set about plotting the downfall of the French. Vo Nguyen Giap, history professor and lawyer, set about building an army.

In 1944, Ho Chi Minh's guerrillas helped rescue US pilots who bailed out in Vietnam to escape to China. The Vietminh provided the Americans with useful intelligence and hosted the Deer Team, an American reconnaissance mission. Major Archimedes Patti, head of the Office of Strategic Services (OSS)-Indochina mission wrote *Why Viet*

Nam? Prelude to America's Albatross, an informative record of the early years of US relations with Vietnam.

Ho formed the Viet Nam Doc Lop Dong Minh Hoi (Viet Nam Independence League), known as Viet Minh, so as to present a broad national united front, rather than a communist one. He wanted broader appeal in the interests of national unity. There was a struggle among rival nationalist movements for members and the Vietminh resorted to what we would today call terrorist measures to gain support. An uncooperative village headman might be executed in order to encourage the village to become supportive. Then the Vietminh would move on to the next village. French efforts to suppress the Vietminh were also brutal with public beheadings and executions without trial practiced in addition to a regimen of torture.

There was a rice shortage in 1943-5 that caused 2,000,000[38] deaths from a national population of perhaps 20,000,000. The suffering was worst in the north, where, of a population of 10,000,000, the death toll reached fifty per cent in some provinces. At best, it could be said that Japanese indifference to the plight of the peasants caused the tragedy. A separate chapter, "Starvation", is devoted to a disaster that is often overlooked when the tribulations and suffering of the Vietnamese is reviewed.

On 9 March 1945, the Japanese turned over control of Vietnam to Bao Dai, the last Emperor of Vietnam.[39] Vietnam was now independent within the Japanese Greater East Asian Co-Prosperity Sphere. It was effectively a puppet government.

The end of World War 2 found Vietnam in an unusual situation: the Japanese were displaced as the local power, the Viet Minh had grown strong and were in Hanoi and Saigon, and French forces were very weak. The Viet Minh had been of assistance to the US Office of Strategic Services (OSS) for several years and Ho was optimistic of gaining support in Washington for an independent Vietnam.

In Hue, the Viet Minh demanded that Bao Dai resign and on 25 August 1945, he transferred power to them. On 2 September 1945, Ho Chi Minh read out the Declaration of Independence, as head of the new Provisional government.

US President Roosevelt, who had been a staunch opponent of colonialism, determined that France should give up her Indochinese colonies[40]:

The question of freedom for all dependent peoples became a major issue during the years 1942-1944, and the Americans championed the cause. Roosevelt and Cordell Hull insisted that the European colonial powers follow our example in the Philippines in laying the foundations for ultimate independence for their colonies. Roosevelt went out of his way to single out France in Indochina and often cited French rule there as a flagrant example of onerous and exploitative colonialism.

Roosevelt died before the end of the war. The gathering fear of communism that led to the Cold War put France in an unexpectedly strong position in that French support was vital for creating a European organization as a buttress against the communist threat. NATO was later formed to meet that objective. The Allies agreed that the French could return to Vietnam.

Halberstam[41] refers to Asia experts in the State Department who, even in 1945-46, tried to have the French engaged in meaningful negotiations with the Vietnamese, only to be rebuffed by the European experts who were preoccupied with helping the French regain the glory and prestige they had lost with their hasty surrender to the Germans a few years before.

The question of dealing with the Japanese surrender and hand-over was resolved by dividing Vietnam temporarily in two: Nationalist China would deal with the northern part and the British the south until the arrival of the French to take charge once more. Both countries bungled their duties: in the north, the Chinese behaved in rapacious fashion, and in the south, the British erred by arming French Foreign Legionnaires who had been imprisoned by the Japanese. They went on a rampage of killing and an already complicated web of factions and gangs got into the action, leading to the British helping the French hurry back to the south.

In March 1946 France recognised Vietnam as a free state within the French Union, but in June 1946 the French High Commissioner violated that recognition by proclaiming a separate government for Cochinchina, roughly the southern third of Vietnam. France was keen to protect as best it could its investments in the south where it had significant rubber plantations and industry. Bao Dai fled to Hong Kong, where he lived for three years.

The French Vietnam War had been put in train as a result of what the Vietminh saw as an act of treachery. All that was needed was an opening salvo. The American Vietnam War would be put in train as a result of what the Vietminh viewed as an act of treachery on the part of major nations in Geneva almost 10 years later.

Hostilities broke out between the Vietminh and the French on 23 November 1946. The French in the meantime continually presented Bao Dai with proposals that appeared to offer Vietnam varying degrees of independence but with France fundamentally in control.

In June 1948, having, as Karnow records, pursued Bao Dai around Europe, where he hid in cinemas during the day and cabarets at night, the French persuaded him to return to Vietnam where the Treaty of Halong Bay was signed. Bao Dai was relegated to the status of witness. This ceded independence of sorts to Cochinchina but Bao Dai was unhappy with the terms.

In 1949 the Elysee Agreement was signed by Bao Dai and the French President confirming the independence of Vietnam and outlined ways to reincorporate Cochinchina into a united Vietnam. China fell to the communists that year, thereby sealing Vietnam's fate. In time the domino theory prevailed in Washington: communism would spread south from China through Vietnam, Thailand and Malaysia even into Australia and New Zealand.

The fall of China to the Communists in 1949 led to a demand in the USA for a strong line against Communism, a sentiment heightened during the McCarthy witch-hunts of the early 1950s.

The US policy changed from supporting Vietnam independence around 1944 to supporting the French against the Vietminh by 1950.

In 1950 China and the USSR recognised Ho's Vietnam while the US recognised Bao Dai's. By the early 1950s, the Vietminh had progressed from small hit and run raids against the French to pitched battles. Superior firepower, uncontested air power and superior training had given the French the edge in earlier years. With the end of the Korean War in July 1953, China provided the Vietminh with a host of captured US equipment, often more modern than that used by the French, who sometimes found themselves outgunned, a new and unwelcome experience. The Chinese were also able to increase the training assistance they had provided to the Vietminh.

The Chinese had learnt a great deal about anti-aircraft gunnery during the Korean War, hard-won expertise that they passed on to the Vietminh along with effective anti-aircraft weapons. This was to make a huge difference at the definitive and final battle at Dien Bien Phu, where French airpower was neutralized, dooming the garrison to defeat. The Vietnamese communist forces retained that skill, contributing to the loss of over 8,000 American aircraft during their war.

The US had considered direct means of helping the French at Dien Bien Phu, including a limited nuclear air attack, but concerns about China's reaction as well as the effect on nearby French troops saw common sense prevail. The British wanted no involvement in Vietnam.

The Vietminh duly crushed the French at Dien Bien Phu on 7 May 1954, the eve of the Conference in Geneva that was to determine how to end the war. The atmosphere at the Geneva Conference was abysmal, according to Karnow[42]:

> The Vietminh's officials avoided Bao Dai's representatives and spurned the envoys from Cambodia and Laos; they also boycotted the French, who did not encounter the Chinese until late in the episode. The Russians dropped disparaging remarks about the Chinese. The Americans had been ordered to shun the Chinese, lest a smile be interpreted as formal recognition, and Dulles even refused to shake hands with Zhou Enlai, conceding sarcastically that they might possibly meet if their cars collided.

It was a complicated scene[43]:

> The French resented American attempts to use them as intermediaries, and the Americans blamed the French for keeping their manoeuvres secret. The Americans also expressed impatience with the British, who they felt were not sufficiently tough. Eden struggled heroically to hold this fragile house of cards together, observing afterward:

> 'I had never known a conference of this kind. The parties would not make direct contact, and we were in constant danger of one or another backing out the door.'

In the end the Geneva Conference produced no durable solution to the Indochina conflict, only a military truce that awaited a political settlement, which never really happened. So the conference was merely an interlude between two wars—or, rather, a lull in the same war.

Ho Chi Minh wanted full independence for his country, but was pressured by China, his main supporter, to settle for less. China was wary of another Korean War and advised Ho to settle for a ceasefire, and a temporary division of the country in two, pending a nationwide election within two years to decide on a leader for a united Vietnam. The Vietminh were war-weary and lacking in diplomatic skills, so they accepted. The US was not a signatory to the Accords but declared "its traditional position that people are entitled to determine their own future and that the United States will not join in an arrangement which would hinder this"[44]. There was murky work afoot as the US set about undermining the Accords almost immediately[45]:

> But in June, according to the *Pentagon Papers*, the US had decided on measures to train and finance a 234,000-man Vietnamese National Army and to 'work through the French only insofar as necessary'.

Vietnam was divided at the seventeenth parallel at the Ben Hai River just north of Dong Ha. It would acquire notoriety as the Demilitarized Zone (DMZ) during the American war, becoming a wasteland that feels eerie even thirty years later. The northerners had to cross the DMZ to fight in the south, and thus came under fire from numerous US firebases in the area, as well as B52 bombing raids and other regular air attacks. They developed the Ho Chi Minh Trail that passed through parts of Laos and Cambodia in order to escape some of the bombing.

About a month before the Conference ended, Bao Dai appointed Ngo Dinh Diem Prime Minister of the Republic of Vietnam, as the south would be known until it was conquered in 1975. The north was known as the Democratic Republic of Vietnam, something of a misnomer for a Communist state.

Diem was the US choice of leader in the south largely due to a lack of rival contenders. He was not without virtue, as Karnow points out[46]:

> Ngo Dinh Diem filled a vacuum, but despite his record of integrity, he lacked the dimensions of a national leader. An ascetic Catholic

steeped in Confucian tradition, a mixture of monk and mandarin, he was honest, courageous and fervent in his fidelity to Vietnam's national cause: even Ho respected his patriotism. But he was no match for Ho, whom even anti-Communists regarded as a hero. Imbued with a sense of his own infallibility, as if he were an ancient emperor ordained to govern, Diem expected obedience. Distrustful of everyone outside his family, he declined to delegate authority, nor was he able to build a constituency that reached beyond his fellow Catholics and natives of central Vietnam.

The US had picked the wrong man. They met secretly with representatives of France on 29 September 1954 to retain Diem in the south, and there was a meeting of US and French military personnel on 13 December 1954 to discuss related issues.

The US was busy during the two-year period leading up to the agreed elections. The defender of democracy set about violating the Geneva Accords in many ways. It trained Vietnamese agents, and sent them north to perform various acts of sabotage. Some were to await instructions at some future date, and weapons were cached in the north for future military operations. It initiated rumours about Vietminh excesses in the north in an effort to lure people to move from the north, bringing about a million new residents to the south. The Geneva Accord permitted free migration north and south for those who wanted to move, and both sides seized the opportunity to place "sleepers" in opposition territory.

Diem was able to maintain US support after cleaning up a number of factions in the south, and, with American help, deposed Bao Dai in a rigged election. Karnow points out that ballot papers for Diem were red, the colour of good luck, while Bao Dai's were green, the colour of misfortune[47].

The US wanted Diem to win sixty to seventy per cent of the vote but he recorded over ninety-eight per cent instead. There were beatings at ballot boxes and in some places Diem's votes exceeded the number of registered voters.

The 1956 election deadline passed and Ho realized his people had been betrayed. Russia even suggested recognition of two Vietnams but the US refused to recognize a communist regime. It may have prevented further warfare, or it may have led to the two Vietnams deciding their future militarily at some time in the future, with the outcome predictable. In the end, this is more or less what happened, with US involvement merely postponing the inevitable result and consigning 3,000,000 Vietnamese to their graves.

The US demonstrated an alarming ignorance of matters Chinese and Vietnamese, although it demonstrated great expertise in handling the Russians. It need not have been so. Halberstam explains in *The Best and the Brightest*, how Washington denied itself expert advice on the Chinese situation along the following lines:

The struggle in China after World War 2 led to a split in that country between Chiang Kai-shek and Mao Tse-tung, with the latter winning, leading to China turning communist in 1949. Whilst this was in progress and a huge defeat for the US loomed, the US ambassador to China resigned, claiming China officers in the US Foreign Service had undermined him.

This led to a purge of an enormously talented group who had their careers thoroughly destroyed during the McCarthy witch-hunt. Halberstam mentions Raymond Ludden, John Carter Vincent, John Stewart Service and the phenomenally talented John Paton Davies, son of missionaries to China. Davies was educated in China, and knew the language, the culture and the history. He had been to school with some of the emerging leaders.

Eisenhower, Kennedy, and Johnson were denied the services of very talented China specialist State Department officers and, as a result, the relationship between China and Vietnam would be seriously misread. Officers who would have acquired extensive knowledge of Vietnamese matters were instead dismissed, or transferred to remote and unlikely places.

Another effect of the McCarthy witch-hunt was that politicians felt pressured to appear tough in the face of any perceived communist threat. Richard Nixon was one who attacked those he perceived were soft on the communists, pressuring normally moderate politicians to act more forcefully. He would have an opportunity to contribute to the Vietnam debacle many years later and wage a secret war in Cambodia.

Diem was initially successful against the Vietminh in the south in the late 1950s and early 1960s, but refused to implement reforms that may have helped increase his popular support base. He was not himself corrupt, but family members and a close circle of friends shared in a staggering variety of benefits that did little to endear him to the peasants of the south. The corruption within the upper echelons of his military became the stuff of legend. The common touch, the Ho factor, was missing.

The US was financing Diem, but missed an opportunity to link aid to performance. Diem took the money and continued on his merry way, as did succeeding governments. In the early years the Americans could not do without him, whereas in later years they were unable to disengage because they were in too deep. Karnow quotes an American official who described Diem as "a puppet who pulled his own strings—and ours as well[48]."

In 1959 the northerners enlarged the Ho Chi Minh Trail and started shifting men and supplies south.

1960 saw the election of John F Kennedy as President of the USA. It also saw the formation in South Vietnam of the National Liberation Front, the NLF, later to be dubbed the Vietcong, or Vietnamese Communists, by Diem. An attempted coup was thwarted by Diem who developed a policy of keeping his better commanders in Saigon where he could keep an eye on them, promoting friends and relatives wherever possible.

Diem was losing ground and the US had to make a difficult decision: take charge or leave. In the end it did neither, simply increasing the number of "advisors" to 12,000 by 1962. By now, Diem's commanders knew he was displeased when his army incurred casualties, so they became adept at avoiding combat, a practice that was to annoy US commanders who had to deal with many additional problems as a result.

1963 was a landmark year. Diem's discrimination against the Buddhists led to public self-immolations and again he was too stubborn to reform. A coup was planned in Saigon, and with US approval Diem was overthrown. He and his brother-in-law were shot dead, a departure the US had probably not approved. Diem was replaced by one of a long line of new rulers in the south, none of whom proved to be particularly effective. President John F Kennedy was assassinated, replaced by an unprepared Lyndon B Johnson who had little previous involvement in the Vietnam War and who was pleased to inherit Kennedy's team.

By 1964 it was clear that the communists were making progress. The army of the south was plagued by desertions and inertia and the campaign for the hearts and minds of the peasants was not working.

The Ho Chi Minh Trail was expanded from what had been a myriad of footpaths into a major road to bring men and supplies in large quantities from the north to the south. It was well hidden, and would be a major problem for the US for the duration of the war.

The strategic village programme was implemented during Diem's reign. Villagers were moved from their hamlets against their will into fortified villages so that they were inaccessible to the Vietcong. They were loath to move from familiar surroundings, leaving their ancestors. The reality of the fortified villages was that the Vietcong gained entry by night and controlled many of them, before heading off to fight early in the morning.

In 1964 President Johnson offered North Vietnam economic aid and diplomatic recognition if they withdrew assistance to the Vietcong. The alternative was attacks on North Vietnam. The northerners wanted American withdrawal, and they wanted to participate in government in the south. No agreement could be reached.

The problem for Johnson was that he needed a declaration of war to bomb the north, but that might cause problems at home. He also wanted a show of strength—a US election was approaching and his opponent, Barry Goldwater, proposed a tough line on Vietnam.

A dubious incident involving the US destroyer Maddox in the Tonkin Gulf did the trick. The Maddox was attacked by small North Vietnamese craft whilst the Maddox was assisting the South Vietnamese in running covert military missions in the north.

A second, bogus, attack on a couple of US Navy vessels during which a commander counted twenty—two torpedoes, much to the surprise of a senior pilot who had been flying overhead, helped complete the theatre. By the time *Life, Time and Newsweek* had published their dramatic eyewitness accounts of this stirring engagement Johnson had no difficulty in having Congress pass his resolution of support. Captain Herrick could not confirm that he had been attacked, but the first US bombing mission took off on 4 August 1964. Karnow is interesting on this issue[49]:

'Subsequent research by both official and unofficial investigators has indicated with almost total certainty that the second Communist attack never happened. It had not been deliberately faked, but Johnson and his staff, desperately seeking a pretext to act vigorously, had seized upon a fuzzy set of circumstances to fulfil a contingency plan.'

Robert McNamara denies that the Maddox incident was staged or misrepresented, but confirms, after a meeting with General Giap in Hanoi in 1995, that there was no second attack[50]. Johnson would have been well aware of that. Authority to bomb North Vietnam was granted on the strength of a bald lie; the truth was a regular casualty of this war.

In February 1965, a Vietcong raid on a US base at Pleiku in the central highlands killed eight Americans and destroyed ten aircraft. Concerns about the defence of the large airbase at Danang led to US Marines landing on Danang beaches later that year, and by the end of 1965 there were 200,000 US personnel serving in Vietnam. The US was now mired in the morass and increased its military presence to stave off military collapse in the south.

General Westmoreland, the senior US commander, wanted even more troops. Halberstam writes of President Johnson's dilemma, meeting with members of Congress to explain that he would have to send more troops to Vietnam. One, Gaylord Nelson, told his good friend Hubert Humphrey that it looked bad[51].

"You know, Gaylord," said Humphrey, "there are people at State and the Pentagon who want to send three hundred thousand men out there." Humphrey paused. "But the President will never get sucked into anything like that."

The number of US military personnel in Vietnam would increase to about 540,000 by 1968.

1968 was a bad year for both sides. The assassinations of Martin Luther King and Robert Kennedy caused shock waves in the US, and the war in Vietnam took on a new dimension with the Communist Tet Offensive.

There was to have been a truce over Tet, the Lunar New Year. Instead, Vietcong units attacked towns, cities and bases throughout South Vietnam in the mistaken belief that this might promote local uprisings, leading southerners to join the communists and overthrow the southern government. It was a bloody affair, and unsuccessful from the Communist military viewpoint as they are thought to have lost up to 50,000 soldiers. It nearly destroyed the Vietcong.

It came on top of the offensive against the Marine base at Khe Sanh that also cost the Communists dearly. That operation had been partly a distraction for preparations for the Tet offensive. The Marines were reinforced, and heavily supported with over 5,000 air strikes. Over 100,000 tons of explosives were dropped within an area of less than five square miles, but more than 500 American lives were lost.

Both these major operations sent shock waves through senior US military ranks, and shook up the folks back home. Nobody thought the Communists could mount operations of such a scale under the noses of the US, especially as the US was supposedly winning the war. The Vietcong took the ancient central capital city of Hue, held it for almost a month, and it was only regained with US help after much damage was done to the graceful old city.

1968 will also be remembered for two atrocities. US soldiers massacred 500 women, children and old men at My Lai in Quang Ngai Province. The Vietcong murdered an unknown number of civilians after taking Hue, some of whom were buried alive. The number is generally thought to be about 3,000.

In the USA, voters elected Richard Nixon to the presidency almost eight months after My Lai but some five months before the story of the atrocity began to emerge.

In 1969 Ho Chi Minh died in Hanoi. That year also saw the commencement of the secret bombing of Cambodia, and the "Vietnamization" of the war, whereby US troop numbers declined as the ARVN took more responsibility for the fighting. US troop numbers decreased from 540,000 to 140,000 by 1971.

In 1970 Henry Kissinger, US security adviser, met secretly with his opposite number Le Duc Tho, founder with Ho Chi Minh of the Indochina communist Party, in Paris to start peace talks. Nixon made a secret offer of war reparations of $3.25 billion to the northerners, an undertaking that was never honoured.

In 1972 North Vietnam crossed the DMZ and captured Quang Tri, at enormous cost, leading to retaliatory bombing of North Vietnam. Kissinger in the meantime had made progress in the peace talks, but found the South Vietnamese president opposed to the proposals.

The US stepped out of the war in 1973, leaving behind massive quantities of armaments for the southerners. Cease-fire agreements were signed and the last US troops left on 29 March, 1973.

On 31 March 1975, the Politburo in Hanoi ordered a push to Saigon and on 30 April, the city fell to Communist forces. The war was finally over, the long journey from the cave at Pac Bo that commenced in 1941 finally completed.

Vietnam invaded Cambodia in 1978, in retaliation for Cambodian attacks on Vietnam, deposing Pol Pot in the process. Vietnam had originally sponsored the Khmer Rouge in partnership with China. In the meantime China, who had continued to support Pol Pot, was trying to foster better relations with a willing US. The invasion thus attracted the wrath of the US and was one of three reasons given for withholding the promised war reparations, the other reasons being the invasion of South Vietnam in 1975, and its poor human rights record.

China invaded Vietnam in 1979. They inflicted significant damage on the northern border states, but resistance was fierce as usual and the Chinese followed that familiar route home once more.

In 1993 the US ceased its opposition to foreign aid to Vietnam, twenty years after leaving. The US lifted its trade embargo in 1994.

Sadly, there is now a Kentucky Fried Chicken outlet near Hoan Kiem Lake in Hanoi.

26. Travel notes

Laos was the first country I visited in Indochina, in 2001. Being on an overdue holiday, I refused to engage with the country to any depth, although my Lonely Planet guide book told me Laos became the most heavily bombed country in history during the Vietnam War. The country was not at war, but Washington donated 2,000,000 tonnes of bombs (the total World War 2 all-nation tonnage) that cost 600,000 lives. Vientiane had quite a display of abandoned, formerly-opulent French residences, but many remained abandoned forty years after their hasty departure. Most have since been converted to other use.

Then I travelled on the back of a pick-up truck to Luang Prabang, the old royal capital. It was while strolling down a road in Vang Vien, a small tourist haven along the way that I noticed the street was particularly wide at about 50 metres, and well-surfaced. A shopkeeper explained it had been an airstrip.

"What for?" I asked him.

"Jets. Helicopters. American." This of course was one of dozens of Air America airfields, with phantom aircraft flown by non-existent pilots on missions that never happened. The reality was not nearly as funny as the movie.

A couple of years later I returned to Laos to visit an old French battle-site. Luang Prabang had captivated the French, and was quite intoxicating. My travel guide back then advised against travelling on the national airline: they flew old Russian aircraft that had little by way of avionics and the airline refused to report accidents in accordance with international convention. Due to tight travel arrangements I was obliged to catch a flight from Luang Prabang to the capital, Vientiane.

As passengers awaited the arrival of the aircraft, there was an ear-splitting sound. A red fire engine appeared out of nowhere, did a high-speed lap of the runway under sirens and alarms, and disappeared whence it came. There was considerable nervous shuffling of feet; most of the passengers appeared to be locals, and if the purpose of the loud demonstration had been to inspire confidence in passengers it was an abject failure.

At boarding time the heavens opened and it started to rain quite heavily. The airport authorities kindly decided passengers should not get drenched as they boarded from the runway, so the aircraft was towed across the tarmac where undercover boarding was possible. We passengers walked across the runway in the rain, but could board the aircraft under shelter.

During the secret war in Laos, the Americans were never there, officially. Nor, of course, were the Russians. That meant that neither side could report the presence of the other. A practical solution to the dilemma was found in Vientiane where they frequented different bars and brothels whenever possible.

At Vientiane airport I met a US Navy Seal, a member of an elite special force, who told me I had missed the official handing-over ceremony of the body of an America pilot the day before. He had been downed some forty years earlier.

"That was one of your men who were never here?" I asked. He nodded his agreement, and moved to the far side of the departure lounge.

Cambodia, or Kampuchea as it is now known, was my next port of call and I was troubled immediately. A visit to Tuol Sleng in Phnom Penh was depressing. A former school, it became a major torture centre en route to the Killing Fields. Perhaps a quarter of the country's population died at the hands of the Khmer Rouge, but only recently have judicial proceedings commenced against the major perpetrators.

There was no way of knowing if the Cambodian who befriended you had atrocities in his background, and there seemed to me to be an aura of violence about the place. Perhaps I sensed a little of what Philip Short described in his excellent history[52]:

"Eighteen months after Pol Pot's death in 1998, when the last of his guerilla armies had laid down their weapons and peace had returned to

Cambodia after three decades of war, a sixteen-year-old girl sat down at a stall in one of Pnomh Penh's markets and ordered rice soup for herself and her three-year-old niece. A well-dressed woman, accompanied by several bodyguards, came up behind her, grabbed her hair and pushed her to the floor, where the men kicked and beat her until she passed out. Two guards then carefully opened a glass jar containing three litres of nitric acid, which the woman poured over the girl's head and upper body. The pain made her regain consciousness and she started to scream—splashing acid on the woman and one of the guards, who fled in a waiting car. People in a nearby house doused her with water, but by the time she reached hospital she had third-degree burns over 43 per cent of her body.

Tat Marina had been a stunningly beautiful young actress who made her living by appearing in karaoke videos. The previous year she had come to the notice of a Cambodian government minister, Svay Sittha, who had seduced her and installed her in a cheap apartment as his concubine. The attack was carried out by Sittha's wife, Khoun Sophal, whom an American woman friend would describe later as 'the gentlest soul you could imagine'.

The young woman survived, her head and body from the waist up made hideous by scar tissue. Her attackers were never questioned, still less charged with any offence.

Scores of teenage Cambodian girls are disfigured and in many cases blinded by rich men's wives. Older Cambodian women say that Tat Marina and girls like her 'steal other women's husbands' and get what they deserve. Men treat them as disposable, 'like Kleenex, to be used and thrown away'.

The parallel with Khmer Rouge atrocities is striking . . ."

The Pol Pot regime liquidated perhaps a quarter of the population whilst enjoying the recognition of Washington and Canberra. Cambodia today has problems with mines and other unexploded ordnance left behind that still takes a toll on the local population, as happens in Laos and Vietnam also. Washington has shown no interest in cleaning up its military detritus, possibly because it is of course distracted today as it sets about winning hearts and minds in Iraq and Afghanistan.

After enjoying a visit to the temples at Angkor Wat I was pleased to head for Vietnam, where I did the usual tourist things, and caught a tourist bus that followed the coastline to Hanoi. Most of the remnants of war one would expect to see have long since been recycled by the canny peasants: concrete emplacements are now road base, and military metal has long since been melted down and converted into more useful objects. There were scores of large American trucks about at the time, their military origin generally visible under the mind-boggling local modifications undertaken on the pavements of city and village to adapt the vehicles to the owner's requirements. They have disappeared in the last decade, although one suspects components are still in use in paddies around the country.

I was distracted by my fellow tourists, and it was not until I came across the Hero Mothers exhibit in Hanoi that the war beckoned to me.

A year later, somewhat better informed about Indochina, I returned to Vietnam in search of underlying messages about the war. I explored parts of the Central Highlands on the back of a motor scooter I had hired in Quy Nhon, a coastal city that had strongly supported the Viet Cong. The rider was perplexed at my careful measurement of distances so that I could follow Bernard Fall's account of the slaughter of French Mobile Group 100 just beyond Mang Yang Pass on the road to Pleiku. The tall elephant grass that concealed the Vietminh from the French has gone now, but I could visualise the horror of that day.

Then it was on to Kontum, scene of much action for the Americans in a region where a couple of Australians earned VCs with the Australian Army Training Team Vietnam, Australia's most highly decorated military unit.

I spent a couple of days around Hue, going on a DMZ (Demilitarised Zone) tour to get a feel for the very heavy action at the point where the country was divided between North and South. An old Catholic Church, sans roof, walls perforated like a colander, said it all. The city of Quang Tri has never been properly restored and the sense of destruction is palpable.

Guides tell tourists that the bridge across the Ben Hai River, where the country was divided, became the site of a painting duel. Southerners painted their half a different colour to distinguish it from the Communist half. At night time the Communists repainted their side to match the Southerners hue, and that apparently continued throughout the war.

In Hanoi I found someone who could help me find the French battle site at Tu Vu on the Black River near Hoa Binh. Once again, Fall's account and maps made it easy for me to participate in yet other French nightmare. Even the sandbank the French forces fled to is still there. I could not understand why they had been allowed to survive there, as their enemy General Giap had little reason to extend mercy to them, as is mentioned elsewhere in this book.

Literature about some aspects of the French war machine intrigued me. Their ranks abounded with colourful characters that appear to be quite happy to die gloriously in battle in remote places. It was not all that unusual for an officer to call artillery fire onto his own position if it was about to be over-run by the enemy, for instance. Elsewhere I read that they celebrate their defeats as much as they do their victories. I travelled to Aubagne, in Southern France, where the Foreign Legion HQ is located.

My day was made when I was met at the gate by a crusty old sergeant with a massive beard. He was a *Pionniere*, a combat engineer, and they are permitted to wear beards. On parade, they wear leather aprons and carry long handled axes by way of uniform—along with their beards, of course. With the unofficial motto *March or die* (and they have done a good deal of both) the unit has a short but colourful history and was active throughout Vietnam.

The main exhibit in the museum at Aubagne is in a glass display case beyond reach of visitors—the wooden hand of Captain Danjou. There is of course a heroic battle of 1863 at Camerone in Mexico behind this relic; a bayonet charge, no less, three surviving Legionnaires against more than three battalions. The senior Mexican officer spared their lives and allowed them to keep their weapons—the only terms of surrender acceptable to the Legionnaires.

In 2003 I visited Vietnam to attempt to interview Hero Mothers, with those events described elsewhere. This was the most significant trip by far as I had time to kill. Purchasing my own motorcycle gave me enormous freedom of movement and I clocked up several thousand kilometres in pursuit of a little background. I could observe without distraction as I described a circle of sorts from Hanoi to Dien Bien Phu, Lai Chau and Sapa to Hanoi via Yen Bai, through territory as pristine as it was brutal during the French period. Then it was time for another circle, from Hanoi to the cave at Pak Bo, back to Hanoi via Cao Bang and Lang Son. That area saw the first of several heavy defeats for the French, who lost some 6,000 men in the region.

I asked one old man if he had any idea where some of the missing French might be, and he suggested close to the river banks might be a good place to look, as stragglers tried to escape. He could have told me a great deal more, had he felt so inclined, but this is an area where stories are closely held.

In Yen Bai, a city that does not cater for tourists, I found an example of the innate grace of the locals. After ten hours in the saddle of my Minsk, I found myself on a muddy back road at night without lights, totally lost. I eventually made it to Yen Bai, tired and famished. The only eatery I could find was rather too splendid, and even sported a neon sign; I was about to ride off when a receptionist approached me with her young male assistant. They carried my bag into the restaurant which was crowded with locals and found me a table of my own in a prominent spot. When I ordered a Heineken I was surprised to be brought a 6 pack in a bucket of ice. They had obviously identified me as an Australian.

I was offered a face cloth, which I declined. Minutes later, when visiting the toilet, I discovered I was covered in mud from the shoulders up. I hastily reclaimed the cloth and spent minutes tidying up as best I could. Then it was back to my table with smiles all round. A magnificent meal followed, laced with plenty of humour, although none of us was certain as to what we were laughing about since we could not communicate—not with language, anyway. The bill was modest, and I realised they did not need my business. They could simply have watched me ride away as I had intended.

Yen Bai was the scene of massive French reprisals for an uprising in 1931 with public beheadings of scores of rebels. It also lay along one of the main supply routes to Dien Bien Phu. They do not encourage Western tourists to come a-calling, although there is a magnificent, massive lake nearby and the area has much to offer visitors.

Near That Khe, along the northern border with China where the French suffered calamitous casualties, I offered to tow a peasant's motorcycle. He had a mechanical problem, but kept declining my offer of help. An occasional Good Samaritan, I managed to over-rule him.

Five minutes later I had wrecked the clutch on my Minsk, causing my towee to shake his head in disbelief at my stupidity.

It was growing dark and I was a little anxious—this was not tourist territory and an awful lot of Frenchmen had disappeared around here. I had pushed my old bike about 5 kilometres through hilly country when an old man arrived on the back of a motor scooter piloted by his son. Word of my plight had travelled fast; an escaping French soldier would have been hunted down here in minutes. The old man had a screwdriver and a sort of shifting spanner, all one requires to manufacture a Minsk as far as I can tell. I continued on my way ten minutes later.

In tough frontier town Cao Bang a group of young men examined my Minsk with great interest. They were amused at my flashy stainless steel Japanese front springs, an expensive optional extra. The next day I hit a rock that broke one of the springs. I was able to make it to a dusty village on a bad dirt road where an ancient mountain man pointed at a nearby tea house—never a good sign. An hour later I waddled back across the road, belly full of green tea. I retrieved my Minsk, now sporting what a dealer in Hanoi called a perfect weld. I have no doubt the old man could have manufactured a serviceable machine gun for me.

Then it was a trip south past Danang to visit My Lai, and the fateful trip to Pleiku and the town where my motorcycle was confiscated and I had a little temporary bother. I returned to Danang via part of the Ho Chi Minh Trail before returning to Hanoi to commence meeting the Mothers, where another accidental meeting gave me further insight into another man's war.

Ambling peacefully along one of Hanoi's busiest roads on my Minsk, I momentarily forgot one of the cardinal local road rules: he who has his nose in front has right of way. The bike next to mine, enjoying a 25mm advantage, turned across my nose as was his right and I ended up face down on the tarmac, which gave me an interesting view of approaching buses. I ended up with one finger pointing at an exotic angle, another in a semi-circle and my knees not functioning quite as they should. The good news was I ended up being treated by a local doctor who had trained in East Germany for ten years. The period of his training bothered me at first—I wondered why it had taken so long—as did the funny little electrical impulse machine he used. I thought I had seen the manufacturer's name on an ancient East German motorcycle many years before.

A damp day on the Ho Chi Minh Trail

It all turned out very well. My doctor had served his internship in war-torn Cambodia, where he performed amputations for two years; there was no shortage of patients. He not only gave me excellent care and further insight into the war, but by the time he had finished I was thrilled as hell to have only broken two fingers and a couple of bits. As he pointed out, I did not have a stellar career as a concert pianist that would have to be cancelled. He was about blessings and arithmetic, as well as healing.

Travelling by Minsk was a highlight of the journey. A 2-stroke of a mere 125 c.c., the machine is not built for speed, but it is practically indestructible. It reigns supreme in the mountains of North Vietnam where it is a beast of burden, often carrying two large pigs to the market in a specially designed basket. A seized engine can be repaired for $20, making it a firm favourite in impoverished areas. Brakes sometimes work, and headlights usually respond to regular blows with the heel of one's hand.

In the cities, people sneer at these unfashionable, smelly machines, especially if they are belching smoke, as is often the case. Japanese scooters are the conveyance of choice for the urban chic.

The Minsk factory has closed down now and the end of an era is approaching: the natty 250 c.c. Japanese moto-cross machines that the young macho types crave cannot stand up to the demands of the mountain men.

A visit to Hanoi in 2011 after a 6-year absence provided a few jolts. Tall office buildings and apartment blocks are springing up all over the place. I counted more Rolls Royces in one day than I have seen in a couple of years in Brisbane. Range Rovers are popular, some fitted with accessories I would not have thought existed. Property developers are doing rather well, it seems, able to purchase land at strangely reasonable prices. Rezoning apparently works well for some and gated community living appears to offer the desired lifestyle for some of the more affluent Vietnamese. It sits awkwardly alongside the community closeness I grew accustomed to seeing during my journey.

Times are changing in Vietnam, but I am grateful to have had the opportunity to glance briefly at aspects of a very special period in the modern history of a remarkable nation.

27. The Sacred Cow Toll—personal reflections

I was raised in small towns in the rural highlands of South Africa. My mother was of French Huguenot stock while my father was the son of a Scottish soldier and an Irish woman, so I straddled both major white language groups. I grew up in territory that had been bitterly disputed during the Anglo Boer War barely 40 years before my arrival, although surprisingly little was said to me even though I was regarded as "English".

At times the straddling was a little awkward—I was a "Rooi Nek" (Red Neck—a term used for British soldiers during the Anglo—Boer War, and still used in some Afrikaner areas for people of British descent) in Afrikaner regions, and a "Boer" (farmer in Afrikaans) in English speaking territory. It wore off with age.

In Clocolan, Ficksburg, Harrismith, and like towns, the major entertainment for most youngsters was a Saturday afternoon film. In the 1950s John Wayne reigned supreme in the local cinema. We watched in wonder as he despatched vast numbers of bloodthirsty Red Indian barbarians, surely the silliest fighters ever; he gunned down hordes of stupid Germans and on numerous occasions reduced the ranks of evil gunfighters, bank robbers, ruthless cattlemen and the like. Wayne was not only heroic, but chivalrous: he never shot anyone in the back and sometimes even expressed a tinge of remorse at ridding the world of yet another wrongdoer. But a man had to do what a man had to do, and when Wayne saddled up we all knew it was curtains for the villains. We invariably rewarded him with a rousing ovation at the end of each adventure.

Blessed with tolerant parents, I started hiking in the mountains in my early teens, usually on my own as other kids had more restrictive parents. I grew to love my country, which grew more isolated each year as international hostility mounted and the prospect of military action became increasingly likely. As I tramped about the place I resolved to become a fearsome warrior and sell myself dearly to any prospective invader, so I eagerly read the few military publications about at the time and worked on my physical fitness.

My ideals matured a little with time, but I found myself in a paratroop unit with the intention of doing well so that I could attend Sandhurst, gain entry to the British Royal Marine Commandos or the British Special Air Services, and return to my country as a very useful soldier. It all seemed very simple to a country boy at that time—other South Africans had followed a similar route. Unfortunately, the day before I had won my wings, the doors of Sandhurst were closed to South Africans. The armed forces of my country were fiercely politicised and my military aspirations died, although my interest in special warfare remained. Then two fine sons appeared in my life and it was time to find another home: South African politics was no longer acceptable. My sons' arrival had opened my eyes.

After migrating to Australia in 1974 I learnt of returned Vietnam Veterans who seemed to be experiencing problems not encountered by their predecessors, but nobody seemed to know much about this new malaise or the war that had caused it. The war had apparently been fought to save democracy in the region, as Communism was bound to spread down even to my home city from a tiny sliver of a country called Vietnam, where the USA had over half a million soldiers at one stage. Again, I could not find anyone who could explain this sinister risk, but of course the USA would not have become so involved without good cause: that is not the Western way. It went without saying that Australia would not have joined them had the cause not been a worthy one. I resolved to find out more about Vietnam but lost track of it until 2001.

Following my first visit to Indochina, in trying to come to grips with Vietnam, I necessarily researched fairly widely and the sacred cows started dropping almost immediately. The Pentagon would probably ascribe this to collateral intelligence. Finding a reason for the whole tragedy was difficult.

I found that although the world was a different shape then, with the Cold War in full swing, the notion of Communism spreading southwards was a product of the panic of powerful, uninformed men—men of formidable education, lacking in wisdom, but with access to unprecedented powers of destruction.

It is very clear now, as it should have been then, that we need not have worried about Mother Gom running around the streets of Perth with an AK-47, spreading Communism. Hell, she couldn't spell it, and her world ended twenty kilometres from her home. Anyway, she had better things to do, like raising her family. She certainly became very handy with a variety of weapons, and like the rest of her countryfolk she did want the French out. When that was achieved at great cost the Americans moved in, and they had to be moved on. It was as simple as that. This had been spelt out to the US delegation during the Geneva Accords process, so it should have come as no surprise. The problem was, of course, that men from Washington are not good listeners.

The critical period for the Vietnamese initially was 1945-56, but this coincided with a difficult period in the US.

Joseph McCarthy, a drunken Senator from Wisconsin, destroyed many a Hollywood career, and others besides, during this period. His only lasting legacy to his nation appears to be the linkage of his name to the process whereby damaging statements are made without evidence. McCarthy wanted to be sure that everyone hated the Commies. One alcoholic politician should not imperil a nation, but the most powerful nation on the planet was distracted by other issues at this time. By the time he self-destructed, or was destroyed after taking on the military, the word was out: any prospective United States government or resident would not want to be seen being soft on the Communists. I wondered how a man like McCarthy was ever allowed to wield so much power, but there was more to come.

It turned out that the hero of Harrismith, John Wayne, never fired anything. He did not serve in World War 2, unlike real-life war hero Audie Murphy. He found it desirable to defer enlistment continuously in order to complete yet another film; his career prospered while he stayed home. Oh, and his name was Marion. He was an ardent supporter of the House Un-American Activities Committee, a right-wing anti-Communist witch-hunt organisation.

He appears on television regularly in re-runs of the *Green Beret* cast as a senior Special Forces officer. It is one of the more absurd castings—an ageing, out of shape actor; however, the film itself is a strange pro-war creation and it is no surprise to find he was also the director.

Wayne was one of several former heroes who bit the dust during my research, although in his case I think someone managed to find that he had a perforated eardrum or something that would have prevented him from enlisting.

The problem with John Wayne did not end there. I vaguely recall him appearing in a film about the Alamo. That was inspiring, the small body of men magnificently defying the evil Santa Anna and his rotten cutthroats. We kids were in awe of the seriously stricken Jim Bowie, taking a heavy toll of really ugly, evil Mexicans from his sickbed.

Suddenly, on 16 August 2011 an article in *The Australian* newspaper caught my eye. The headline read: **Alamo myth a load of Crockett.** The story read:

Davy Crockett's defiant stand at the Alamo is cherished in the US as a moment that defined a young nation's pursuit of liberty. It is also utter fantasy.

Legend describes a tenacious and lengthy defence of the garrison in March 1836 that continued even when defeat was assured. A new book, however, shows the Alamo was routed after a surprise night attack that left many Americans dead—as they tried to escape.

Philip Thomas Tucker, in Exodus from the Alamo, says the popular version took hold as no Americans survived and the Mexican version was ignored.

"A culture of chauvinism disregarded the accounts of the Mexicans. The power of the myth was so strong it transcended the truth," he said.

Using Mexican reports, diaries and newspaper accounts, Dr Tucker built a picture of a battle that might have lasted only 20 minutes. It was "but a small affair" said General Antonio Lopez de Santa Anna, who led the assault.

Scores of Mexican soldiers breached the walls before most inhabitants were even out of bed. There was no evidence of the drawn-out defence popularised by John Wayne and Hollywood. Most of the modest Mexican casualties were sustained inside the garrison walls, many as a result of "friendly fire".

Dr Tucker writes: "A large percentage of the garrison fled . . . to escape the slaughter." He depicts a group hoping to profit from new land in which they could use slaves on plantations, but only if they could defeat the Mexicans who had abolished slavery.

Casemate, the publisher, says the book received a hostile reception in Texas, where the story is said to embody the spirit of the state. "Texans have rallied en masse . . . in the most vitriolic criticism any of our military history books has ever received," a spokesman said.

William Galston, of the Brookings Institute, said the myth was likely to prevail: "Myths are powerful because they say things about people that they want to believe."

The Alamo would make a marvellous Kentucky Fried Chicken site.

The day after the annihilation of that sacred cow, an even heavier blow struck me.

I had come across the name of David Hackworth, a career soldier with the US forces in Vietnam. This had led to my purchase of a couple of his books that were excellent reading. Hack was the most decorated living US soldier at the time, apparently, although he had missed out on the Congressional Medal of Honour despite two commendations. A third commendation was made quite recently, but was not acted on. I contacted him as I was researching my book and found him pleasant, helpful and approachable.

Hack retired prematurely for reasons outlined in "About Face," and came across as a brave and honourable warrior. His third commendation for the big medal came through as I communicated with him, but he did not expect the award as he had trodden on too many toes. He passed away a couple of years ago, a legend to the many men who served under him. A day after my Alamo shock, I opened my latest acquisition, a copy of *War Without Fronts,* by Bernd Greiner, a professor at the University of Hamburg who directs the research programme on the theory and history of violence at the Hamburg Institute of Social Research.

There, on page 164 Greiner lays it out: Tiger Force, which features in the My Lai chapter in this book as an utterly shameful collection of murderous misfits, was founded by David Hackworth. Elsewhere within the book Greiner raises some unsavoury allegations against Hackworth regarding an operation Speedy Express, as well as other serious misconduct. In effect, says Greiner, Hack's early retirement suited everyone, ensuring that the 8-volume dossier compiled by the authorities was never required in a court of law.

Now, Hack died a couple of years ago and cannot defend himself, but it is hard to believe Greiner's allegations are totally unfounded.

Hell, are there any heroes in the West?

The civilian death toll in Vietnam bothered me from the outset. Whilst researching civilian casualties during recent wars I looked into the Anglo Boer War in South Africa, my birth-place. My parents had been strangely reluctant to discuss the war with me, as had been my extended family. I had, however, grown up believing the British had fought fairly and honourably, as always. That turned out to be a little fanciful.

The discovery of gold towards the end of the 19th century in the Boer Republics suddenly saw Great Britain take a renewed interest in democracy in the region, rather as oil reserves bring out the philanthropists in Washington DC. Soon with help from the Empire there were 500,000 soldiers matched against two small farmers' republics with a total population of 200,000 and a maximum of 50,000 part-time farmer warriors.

The British hero of the war, Lord Kitchener, authorised the erection of concentration camps that caused horrific deaths among the women and children who were afforded "sanctuary" there. By the end of the war 6,000 women and 22,000 children under the age of 16 years had died in those "sanctuaries". At 14% of the total population, a similar disaster in Australia today would see 600,000 women and 2,200,000 children dead, 28 times the total of our entire war dead. Sadly, our main memory of the war seems to be the execution of Harry "Breaker" Morant, an Englishman guilty of the murder of several civilians. At the time of writing there is movement afoot to fight for a pardon for Harry and friends. It seems we Australians are outraged that this magnanimous little crew represents the only Australians executed for war crimes. Perhaps we could simply legislate against our nationals being tried for such offences, or ban people from ever reporting them. Or ban people from reading the reports, should someone inadvertently allow one to slip through the cordon.

Parents and teachers in South Africa had neglected to tell me about this, presumably for fear of the divisions it might cause in a fragile society, but I still feel utterly betrayed at the highly selective history lessons.

I started researching concentration camps, but when I found they probably originated in the US when the indigenous population was being, ah, dealt with, and were later in use about the same time (1899-1902) by Britain and the USA in South Africa and the Philippines respectively, I shut the book. But Kitchener should have hanged. Instead he left a useful blueprint for some rather unpleasant Teutons.

This all in turn led to general disillusionment about the moral rectitude of democracies that would like to be considered great and that would certainly lay claim to being so regarded.

As an example, I mourn the lack of greatness among the great nations. To me, one of the great stories of the 20th century was the way in which the Allies helped rehabilitate Germany and Japan after World War 2, a process during the vanquished enemy recovered quicker and better from the ravages of war than Britain. This followed the disgracefully merciless treatment of Germany after World War 1 that led to the second war. So it is hard to understand why Nixon's promise of $3.25 billion to Vietnam has still not been paid.

The case for Vietnam is so much stronger—they presented no threat to the US, they did not practice genocide. Hell, they didn't even attack Pearl Harbour—they probably could not have found it, but if they had, they had no air force. Plus, of course, they had no interest in attack and conquest. One suspects Washington will never pay because of the emotional issue of some 2,000 US service people still missing in action in Vietnam. Perhaps that might change when Hanoi hands over the vapourised remains of the last pilot to nosedive into the ground in his fully armed Phantom at Mach 1.5 in some dense patch of jungle, or one who bailed out 10 miles out to sea.

Then there were the secret wars—Laos and Cambodia. Knowing the American people would not countenance the butchery of tiny nations, incumbents in the White House decided not to burden the populace with knowledge of what had been authorised in distant lands. Or what was being done there. However, almost forty years after those shameful events, no US President has made any effort to address the wrongs. Another notion of greatness utterly destroyed.

My other major concern is about the difficulty of matching great power with great wisdom, a match that was never evident during the Vietnam War. There were certainly men of great education about, but education is not wisdom, any more than it is intelligence. I was shocked when watching a documentary, *American Holocaust,* to see Robert McNamara speaking during a visit to Vietnam as an old man. He actually berated the Vietnamese for being prepared to pay such a huge price for freedom. After all those years and all that bloodshed, that highly-educated and highly-credentialed man still did not understand his old enemy. McNamara was of course a mathematician, not an historian.

28. The Road to Platypus

The problem with travelling around Vietnam beyond the main tourist routes is that inevitably a few burning questions recur. Visiting an idyllic island, passing through a remote village on the Laos or Chinese borders, enjoying a beer on the deck of a junk in Halong Bay or cycling around a dusty little mountain town, inevitably one wonders how on earth a small country with such great charm was singled out for such unwarranted savagery by two allegedly civilised countries that ought to hold a special place in our world: one practically invented democracy, and the other loudly and regularly trumpets its support of that fine system to the rest of the world. Then when one reads about events there, it all falls apart. My sense of horror at what great, Christian nations inflicted upon the Vietnamese was exacerbated by regular Washington pronouncements about the sanctity of human life and the importance of human and civil rights as it addresses crises around the world. It sometimes sounds just a little hollow.

However, one can only wallow about in a trough of anger, indignation, outrage and the like for so long. Eventually one has to either move on or address the issues of concern. The war cannot be unfought, casualties cannot be undone and the dead returned happy and healthy to their glowing families. Nobody understands this better than the Vietnamese. Apologies are inadequate, although the nations that participated in this pack attack do not apologise: we are never in the wrong. That is also why we do not help clean up the wreckage: the neighbours might think we behaved badly.

On the basis that even a tiny insect can provide a little comfort by removing a flea from an elephant's backside, I sought to try and do something to ameliorate some of the damage done. Young people hold a special place in Vietnamese society, so that seemed the place to start. Besides, I had seen for myself that youngsters and their families could use a hand. I had seen this first hand in Hue.

Upon reaching my hotel in Hue during my third visit to Vietnam, I was approached by a dignified man of perhaps 50 years who offered his services as a cyclo (three-wheel cycle) guide for the day. He had excellent English, and knew his city intimately, so we enjoyed a fine day. He was quite an adventurous cyclo, but I was able to extract revenge for some of his hair-raising navigation in heavy traffic: when he tired of pedalling I would take over, and the sight of his hands clasping the carriage provided me with much perverse satisfaction. After a fine day we dined together.

I learned that like almost all operators around Vietnam, he rented his machine. His average daily earnings were about $5, of which $2 went to the owner of the vehicle by way of a rental. A good, used cyclo cost about $200.

He knew, of course, that his rental could buy more than 3 cyclos per year, but he did not have the $200 capital required to buy his own machine. He was working on it, and told me proudly that he had $70 saved up. It would have been more, but bad floods the year before had cost him his house. However, he said, his family had been lucky as they all survived—a typical Vietnamese attitude to disaster.

When I came across him the next day, having had a few hours to mull over what he had told me, I told him I would wire him $130 (my funds were running low as I was self-funding my research) so that he could buy his cyclo. In return he would someday help a stranger. We shook hands and parted company.

A year later, during a follow-up trip to Hue, I found him on his cyclo. It was now sprayed a splendid metallic purple, and sported a new soft seat and chrome mudguards. Mr Dong was a very happy man. His small business was doing fine, but more importantly, he had of course saved $2 per day for the previous year, which plucked his family out of the poverty trap they had been caught up in.

During my last visit to Vietnam the following year, I found him astride a small motorcycle. He and his brother-in-law had pooled resources. His successful cyclo business had enabled them to raise money for the motorcycle, and they now alternate between vehicles. Brother-in-law's 2 children are assured of education also, and of course his family is now also out of the poverty trap. The $130 was worth $750 a year, for life, to him in rental savings alone but had brought 2 families financial independence and freedom.

Friends had suggested that Mr Dong might gamble or drink away the money, but he just did not look the type. I had an idea by then of just how deeply the commitment to family runs amongst the Vietnamese, and was confident the money would be put to good use. That was how I learnt you can change 7 lives or more in a major way for $130.

The old adage about teaching someone how to fish rather than buying him a meal was uppermost in my mind when I first dined with Mr Dong and I am delighted at the successful outcome. The Viet we seek to help need no lessons in fishing, but fishing rods are in desperately short supply. The most effective rod one can offer is education.

When you hand an Annamite a spark plug, he may build a car around it. Or he may pass it on to his wife, who will build a motor scooter for family use in her spare time. Platypus wants to be in the business of spark plug supply. The problem lies in funding those spark plugs as my funds are exhausted.

I soon found that many of my countrymen were a little incredulous at the thought of being asked to contribute to the cause of a former enemy so thoroughly demonised in the west. No matter how we try, we can extract no glory from our role in Vietnam: it became an unpopular cause the moment we found we could not win. Even carrying on about Long Tan and the indomitable spirit of the Digger wore thin. Another problem was I seldom met anyone who had any idea of what really caused the Vietnam War or what really happened on the ground.

I was confident that my fellow Australians, armed with more knowledge of events there, would support a good cause. It would be part of the fair go that is so deeply embedded in the Australian psyche. I would write a book and relate what I had discovered.

Then I would start a foundation. Kangaroo and Koala were obvious names for an Australian foundation, far too well known. The platypus is a quiet creature, seldom seen, that has been around for a long time and is likely to remain a lot longer. It quietly goes about the business of survival. Platypus will quietly go about the business of lending a helping hand, hopefully for a long, long time with public support.

It became necessary for me to work casually so that I could research and write *Journey*. That presented a couple of problems: I now had a

5-year hole in my CV with Vietnam written all over it, leading some to assume I might be a Vietnam Veteran haunted by the war, and thus not to be employed or even interviewed under any circumstances. Or even worse, a non-Veteran haunted by the war. My age meant that none of the 30 job applications I completed even resulted in an interview: a former financial controller, I was adjudged unsuitable for employment in even the most junior capacity. I became a baggage handler at Perth airport until my forearms played up. I moved to Brisbane where none of the 64 job applications I completed won me an interview. Funds exhausted, at 64 I became a traffic controller, holding my STOP/SLOW bat with precision and poise on the Gateway Bridge for $21 per hour, or $26 on night shift.

I used the proceeds to have copies of the manuscript bound, and, in a moment of madness, elected to have presentation boxes made up in the hope that recipients might recognise the effort that had gone into the contents of the envelopes that had arrived by courier unexpectedly. At $200 excluding courier fees, it was a major investment. A friend tipped in generously, and it was with quiet optimism that I saw off this major investment. What a naïve old bugger I was!

The great Foundations in the USA responded fairly quickly. They were working on ridding the world of cancer, AIDS and other nasties, and, unsurprisingly Vietnam did not form part of their territory. Vietnam forms no part of anyone's territory. There was some humour in packages sent separately to a Hollywood couple well known for their philanthropy, at the website address of their Foundation. His copy was returned to me some weeks later, under cover of a letter from an irate Hollywood lawyer, who indignantly informed me it was not his policy to read unsolicited manuscripts! At least, I think that was what he wrote—I think he may have gone to a top law school—possibly Harvard—as the letter was confusing. Disappointed, I gritted my teeth, wrote another letter, and sent off the book at a cost of another $100. That was some months ago and I have heard nothing, but I am confident a lawyer will be in touch presently, possibly with a restraining order.

Other celebrities remained silent, as has the richest man in the world. I understand reading *Journey* is not a burning priority for anybody, but I had hoped some star's assistant secretary's media consultant might have sent me a standard letter as a matter of form, thus providing me with wallpaper for whatever might pass for an office some time in the future.

And so it went on. Out of it all, though, I had a promising call from a Queenslander. That is still live, and it may take only one supporter to achieve lift-off. But I had to keep going in order to complete the Australian legal formalities. Here I had great joy.

In my home city of Perth, six friends from whom I had grown estranged because of the journey stepped in to help. Five agreed to become members of Platypus Inc, an association formed to help improve the quality of life of peasants in Vietnam who are doing it tough. We chose education as the best way to help, and have incorporated the legal entity that will enable us to raise funds, set about establishing good relationships with organisations in Vietnam that will support us, and just get down to it.

A trip to Hanoi in August 2011 revealed an enormous amount of goodwill towards Platypus, and good advice was offered by officials who work with those doing it tough. Rather than rush about sprinkling school fees all over the place, a more selective approach will be employed whereby people will receive what they need.

A family may only need help in purchasing uniforms, or for purchasing food since their child could only perform limited paid work to assist family finances. In some cases education will be a joint project involving the child, the family, the education authorities, the Women's Union, Platypus and perhaps the local hamlet or village. I have seen such a strange partnership work very well in a hamlet in Hoa Binh Province, where Huong brought to my attention the plight of 10 year-old Tam, a youngster I had helped in a small way the year before.

Bright as a button, Tam faced problems in remaining at school. Her father has a few issues and is unable to productively cultivate their land, or undertake regular paid work. Her mother is unusually diminutive, sometimes has difficulty in expressing herself, and suffers from occasional depression. I take care of her school fees.

In the past year, Tam has topped her class with progressively-improving marks. Studying in a single-room little house is difficult, especially when father is home, clouding up the place with smoke. However, the whole hamlet is proud of Tam, pleased to see her receive the support she needs and deserves, so she has several work places she can choose from. The school has entered into the spirit of things: Tam receives extra classes in English and mathematics, her favourite subject.

It does not end there. Her family needs income and father is unable to work well consistently, so the hamlet keeps an eye open for employment opportunities for both parents. Huong's parents help out from time to time, as do neighbours. Tam has become a community project and she will go to university so she can return to her village as a teacher and care for her parents. That is all in train and it will happen.

There is so much more to what Platypus proposes doing. In tough territory, in tough times, it is not only a matter of helping a child attend school. Lift a child and lift a family, a hamlet, a village, a district. You give a lot of people a lot of joy and hope, and something to look forward to with good reason. It's about time foreigners gave them something good.

It was an unexpected ending for me. I was embarrassed to travel to meet Tam—I didn't feel the little I had done entitled me to any special thanks. A few people know mine has been a long journey and I tire sometimes, and this I guess was a very special thank you that had the desired humbling effect.

We go on. My journey has in a sense ended in a little hamlet in Hoa Binh, but there are many little side roads to be navigated yet. Platypus is on its way.

Appendix A—Geneva Accords

The major nations attending the Geneva Conference on Indo-China to bring an end to hostilities in the region sent senior representatives:

France: M Mendes-France   President of the Council of Ministers (Prime Minister)

Britain: Mr Anthony Eden	Foreign Secretary
USA: Mr Bedell Smith	Under-Secretary of State
USSR: Mr Y Molotov	Foreign Minister
China: Mr Chou En-lai	Foreign Minster
Laos: Mr Phoui Sananikone	Foreign Minster
Cambodia: M Tep Phan	Head of Cambodian military delegation

Democratic Republic of Viet Nam: Mr Pham van Dong—Minister of Foreign Affairs

State of Viet Nam: Mr Tran van Do

At its final meeting in Geneva on 21 July 1954 the Chairman for the day was Anthony Eden and he presented documents relating to the discussions and agreements. Tabled below are selected extracts—a good deal of the resolutions relate to Laos and Cambodia or unrelated issues regarding Viet Nam. Author's comments follow the last agreement at Article 43.

Final Declaration of the Geneva Conference on the problem of restoring peace in Indo-China, in which the representatives of Cambodia, the Democratic Republic of Viet Nam, France, Laos, the People's Republic of China, the State of Viet Nam, the Union of Soviet Socialist Republics, the United Kingdom and the United States of America took part

July 21, 1954

4. The Conference takes note of the clauses in the agreement on the cessation of hostilities in Viet Nam prohibiting the introduction into Viet Nam of foreign troops and military personnel as well as of all kinds of arms and munitions . . .

6. The Conference recognises that the essential purpose of the agreement relating to Viet Nam is to settle military questions with a view to ending hostilities and that the military demarcation line is provisional and should not in any way be interpreted as constituting a political or territorial boundary. The Conference expresses its conviction that the execution of the provisions set out in the present declaration and in the agreement on the cessation of hostilities creates the necessary basis for the achievement in the near future of a political settlement in Viet Nam.

7. The Conference declares that, so far as Viet Nam is concerned, the settlement of political problems, affected on the basis of respect for the principles of independence, unity and territorial integrity, shall permit the Vietnamese people to enjoy the fundamental freedoms, guaranteed by democratic institutions established as a result of free general elections by secret ballot. In order to ensure that sufficient progress in the restoration of peace has been made, and that all the necessary conditions obtain for free expression of the national will, general elections shall be held in July 1956, under the supervision of an international commission composed of representatives of the Member States of the International Supervisor Commission, referred to in the agreement on the cessation of hostilities. Consultations will be held on this subject between the competent representative authorities of the two zones from July 20, 1955, onwards.

12. In their relations with Cambodia, Laos and Viet Nam, each member of the Geneva Conference undertakes to respect the sovereignty, the independence, the unity and the territorial integrity of the above-mentioned States, and to refrain from any interference in their internal affairs.

13. The members of the Conference agree to consult one another on any question which may be referred to them by the International Supervisory Commission, in order to study such measures as may prove necessary to ensure that the agreements on the cessation of hostilities in Cambodia, Laos and Viet Nam are respected.

Document No. 5
Agreement on the Cessation of Hostilities in Viet Nam
Chapter 1
Provisional Military Demarcation Line and Demilitarised Zone

Article 1
A provisional military demarcation line shall be fixed, on either side of which the forces of the two parties shall be regrouped after their withdrawal, the forces of the People's Army of Vietnam to the north of the line and the forces of the French Union to the south.
Chapter 2
Principles and procedure governing implementation of the present agreement
Article 14
Political and administrative measures in the two regrouping zones, on either side of the provisional military demarcation line:-
Pending the general elections which will bring about the unification of Viet Nam, the conduct of civil administration in each regrouping zone shall be in the hands of the party whose forces are to be regrouped there in virtue of the present Agreement.
Chapter 5
Miscellaneous
Article 27
The signatories of the present Agreement and their successors in their functions shall be responsible for ensuring the observance and enforcement of the terms and provisions thereof.
Chapter 6
Joint Commission and International Commission for Supervision and Control in Vietnam
Article 28
Responsibility for the execution of the agreement on the cessation of hostilities shall rest with the parties.
Article 29
An International Commission shall ensure the control and supervision of this execution.
Article 34
An International Commission shall be set up for the control and supervision over the application of the provisions of the agreement

on the cessation of hostilities in Viet Nam. It shall be composed of representatives of the following States: Canada, India and Poland.

It shall be presided over by the representative of India.

Article 43

If one of the parties refuses to put into effect a recommendation of the International Commission, the parties concerned or the Commission itself shall inform the members of the Geneva Conference.

If the International Commission does not reach unanimity in the cases provided for in Article 42, it shall submit a majority report and one or more minority reports to the members of the Conference.

The International Commission shall inform the members of the Conference in all cases where its activity is being hindered.

It would seem that the chances of a successful outcome to the Geneva meeting were remote indeed for a number of reasons:

The Vietminh had defeated France and the French had agreed to accept the independence of Vietnam. The major countries represented at the Conference had their own preoccupations and distractions, including, *inter alia*:

The USSR: Stalin had died a year before after a long and bloody reign. Kruschev was coming to terms with his new office and was not interested in a conflict with the USA over Vietnam.

China: The savage and costly Korean War had ended the year before. China had paid a heavy price for its involvement and was anxious to avoid further conflict in Vietnam since it had also been the major sponsor of the Vietminh. China persuaded the Vietminh to accept the terms of the Geneva Accords and rely on the promised free elections to achieve unification of Vietnam.

Britain: Struggling to come to terms with massive war debt, the crumbling of its Empire and problems with Egypt, by 1956 Britain would become involved in the Suez Crisis. By secret agreement between Britain, France and Israel, and without the knowledge of the USA, Israel would invade Egypt through Sinai. Britain and France would send in troops to be seen to save the day in order to help achieve its goals in the region. The operation went disastrously wrong and Anthony Eden, who had represented Britain at the Geneva Accords as Foreign Secretary was Prime Minister at the time of the invasion. He had no choice but to resign.

France: In South Vietnam, the French constantly struggled against American influence and CIA and other intelligence operatives. France also was becoming preoccupied with nationalist movements in its North African territories, particularly Algeria.

The USA: It was only at the end of 1954 that Joseph McCarthy, a drunken and corrupt senator who stirred up Communist witch hunts to strengthen his political base was dealt the final blow that brought several years of insanity to a close. The fall of China to the Communists in 1949 had been a massive blow for Washington so that in future vast sums of money and resources were invested to combat Communism wherever it surfaced or was thought to be likely to surface. Nobody wanted to appear to be soft on communism. By refusing to sign the Accords the USA was signalling its intentions.

These, then, were the power brokers who said to the Vietminh in effect: settle for less than you wanted initially, and we'll sort it out with free elections in two years' time. Trust us!

During Eden's meeting the Accord documents reveal the following statement from Bedell Smith, representative of the United States:

Mr Chairman, Fellow Delegates, as I stated to my colleagues during our meeting on July 18, my Government is not prepared to join in a Declaration by the Conference such as is submitted. However, the United States makes this unilateral declaration of its position in these matters:-

In conexxion with the statement in the Declaration concerning free elections in Viet Nam, my Government wishes to make clear its position which it has expressed in a Declaration made in Washington on June 29,1954, as follows:-

"In the case of nations now divided against their will, we shall continue to seek to achieve unity through free elections, supervised by the United Nations to ensure they are conducted fairly.

With respect to the statement made by the Representative of the State of Viet Nam, the United States reiterates its traditional position that peoples are entitled to determine their own future and that it will not join in an agreement which would hinder this. Nothing in its declaration just made is intended to or does indicate any departure from this traditional position.

We share the hope that the agreement will permit Cambodia, Laos and Viet Nam to play their part in full independence and sovereignty, in the peaceful community of nations, and will enable the peoples of that area to determine their own future."

Even before Bedell Smith's fine endorsement of the free election process echoed around the chamber, Washington had commenced plotting to split Vietnam in two in order to avoid the democratic process it would later endorse. Diem, a strong anti-Communist was selected by Bao Dai as Prime Minister in South Vietnam on 16 June 1954.

In May 1955 Diem deposed Emperor Bao Dai with American help. The USA could hardly have been unaware this was a major breach of clause 12 of Document 2. Within two months he declared that the elections were impossible because of "the oppressive regime that reigned in the occupied zone by the Vietminh". This was a full year before the elections were due, and none of the members of the Accord could have been unaware of his stated intentions.

None of the attendees moved to correct the blatant breach and the road to the American War was opened wide.

In there somewhere was the International Commission which did on occasions report breaches but trying to achieve satisfaction from the major powers would have been hopeless, especially since the most powerful major power was hell bent on destroying the Accords.

In theory, even if nobody heard Diem announce he would ignore the Accords and if they somehow managed to miss all the press coverage, the people of Viet Nam could rely on the International Commission (Canadian, Indian and Polish) to take steps to correct the breach: in theory as a last resort the members of the Geneva Accord would be notified and they would by some process resolve the breach.

In the case of Diem's fatal breach, the one that cost 3,000,000 Vietnamese lives, all that was required was a meeting at which the Soviet delegate could stretch his legs under the table and kick his American counterpart sharply on the shin. There should have been no need to say anything—everyone would have known exactly what was happening.

The disgust of the Vietnamese at this betrayal by the major powers was evident from the way they set about peace negotiations with the USA. They refused any offers of international assistance and negotiated directly with the Americans, who found them extremely difficult to deal with. In 1954 Vietnam needed help—the French had destroyed the mandarin system of government and replaced it with French bureaucrats. Ho Chi Minh had nobody with international diplomatic experience and was pleased to receive assistance from Beijing, although the outcome is thought to have cost him dearly in terms of credibility as well as human life, and probably changed the nature and mood of government in Hanoi.

There may be doubt about the validity of statehood of both North and South Vietnam due to concessions by the Japanese and French in 1945-1949 but the intent of the Accords seems very clear.

The Geneva Conference seems to have been held to end the hostilities and silence the Vietnamese so that the major powers could tick off other items on their long agenda.

Bibliography

Allen, George W. *None So Blind*, Ivan R Dee, Chicago, 2001

Berman, Larry. *No Peace, No Honor*, The Free Press, New York, 2001

Bilton, Michael and Sim, Kevin. *Four hours in My Lai*, Penguin, New York, 1992

Buzzanco, Robert. *Masters of War*, Cambridge University Press, 1996

Chong, Denise. *The Girl in the Picture*, Scribner, London, 2001

Currey, Cecil B. *Victory At Any Cost*, Brassey's, Dulles, 1999

Duiker, William J. *Ho Chi Minh*, Theia Books, New York 2000

Fall, Bernard B. *Street without Joy*, Stackpole, Mechanicsburg, 1994

Fall, Bernard. *Hell in a Very Small Place* The Siege of Dien Bien Phu, Da Capo Press, 1985

Fall, Bernard. *Last Reflections on a War*, Stackpole, Mechanicsburg, 2000

Goldstein, Gordon M. *Lessons in Disaster*, Times Books, New York, 2009

Greiner, Bernd. *War Without Fronts*, Bodley Head, London, 2009

Hackworth, David. *Steel My Soldiers' Hearts*, Rugged Land, New York, 2002

Hackworth, David and Sherman, Julie. *About Face*, Touchstone, New York, 1990

Halberstam, David. *The Best and the Brightest*, Modern Library, New York, 2001

Hamilton-Paterson, James. *The Greedy War*, David McKay, New York, 1972

Kaiser, David. *American Tragedy*, The Belknap Press, Cambridge, Mass, 2000

Karnow, Stanley. *Vietnam: A History*, Penguin, New York, 1997

McMaster, HR. *Dereliction of Duty*, Harper Perennial, New York, 1998

McNamara, Robert S. *In Retrospect*, Vintage, New York, 1996

Maclear, Michael. *Vietnam: The Ten Thousand Day War*, Thames Mandarin, London, 1990

Mangold, Tom and Pennycate, John. *The Tunnels of Cu Chi*, Berkley, New York, 1986 Cassell, London, 2005

Patti, Archimedes L A. *Why Viet Nam?* University of California Press, 1980

Porch, Douglas. *The French Foreign Legion*, HarperPerennial, New York, 1992

Prados, John. *Operation Vulture*, ibooks, New York, 2002

Sallah, Michael and Weiss, Mitch. *Tiger Force*, Hodder & Stoughton, London, 2006

Sheehan, Neil. *A Bright Shining Lie*, Vintage, New York, 1989

Short, Philip. *Pol Pot*, John Murray, London, 2006

Sorley, Lewis, *A Better War*, Harcourt, Orlando, Fl, 1999

Tang, Truong Nhu., *A Vietcong Memoir*, Vintage, 1986

Turner, Karen Gottschang with Phan Thanh Hao., *Even the Women Must Fight*, Wiley, New York 1998

Windrow, Martin. *The Last Valley*, Cassell, London, 2005

Notes

1   Duiker, William J., Ho Chi Minh, Theia Books, New York, 2000, p244

2   Tang, *Truong* Nhu., *A Vietcong Memoir*, Vintage, 1986, p71

3   Karnow, Stanley., *Vietnam: A History*, Penguin, New York, 1997, p245

4   Bui Minh Duong, J Stor file (http://www.jstor.org) containing Modern Asian Studies Vol 29, No.3 (Jul 1995) Cambridge University Press p573-618

5   Karnow, Stanley., *Vietnam: A History*, Penguin, New York, 1997 p160

6   Sheehan, Neil. *A Bright Shining Lie*, Vintage, New York, 1989, p686

7   Ibid, p540,541

8   Ibid, p541

9   Bilton, Michael and Sim, Kevin. *Four hours in My Lai*, New York, 1992,

10   Ibid, p356

11   Ibid, p138,139

12   Ibid, p334

13   Sallah, Michael and Weiss, Mitch. *Tiger Force*, Hodder & Stoughton, London, 2006,

14   Ibid, p213

15   McNamara, Robert S. In Retrospect, Vintage, New York, 1996, p322

16   Currey, Cecil B. *Victory At Any Cost*, Brassey's, Dulles, 1999, p44-45

17   Duiker, William J., Ho Chi Minh, Theia Books, New York, 2000, p143

18   Ibid, p185

19   Ibid, p225

20   Ibid, p555

21   www.utvetdsp.com/agentorange.htm

22   Turner, Karen Gottschang with Phan Thanh Hao., *Even the Women Must Fight*, Wiley, New Yor,1998, p55

23   Mangold, Tom and Pennycate, John., *The Tunnels of Cu Chi*, Berkley, New York, 1986 Cassell, London, 2005, p228-237

24 Tang, Truong Nhu., *A Vietcong Memoir*, Vintage, 1986, p130

25 Turner, Karen Gottschang with Phan Thanh Hao., *Even the Women Must Fight,* Wiley, New York 1998, p20-21

26 Currey, Cecil B. *Victory At Any Cost*, Brassey's, Dulles, 1999

27 Fall, Bernard., *Hell in a Very Small Place* The Siege of Dien Bien Phu, Da Capo Press, 1985, p54

28 Turner, Karen Gottschang with Phan Thanh Hao., *Even the Women Must Fight*, Wiley, New York 1998, p31

29 Fall, Bernard., Hell in a Very Small Place The Siege of Dien Bien Phu, Da Capo Press, 1985, p54bid, p451

30 Maclear, Michael. *Vietnam: The Ten Thousand Day War*, Thames Mandarin, London, 1990, p478

31 Tang, Truong Nhu., *A Vietcong Memoir*, Vintage, 1986, p167

32 Ibid, p168-169

33 McNamara, Robert S., *In Retrospect,* Vintage, New York, 1996, p323

34 Ibid, p322

35 Ibid, p322

36 Lonely Planet Publications. Vietnam, 2003 p12

37 Karnow, Stanley., *Vietnam: A History*, Penguin, New York, 1997 p136

38 Currey, Cecil B. *Victory at any cost*, Brassey's, Dulles, 1999 p99

39 Duiker, William J., *Ho Chi Minh*, Theia Books, New York, 2000 p288

40 Patti, Archimedes L A. *Why Viet Nam?* University of California Press, 1980, p51

41 Halberstam, David. *The Best and the Brightest*, Modern Library, New York, 2001, p94

42 Karnow, Stanley., *Vietnam: A History*, Penguin, New York, 1997 p215

43 Ibid, p215

44 Maclear, Michael. *Vietnam: The Ten Thousand Day War*, Thames Mandarin, London, 1990, p64

45 Ibid, p64

46 Karnow, Stanley., *Vietnam: A History*, Penguin, New York, 1997 p229

47 Ibid, p239

48 Ibid, p251

49 Ibid, p380-392

50 McNamara, Robert S., *In Retrospect,* Vintage, New York, 1996, p129-143

51 Halberstam, David. *The Best and the Brightest*, Modern Library, New York, 2001, p650

52 Short, Philip. *Pol Pot*, John Murray, London, 2006, p11,12

Special thanks

To the six good men and true without whom Platypus, Inc would never have seen the light of day:

Jeff Burch. Friend, former employer and industrialist, now in semi-retirement as he pursues the perfect pinot at his iconic Howard Park Winery. Financial support at a critical stage encouraged me to pursue the dream. A Member of Platypus.

Humphry Faas. A partner in Anchor Legal, who completed all the legal incorporation formalities at no cost to Platypus. There were no funds left to incorporate. A Member of Platypus.

Peter Kyi. A long-term friend and business manager who offers sage and practical advice and support. A Member of Platypus.

Mark McCarthy. An IT wiz, Mark is creating the Platypus website and contributes as always across several fields. A Member of Platypus.

Andre Sweidan. A partner in Anchor Legal, who completed all the legal formalities at no cost to Platypus.

Craig Yaxley. A partner at KPMG, who assisted generously with the many legal and taxation formalities that go with incorporating a charitable entity. A Member of Platypus.